POCKET
BEER
BOOK

3RD
EDITION

Dedication, from Stephen Beaumont

For my father, Dick Beaumont, who taught me that it's worth going the extra distance for good beer.

An Hachette UK Company
www.hachette.co.uk

First published in Great Britain in 2017 by Mitchell Beazley,
a division of Octopus Publishing Group Ltd, Carmelite House,
50 Victoria Embankment, London EC4Y 0DZ
www.octopusbooks.co.uk

ISBN: 978-1-78472-336-1

A CIP record for this book is available from the British Library.

Printed and bound in China.

10 9 8 7 6 5 4 3 2 1

Group Publishing Director Denise Bates
Art Director Juliette Norsworthy
Senior Editor Leanne Bryan
General Editor Jo Copestick
Copy Editor Jo Richardson
Designer Geoff Fennell
Picture Research Manager Giulia Hetherington
Senior Production Controller Allison Gonsalves

POCKET
BEER
BOOK

STEPHEN BEAUMONT
& TIM WEBB

3RD
EDITION

MITCHELL
BEAZLEY

CONTENTS

A NOTE ABOUT BREWERY LISTINGS

We believe that brewery ownership matters. As such, where previously independent breweries have been purchased by much larger entities, we have listed the owning company in parentheses after the brewery name. Such is the pace and frequency of these deals today, however, that the odd acquisition may have escaped our notice and, of course, further purchases may have occurred between the finalization of the text and the moment this book reached your hands. Until such time as regulations require that the name of the company responsible for brewing the beer you buy be listed on the label, we can only advise careful research.

THE BEERS

INTRODUCTION

A VERY DIFFERENT BEER GUIDE FOR
A VERY DIFFERENT BEER MARKET

No one today knows for certain exactly how many breweries are active throughout the world. We have estimates for various countries, but some of those, like the Brewers Association tally for the USA, are far better and more reliable than others, such as the "guesstimations" for Brazil and China.

Our own very conservative estimate places the global brewery total at over 20,000, but it is likely that there are many more than that. And if we take the equally conservative average of a dozen different labels per brewery, knowing that in this day and age of one-offs, special editions and collaborations any given craft brewery can probably boast in excess of 30, 40 or 50 brands, then the worldwide count of regular beers is fast closing on a quarter-million, and when one-offs are included, doubtless well beyond it.

In this context, the number of beers we assessed in the 2015 version of this book seems minuscule. For while 4,300 beer reviews is by any measure an impressive achievement, it represents but a very tiny fraction of the world's total beer supply.

So, you might ask, why create a book that features even fewer beers? The answer is focus.

We recognize that more people are enjoying more beer than ever before, and that in many cases they are also paying higher prices than ever before, from the special release that retails for $30 per highly coveted bottle to the extremely limited edition that sells for hundreds of pounds or yen or euros. We also recognize that when people open and drink such beers, they may be moved to quote the bittersweet refrain from the Peggy Lee standard "Is That All There Is?"

Hence this new approach. Rather than attempt to deliver a cross section of breweries spanning the globe, we have assembled a carefully selected group of what we firmly believe are the best minds in beer – you can meet them beginning on page 316 – and tasked them to deliver detailed reviews of the absolute best beers their native lands have to offer. Not the most talked about or the rarest or the most obscure, but simply the finest ales and lagers and mixed-fermentation beers that eager enthusiasts might actually be able to get their hands on. Star ratings have been dispensed with because all the beers we have featured are at the top of their class.

Along the way, we have tasted beers beside many of our experts to affirm that the high standards we have set are being rigorously maintained. Where possible, we have travelled with them to sample in situ, and where not we have assembled local and international beers to evaluate as one, making sure that just because a beer comes from a less developed beer culture, that doesn't mean it might disappoint a more seasoned beer aficionado.

We also introduce in this edition three categories of special merit: ICONIC BREWERIES, CAN'T-MISS BREWERIES and BREWERIES TO WATCH.

The ICONIC BREWERIES designation is in many ways self-defining and has been awarded in a most miserly fashion, as we feel is only proper. An Icon is not only a brewery that has to some extent perfected or even invented a style or styles, it is also one that brews splendid beer throughout its range and, most importantly, has acted as a major influencer in its national and, in many cases, international markets.

The CAN'T-MISS BREWERIES accreditation is reserved for those breweries that craft great beers across a variety of styles, with each being as good as or better than the rest of its portfolio kin. Essentially, it means what it declares, which is that if you buy a beer with this brewery's name attached, it is almost guaranteed to be a good if not great taste experience.

Finally, BREWERIES TO WATCH are those breweries under three years of age at the time of writing that show tremendous potential for the future. They can be already well-known operations or under-the-radar gems, but each and every one is a potential Can't Miss or even a future Icon, as chosen by our experts and vetted by ourselves.

And there you have it. You may not agree with every assessment of every beer mentioned in the following pages, taste being the subjective entity that it is, and it is equally likely that you will wonder why a favourite beer is absent or a cherished brewery denied Can't Miss status. But we can guarantee that the beers and breweries noted here will delight almost any beer enthusiast, from tentative novice to seasoned beer-hunting veteran, and that in the deliciously, delightfully crowded beer marketplace we face today, the selections we and our experts have presented will make your next beer-drinking experience just that much more interesting and enjoyable.

Cheers,

Stephen Beaumont and Tim Webb

BEER STYLES

The idea that a beer should be considered of a particular style was anathema to the 20th-century industrialists who forged the notion of the universal beer. For them, the ideal was light gold, grainy sweet, almost bereft of bitterness and served as cold as possible to hide flaws. The key was marketing.

The rise of modern craft breweries, on the other hand, has provoked a need for reliably recognizable terms to describe, distinguish and explain the myriad types of beer, old and new, that now adorn the shelves of bars, stores and home refrigerators around the world. The questions that remain are which terms to use and how to apply them.

We believe it was Michael Jackson, in his 1977 book *The World Guide to Beer*, who first attempted to catalogue global beer styles, introducing readers to such beer types as "*Münchener*", "*Trappiste*" and "(Burton) Pale Ale". His goal then was to provide a context through which to discover — or rediscover — these beers. Our challenge, although addressed to a more beer-aware public, remains in essence the same.

While we would love to report that we have solved all the issues surrounding the current confusion and can provide readers with a simple map of the major beer styles of the world, this is not currently possible and, we admit, may never be. What we offer instead is a rough guide on how to pick your way through a linguistic and conceptual minefield in a fashion that adds to rather than detracts from understanding.

START WITH TRADITION

We believe the most reliable stylistic imperatives to be those based on centuries of brewing tradition, and that most modern derivations are merely modifications of existing beer styles, however inventive or ingenious. Hence our first separation is according to method of fermentation.

Historically, the term **ale** has referred to a beer fermented at room temperature or higher, causing its *Saccharomyces* yeast to rise to the top of the wort, or unfermented beer, hence references to top-fermentation or, sometimes, warm-fermentation. In contrast, a **lager** was fermented at a cooler temperature, causing its yeast to sink, thus known as bottom-fermentation or, sometimes, cool-fermentation.

These main beer classes, comparable to red and white wine, still serve to define the overwhelming majority of beers, despite the temperature and yeast manipulation possible in a modern brewhouse. As a general rule, a beer fermented at warmer temperatures with a yeast of the family *S. cerevisiae* and conditioned at warm temperatures for a short period – an ale – should tend toward a fruitier character. Those fermented at cooler temperatures with a yeast of the family *S. pastorianus* and cold-stored (or "lagered") for a longer period at cold temperatures – a lager – should not. Combine ale yeast with a lager-style conditioning and you have the hybrid styles of **kölsch** and **altbier**, as well as the American cream ale. Flip it to lager yeast and ale-type conditioning and you have **steam** beer, also known as **California common beer**.

Beers that have no yeast added to them, most famously the **lambic** beers of Belgium, are said to undergo spontaneous fermentation, effected by a combination of airborne and barrel-resident microflora, including *Brettanomyces* and *Pediococcus*, which yield complex flavours from mildly lemony to assertively tart. Those fermented with the same types of microbes introduced deliberately are becoming known variously as wild beers, mixed-fermentation beers or, more crudely, sour beers.

ADD COLOUR

Colour is a powerful force in beer and often used to define beer by style, with some references to hue reserved exclusively for certain types of beer, such as "white" (*blanche*, *wit*, *weisse*) for **wheat beers**. "Pale" and "light" (in colour, not alcohol or calories) are also popular adjectives, yielding the now-international **pale ale** and **India pale ale**, or **IPA**, the German *helles* and the Czech *světlý*.

"**Amber**" in North America was and to some extent remains synonymous with otherwise ordinary ales or lagers with a blush of colour, while "**red**" has a questionable degree of Irish authenticity often used to describe a beer of uncertain style. The same tint trait among lagers may be termed *Wiener* or **Vienna**.

"Dark" is often also used in fairly random fashion in the English-speaking world, but retains validity in Bavaria where its literal translation, *dunkel*, should indicate a brownish lager of a style, *Münchener*, once strongly associated with Munich – unless it is combined with *weizen* or *weisse*, in which case the reference is to dark wheat beer. In the Czech Republic and across Europe's eastern half, the term is *tmavý*.

"Brown" implies the use of more roasted malts and is historically associated with **old ale**, a class of fairly winey ales aged in oak still seen in the tart, fruity *oud bruin* style from northern Belgium and the fresher English **brown ale**. Now, however, it is applied to a wide variety of creations, from sickly sweet to forcefully bitter, mild to alcoholic.

"Black" is usually reserved for **porters** and **stouts**, though also applied to bottom-fermented German *schwarzbier*.

CONSIDER STRENGTH

Brewers have for centuries used subtle nudge-and-wink systems to highlight alcohol content. One well-known remnant of this practice is the Scottish shilling system whereby ales are measured from **60 shilling**, or **60/-**, for the lightest, to **80/-** or **90/-** for stronger beers (*see* page 91), the last also referred to as **"wee heavy"** or **Scotch ale**. In the Czech Republic and elsewhere, the old Balling system of measuring wort gravity defines beers by degrees, from **8°** for the lightest to **12°** for a beer of premium strength and on up into fermented-porridge territory.

Few words are less useful to a beer description than "strong", the difficulty being context. In Scandinavia, strong beer (**starkøl**) is above 4.5–4.7% ABV, not far from where the British would place the definition were the word not banned from beer names. In contrast, few Belgians, North Americans and Italians would consider anything below 6–7% "strong".

The terms **dubbel/double** and **tripel/triple** are medieval in origin and have proved both durable and international, in the past used to indicate a beer fermented from a mash with greater malt content – often the "first runnings" of grain then reused to make a second beer. The modern context of *dubbel*/double generally indicates a beer of 6–8% ABV. Most eminently, it appears in reference to the malty and sweet Belgian abbey style *dubbel*, the German **doppelbock** and related Italian **doppio malto** (although use of the latter term appears to be waning) and the American **double IPA**, usually an ale of significant strength and aggressive bitterness.

The current use of *tripel*/triple owes its origins to 20th-century monastery breweries and typically describes a specific type of blond, sweet-starting but usually dry-finishing strong ale, although modern usage extends to **IPA** to suggest an even stronger and hoppier brew.

Quadrupel/**quadruple**/**quad** is a 21st-century affectation, the first variant originally used by the Dutch Trappist brewery La Trappe to designate its new high-strength ale in 1998. The Dutch spelling is employed to imply heritage.

Historically, the term **barley wine** was used to indicate a beer of wine strength, often undergoing some period of bottle-ageing. Modern interpretations vary from a high-hopped, fully carbonated US style to a virtually uncarbonated, fully attenuated Italian form that retains residual sugars and resembles Madeira made from grain. Barrel-ageing is increasingly common.

The adjective **"Imperial"** has experienced a recent transformation from its original deployment in **Imperial Russian stout** designating a strong, intense, sometimes oily stout to the suggestion that any style may be "Imperialized" by being made bolder and more alcoholic, sometimes also hoppier. Thus we find **Imperial pale ale** as a synonym for **double IPA** and confections such as **Imperial pilsner**, **Imperial brown ale** and so on.

FACTOR IN THE GRAINS

Besides the basic four ingredients of beer – water, barley malt, hops and yeast – numerous other grains are used with varying degrees of regularity, in all but a handful of specialized cases in combination with barley malt.

Wheat is the most common of these, creating whole categories of beer such as the German-style wheat beers variously known as *weizen* or *weisse*, prefixed *hefe-* when indicating that the beer is unfiltered and *kristall* when clear. Also included in this family are the derivatives

dunkelweisse and ***weizenbock***, respectively meaning dark and strong wheat beers, and in an emerging category of hoppy versions pioneered by a US–German collaboration and known as ***hopfenweisse***.

Different local traditions of light (typically 2.5–3.5%), quenching wheat beers have survived or been revived, such as ***Berliner weisse***, made tart through lactic acidification and sometimes *Brettanomyces* during fermentation; salted, coriander-laced and tart *gose* (sometimes ***Leipziger gose***); the smoked wheat ***grodziskie*** from Poland (*see* Style Spotlight, page 189) and northern Germany's tart, smoked ***lichtenhainer***.

Spontaneously fermented Belgian **lambic** is by law a wheat beer, though more common in Belgium and elsewhere is ***witbier*** or ***bière blanche*** (white beer) brewed with unmalted rather than malted wheat and spiced with orange peel and coriander, sometimes in conjunction with other spices.

Once ubiquitous but now more seldom seen are simple **wheat ales**, blond beers that have been made lighter of body just through the use of malted wheat, although there is increased North American interest in well-hopped interpretations called **hoppy wheat beers**. Some craft brewers in the USA and elsewhere have started to make strong wheat beers called **wheat wines**, referencing barley wine.

Other grains in general usage include oats, which bring sweetness and a silky mouthfeel to **oatmeal stout**, and other, less conventional beers, such as: oatmeal brown ales; rye, which bestows a spiciness upon **rye pale ale** and **rye IPA**, as well as the odd lager-fermented ***roggenbier*** of German origin; buckwheat, blackened and used in the Breton beer style ***bière de blé noir***; and an assortment of non-glutinous grains employed to create the growing class of **gluten-free beers**.

Malt and grain substitutes are mostly there for fermentable sugar to increase alcoholic strength, with or, more commonly, without adding flavour characteristics. The likes of maize (corn), rice, starches, syrups and candi sugar may bring balance to heavy beer by ensuring that it is suitably strong in alcohol, but are not seen as creating styles in their own right – though **Japanese rice beers** and a handful of related beers in the USA are having a go.

The exception to this rule is where unfermentable sugars are used with the intention of adding sometimes considerable sweetness without alcoholic strength, fructose creating **sweet stout** and lactose contributing to **milk** or **cream stout**.

HOPS AND OTHER FLAVOURINGS

Hops have been the primary flavouring agent in beer since the Middle Ages, but only in the last century or two have beer styles begun to be defined by the variety of hop used.

Perhaps most famously, what the world knows as the **Czech-style pilsner** is seasoned with a single variety of hop, the floral Saaz, grown near where the style was invented. Equally, the typical hops used in a **British best bitter** (*see* Style Spotlight, page 88) have always been Fuggle and Golding (with a wider variety employed in **Extra Special Bitter**, or **ESB**).

When what we now recognize as the **US-style pale ale** was established in the 1970s (*see* Style Spotlight, page 223), the hop used to give the beer its trademark citrusy bite was Cascade, although these days a variety of other so-called "C-hops" are considered acceptable, including Centennial, Chinook and Citra. By extension, these hops have also grown

to be emblematic of the **US-style IPA** and its rapidly developing family, including the double, triple and **Imperial IPA**; **black IPA** – a **hoppy porter** bereft of ample roastiness, lower-strength **session IPA**; fruit- and/ or juice-fuelled **fruit IPA**; spicy **white IPA**; the yeast-defined **Belgian IPA**; and whatever else IPA-obsessed brewers and brewery marketing departments have developed since this writing.

More recent hop-defined beer styling includes the use of **New Zealand** to denote beers flavoured with grapey, tropical Kiwi hops, notably Nelson Sauvin and Motueka (*see* Style Spotlight, page 265), **Australian** for beers flavoured with Galaxy and its derivatives or **South Pacific** where these are mixed. As hop cultivation becomes increasingly scientific and additional varieties are created, more beers are being identified by the single hop variety used.

Hops can be considered a core ingredient of any beer, other flavourings being distinctly optional, including herbs and spices. While we still see the odd beer identified as ***gruit*** (sometimes *grut* or *gruut*), which is to say seasoned with a selection of dried herbs and flavourings but no hops, certainly the most famously spiced beer is the **Belgian-style wheat beer**.

Although all manner of herbs and spices were employed prior to the widespread use of hops in brewing – before Pierre Celis pitched coriander, cumin and dried Curaçao orange peel into the beers of Hoegaarden in 1966 – the extent to which brewers, Belgian or otherwise, spiced beers is questionable. Today, however, beers can be and frequently are flavoured with all manner of ingredients, to the extent that lumping them all into a single **spiced beer** category seems to us rather random. Unfortunately, in the absence of acceptable sub-categories based on which of these additives actually improves what beer, it remains the best available option.

Another area of contention is the addition of fruit syrups to beer. While cherries and raspberries have for centuries been steeped whole in Belgian lambic beers to create respectively **kriek** and **framboise**, the rash of beers made by adding juice, syrup, cordials or essence to ordinary lagers and ales is mostly a post-1980 phenomenon. Although these are collectively known as fruit beers, this can be a misnomer, as the additives are sometimes a considerable distance from their time on the tree.

Dark ales such as brown ale, porter and in particular stout are increasingly having vanilla, cocoa, liquorice and coffee added to them in formats that range from whole pods or stems to syrups and essences, with varying degrees of success. A recent outbreak of coffee-flavoured pale ales suggests that may be a future category to watch.

One of the most curious additives is salt, once commonly and still variously used in (Irish) **dry stout** to fill out the palate, achieved with greatest aplomb in the 19th century by filtering the wort through a bed of shucked oyster shells, hence **oyster stout**. East German *gose* is essentially a salted wheat beer.

Italian brewers have sought to make a style out of adding chestnut to their beer, whether in whole, crushed, honey or jam form, but have more recently, and more successfully, turned their attentions to **Italian grape ale**, indicating a beer flavoured with wine grapes, lees and/or aged in a disused wine barrel (*see* Style Spotlight, page 126). Japanese brewers evoke their own national drink with **sake-influenced beer** made with sake rice, fermented with sake yeast and/or conditioned in cedar sake barrels (*see* Style Spotlight, page 276).

Beyond these, there exists a multitude of other additives and seasonings currently in use – from root vegetables to nuts to flowers

and even Traditional Chinese Medicine herbs, known as TCM herbs. Whether these stand the test of time remains to be seen.

NATIONAL ADJECTIVES

Various national and regional markers have grown in recent years into beer-style descriptors. While some rankle – the term "Belgian" for a beer fermented by US-designated yeast that imbues a spicy or earthy character, for example – they do in most cases provide the buyer with useful information.

Thus **Belgian style** has come to mean a spicy or sometimes somewhat funky take on an understood beer style, as in **Belgian pale ale**, **Belgian IPA** and so on.

In contrast, **US** or **American** almost invariably refers to hop-forward styles in pale ales, IPAs (*see* Style Spotlight, page 223) and others seasoned with Cascade and other such related hops, and **New Zealand** (sometimes **Aotearoan**) pilsner and pale ale references those styles seasoned with Kiwi hops (*see* Style Spotlight, 265). **British** or **English** is usually used in conjunction with pale ale, IPA or barley wine, generally indicating a less aggressive hop character, but also a pronounced maltiness.

Scotch ale or **Scottish-style ale** suggests a beer of quite significant maltiness, with a strength of up to 8% ABV indicated by the former. Long-standing confusion about Scottish brewing methods means that beers so described sometimes also feature a potion of peated malt.

Other geographical qualifiers are more restricted. **Baltic porter**, for example, defines a beer that is not a porter at all, but rather a strong, dark and usually sweet bottom-fermented brew; **Irish red ale** is a popular

descriptor of questionable authenticity; **Irish stout** has both legitimacy and utility in describing a low-strength, dry, roasty form of stout; while **Bohemian** or **Czech style** generally modifies pilsner and suggests one more golden than blond, softly malty and floral; and **Bavarian** or **German** implies crisper, leaner and blonder when referencing pilsner, clove-y and/or banana-ish when applied to a wheat beer.

SEASONAL OFFERINGS

Before 1870 and the coming of affordable large-scale refrigeration, much of mainland Europe enjoyed a brewing "season" that lasted from Michaelmas (29 September) to St George's Day (23 April), fermentation in the summer months being rendered unsound by infestation and insect life. The need for beer during the non-brewing months of summer led historically to the creation of somewhat related styles such as *märzen* in Germany, *bière de garde* in France and *saison* in southern Belgium, each brewed to last the summer months and deploying increased hopping for preservative effect.

Come harvest, German, Austrian, Dutch and Norwegian brewers would clear the stocks of malt from the previous year's barley by brewing a dark *bok* or *bock* and an additional Christmas beer (Scandinavian *Juløl*). This custom was mirrored in the spring in all but Norway with a pale *maibock* or *lentebok* that might see off grain felt unlikely to survive the summer untainted.

There are also beers named after other occasions or seasons, including winter ales, summer beers and harvest ales, suggesting general character traits — heavier in winter, lighter for summer — but little else.

AND LOCAL BREWS

The great unsung charm of German beer is the host of local variants, typically on blond lagers, which are only partially filtered. Sometimes known collectively as *landbier*, they include types that are simply cloudy (*zwickelbier*), some that are cellar-conditioned (*kellerbier*) and a few in which carbon dioxide is vented during lagering (*ungespundetes*).

Franconian brewers claim a slice of history by perpetuating the use of wood-smoked malt in their *rauchbier* – at the same time inspiring a host of new wave smoked beers from Alaska to Poland.

Finnish and Estonian farmhouse brewers create respectively *sahti* (*see* Style Spotlight, page 160) and *koduōlu*, beers filtered through juniper boughs and fermented with bread yeast, served by necessity young and fresh for the lack of hops.

Lithuanian brewers celebrate their curious history with *kaimiškas* (*see* Style Spotlight, page 185), individualistic for a number of reasons, but most notably for adding "hop tea" to rapidly fermented wort post-mashing.

Finally, the craft brewing renaissance has witnessed the emergence or re-emergence of a cacophony of new methods of beer making, both authentically recreated and imagined. In the first group we place **barrel-aged** and **barrel-conditioned beers**, beginning in a multitude of styles and spending time in a variety of different barrels, including those that previously held wine, bourbon, single malt whisky, Cognac, Calvados or, in at least one case, barrels previously used to age maple syrup. Of particular interest in this area, we find, is what Brazilian brewers are currently doing with the exotic woods of the Amazon and Italian brewers with disused wine barrels.

In a similar vein, fresh or unkilned hops are used in a new class of **wet hop beers**, mostly ales and primarily in the USA, but otherwise of almost any hop-driven style the brewer wishes to brew.

At this stage in the development of beer, we see no end to new inventions and possibilities.

SUSPECT STYLES & TENUOUS TRENDS

Very few observers in the mid-1990s would have predicted the rise of IPA as the dominant craft beer style of the new millennium thus far. Too bitter, most would have said – as many did – and in a culture where healthy eating and increasingly moderate drinking were the dominant themes, surely a 7% alcohol content would be considered too high?

What did they know? *What did we know?*

The fact is that beer trends have become pretty much unpredictable over the last two or three decades. Just when you think that IPAs may have maxed out their strength and bitterness, along come double IPAs. Imagine that every long-forgotten beer style that could be revived has been, then sit back and watch the rise of an obscure Polish beer called *grodziskie* (*see* Style Spotlight, page 189). Figure that so-called "sour beers" are too laborious and time-consuming to create in large quantities, and no sooner do brewers develop kettle souring to make the cruder flavours of a months-long process achievable overnight.

That said, craft beer is not immune to the fads, fashions and flights of fancy that have long beset mass-market beer (remember ice beer?). And those, it must be noted, are usually a bit easier to identify.

FRUIT IPA

Occasionally it is possible to place the credit – or blame – for a beer trend at the feet of a single brewery, and so it is with fruit IPAs. For while some might argue that Vermont's Magic Hat Brewing actually kicked things off with their apricot-flavoured "not quite pale ale" #9, it was in fact California's Ballast Point Brewing that really started the ball rolling when they brought out a grapefruit-charged version of their Sculpin IPA in 2013.

It is still unknown if the grapefruit was originally added as a substitute or supplement to the citrusy hops that characterize regular Sculpin (*see* page 221), but either way the modified beer was an immediate hit. In short order, Grapefruit Sculpin went from being a novel curiosity to the sort of beer that sold out the same day a keg was tapped at the local beer bar.

Other fruit IPAs naturally followed, and then the onslaught began. Soon, it was not only commonplace for US breweries to have one, two or more fruited IPAs in their portfolio, but the trend spread to Canada, England, Continental Europe and even Australia.

The problem is that the "style" has now gone from the natural progression of adding grapefruit peel or juice to already grapefruity IPAs to the addition of all sorts of not-necessarily-logical fruits, from pineapple to mango to kiwi. Some of these odd interpretations work, but many more fall out of balance and wind up tasting like bitter fruit beer rather than well-rounded fruity-hoppy ale, which may well signal that this is a trend that will burn itself out sooner rather than later.

KETTLE SOURS

Only a few years old, kettle souring is the process of inoculating wort with various bacteria to lower its pH and then boiling it so that further bacterial growth is inhibited. This brings a level of tartness to the fully fermented beer and so has become a popular short cut, fuelling the growth of the so-called "sour beer" market. In particular, the process has proved popular in the production of low-strength styles such as *Berliner weisse* and *gose*.

The problem with kettle sours, however, is two-fold. On the one hand, many such beers are being sold for the same sort of elevated prices

commanded by beers that spend many months in oak barrels to achieve a similar effect, while on the other, the process has a tendency to result in beers that are relatively simple in their profiles, with chemically slanted lactic flavours and negligible complexity.

And indeed, when compared with the depth and nuance of a beer that undergoes months or years of conditioning in wooden barrels, a kettle-soured beer cannot help but appear as a "one-trick pony" of acidity and little else. Given enough time, it is likely that even those beer drinkers who explore beyond their first couple will tire of such brews, particularly if they continue to be sold at inflated prices.

EXTREME TURBIDITY

With some exceptions, German- and Belgian-style wheat beers most prominent among them, cloudiness in modern beer has been generally frowned upon. In fact, since the advent of transparent glassware, clarity, or what is known in beer circles as brightness, has been prized above all as an indication of a well-made beer.

Then came the New England IPA, sometimes known as the NEIPA or the Vermont-style IPA, a much more extreme version of what started out as "unfiltered" blond lagers in Europe some decades ago (their principle being that a bit of flour in the body of the beer added to the otherwise less impressive flavour). These new interpretations are turbid in the extreme and nothing like that which has gone before.

Typically cloudy in appearance and loaded with fruity esters from both hopping and fermentation, New England IPAs rose to fame on the back of a beer called Heady Topper from The Alchemist brewery in northern Vermont (*see* page 209). Other northeastern US and central Canadian breweries soon started to emulate the massively successful beer, and from there this new style spread westward and eventually overseas.

Along the way, the appearance of these beers gradually evolved, growing first densely cloudy, then turbid and finally reaching something resembling orange juice with a head on it. As the "turbidity stakes" grew hotter, it came out that some breweries were adding flour and fruit purées to increase the cloudiness and "juicy" character of their beers.

Surprisingly, the principal difficulty with such ales is not that their appearance might put drinkers off – a dense cloudiness has, in some circles, come to be perceived as a mark of quality – but that some of these ales lack the flavour stability necessary in a market where competition is growing and kegs or cans of beer might not wind up being consumed within an optimal time frame. As such competition grows further and the bloom starts to come off the turbid beer rose, it seems likely that this will become an even greater issue.

THE TWO WORLDS OF BEER

The division of beer into the two broad categories of fast and industrial versus traditional and craft – dull versus interesting, if you prefer – began in earnest with the commencement of a consumer backlash against homogeneity that started building in the 1970s.

Since then, more than 60 countries have seen the revival, or increasingly the arrival, of a vibrant, local beer culture, often boosted by a growing import–export market. But how much impact is this having?

By 2017, the schism between these two philosophies of beer making seemed more pronounced than at any time in its commercial history. Global beer giants continue to see the job of a beer company as to spend as little money as possible making stuff that people can be persuaded to buy through branding and marketing.

In contrast, the massively growing number of craft or traditional brewers, be they tiny local concerns or companies now producing beer in brew runs the size of an Olympic swimming pool, concern themselves more with offering flavour, choice and authenticity – aims contrary to cost-cutting culture.

In 2016, the value of the US domestic beer market was around US$106 billion or 1.5% of the USA's GDP. Of this amount, over US$23 billion constituted "craft beer" as defined by the US Brewers Association, a figure matched in growth and significance by the sales of imported beers. Sales of both continue to rise impressively year on year despite the overall volume of beer consumed falling. The brunt of the fall was borne by mostly well-known industrial brews.

A similar pattern exists around a world in which the number of commercial breweries has risen from roughly 4,000 in 1977 to more than 20,000 in 2017.

It is hard to define the proportion of beer produced that might be termed non-industrial, for three main reasons.

Firstly, what actually counts as craft, traditional or special beer? Does one include a blond lager simply because it is made by a small brewery that has existed since before 1960? In the UK and Germany, it is clear that some longer-standing and traditionally inclined producers are engaged in a race to the bottom on price, hiding behind pedantic definitions of quality rather than challenging consumers with the sort of more assertive flavours that are one of the hallmarks of the craft beers that are shaking up the market everywhere.

Secondly, should we be considering the proportion of total beer volume or of total sales, and if the latter, should this be the amount received by the brewers or by the end-point sellers? Craft beers tend to be both stronger and more labour intensive, factors that contribute significantly to the fact that the same measure of a craft beer will probably cost 30–50% more than an industrial brew. Which is not to deny that some retailers have a propensity to pimp the c-word in order to raise their margins.

Thirdly, there is the question of ownership versus intention. Can a global brewing company with a business built around shipping vast volumes of consumable liquids cheaply be expected to make carefully crafted beers in small quantities? Or if a global brewer buys a craft brand, is it ever going to be likely to retain craft production principles long-term?

Staking out how much of the beer in the world should now be considered "craft" is a matter of educated conjecture, though one Californian market analyst suggested early in 2017 that current global sales at the brewery gate stand at around US$85 billion per annum – a figure

that in many countries will quadruple by the time the beer hits the glass —
and projected a six-fold rise by 2025, based on current global trends.

In less than 15 years, craft and traditional beers have switched from
being quaint niche products to mainstream commodities, acknowledged
as an essential and prominent part of the portfolio of any beer-selling
company that wants to stay in business. Not bad for a small industry born
out of taste, hope and individuality.

Meanwhile, AB InBev has now become the world's largest brewer by
far, by January 2017 holding 30% of global production and 50% of the
profit from beer making, and posting a projected EBITDA (earnings before
interest, tax, depreciation and amortization) of 38%. Yet in reality, the
volume of industrial beer being drunk is falling steadily in most established
markets and even in places like China, once seen as the key area of
hoped-for expansion. The African market, a large percentage of which was
acquired through the bank loans that enabled it to buy SAB Miller in 2016,
is in effect their last throw of the dice.

Be in no doubt that we live in interesting times.

THE BEERS

WESTERN EUROPE

BELGIUM

Long considered a Mecca for beer aficionados, Belgium's brewing greatness lies in the sheer variety of what is brewed within its borders, from spontaneously fermented lambics to monstrously strong and complex dark ales. A new generation is now appearing on the scene to evolve and define further the country's brewing culture, which is a delightful bonus.

IV SAISON

Jandrain-Jandrenouille, Jandrain-Jandrenouille, Wallonian Brabant; 6.5%

Arriving fully formed at the inception of its brewery in 2007, IV Saison is the beer that enhanced the most popular Wallonian *saison* style by using US hop varieties.

ALPAÏDE

Nieuwhuys, Hoegaarden, Flemish Brabant; 10%

Just up the road from Hoegaarden's only independent brewery is a small brewhouse serving the family pub and a few distributors, creating a highly accomplished, strong and dark brown unclassifiable brew.

AMBRÉE

Caracole, Falmignoul, Namur; 7.5%

Arguably the classic contemporary take on an old-fashioned Wallonian *ambrée*, managing a neat balance of subtle fruity flavours, some with light caramel and a slightly burned edge.

ARDENNE STOUT

Bastogne, Sibret, Luxembourg; 8%

A strong stout that offers remarkably easy drinking by being softened with spelt, then smoothed out further in oak casks. The best of a good range from a rising star of the Ardennes.

AVERBODE

Huyghe, Melle, East Flanders; 7.5%

A brewery renowned for its massive range of gimmick beers has managed to epitomize the so-called abbey style in this clean and direct, unmistakably Belgian, medium-strong pale ale.

BLACK

Bellevaux, Malmedy, Liège; 6.3%

Dark winter ale based on the brewery owner's taste memory for the UK brew Theakston's Old Peculier from way back in 1975. And it comes eerily close.

BLACK MAMBA

Sainte-Hélène, Florenville, Luxembourg; 4.5%

This slowly evolving tiny Ardennaise brewery is finally settling down after playing about for 20 years. Progress is typified by this US-hopped, UK-styled simple but tasty stout.

BLOSSOMGUEUZE

Lindemans, Vlezenbeek, Flemish Brabant; 6%

This seventh-generation brewery has engulfed the family farm, turning it over to making lighter, sharp lambics that now include both a basil version and this one, with elderflower.

BRUNE

Abbaye des Rocs, Montignies-sur-Roc, Hainaut; 9%

Complex all-malt, delicately spiced ale that starts sweet but gains depth down

ICONIC BREWERY

WESTMALLE

Malle, Antwerp

The first and largest of the breweries that operate within the walls of a Trappist abbey, overseen by members of the Order and for the purpose of supporting the Order and its charities. Important to the development of the modern *dubbel* and *tripel* styles of Belgian ale. Best known for its deep, roasted, medium-strength **Westmalle Dubbel** (7%) and the heavier, cellar-evolving, almost honeyed golden blond **Tripel** (9.5%), but also able to craft **Extra** (4.8%), a delightfully simple blond ale once reserved for the abbey's refectory.

ICONIC BREWERIES

CANTILLON

Anderlecht, Brussels

Not the largest or oldest lambic brewery, but by far the most expressive, notable for their provocative style, originality in new products, openness to brewery visits and sheer persistence. Beers, mostly bottled, include fermented-out old lambic **Grand Cru Bruocsella** (5%); the rule-breaking, all-malt and spontaneously fermented **Iris** (6.5%); a delightfully delicate cherry-steeped **Kriek** (5.5%); and the ground-breaking **Saint Lamvinus** (6.5%), steeped with grapes from Bordeaux.

RODENBACH [BAVARIA]

Roeselare, West Flanders

The largest-remaining creator of historically commonplace, recently near-extinct oak-aged brown ale, housed in large oak tuns for expert blending with younger brews. A work of distinctively Flemish preservation best expressed in sharp and caramelly, filtered and bottled **Rodenbach Grand Cru** (6%); upstaged occasionally in the single-cask **Vintage** (7%); and joined by cleverly cherry-steeped variants, including the recently revived **Alexander** (6%).

the bottle. Made by one of Belgium's first "new wave" breweries, founded back in 1979.

BUFFALO 1907

Van den Bossche, Sint-Lievens-Esse, East Flanders; 6.5%

Pure nostalgia drives the support for this authentic early-20th-century burned variant on a routine brown ale, from a fifth-generation family brewery better known for its stronger exports.

BUSH PRESTIGE

Dubuisson, Pipaix, Hainaut; 13%

Dubuisson has brewed an English barley wine since 1933, and Bush Prestige (aka Scaldis Prestige in some markets) is the late-bottled variant that spends an additional six months in oak casks before bottling to smooth out and evolve its character.

CUVÉE DES JACOBINS ROUGE

Omer Vander Ghinste, Bellegem, West Flanders; 5.5%

Created by injecting cultured wild yeast into a beer that then spends 18 months in oak, and originally only a mixer beer used in blending, it was released raw when a US importer tasted its potential.

CUVÉE VAN DE KEIZER BLAUW

Het Anker, Mechelen, Antwerp; 11%

Brewed annually on 24 February, the birthday of Hapsburg Emperor Charles V, who grew up in the town. No-holds-barred brewing makes a strong dark ale that improves on cellaring for a decade at least.

DE KONINCK

De Koninck [Duvel-Moortgat], Antwerp; 5.2%

The beer of the city of Antwerp is this light, sweetish pale ale that dates back centuries. It is always best when drunk locally and on draught in its synonymous glass, known as a *bolleke* (pronounced "ball-e-ke").

EXTRA BRUIN

Achelse Kluis, Hamont-Achel, Antwerp; 9.5%

The standout beer from the newest of Belgium's six Trappist breweries. A hearty, near-black winter ale noted for its intense malt, a little sherrying and a dab of hop.

GOUDENBAND

Liefmans [Duvel-Moortgat], Oudenaarde, East Flanders; 8%

Now brewed elsewhere but still matured at the Liefmans warehouse to create a somewhat sanitized yet evolving recreation of the softer type of aged brown ale.

GRAND CRU

St-Feuillien, Le Roeulx, Hainaut; 9.5%

Famed for making beers in huge bottles and able after decades to be self-sufficient, this massive but strangely delicate, golden-blond top-of-the-range ale is the must-try brewery statement.

GRANDE RÉSERVE

Chimay, Baileux, Hainaut; 9%

The bigger-bottled version of Chimay Blue, the strongest and consistently best regular beer from Belgium's second-largest Trappist brewery.

GULDEN DRAAK

Van Steenberge, Ertvelde, East Flanders; 10.5%

Try to ignore the white plastic bottle wrapping and get to the ruby-brown strong ale inside to find, from an ardently Flemish brewer, a lusciously near-sweet brew of balanced ferocity.

HERCULE STOUT

Légendes, Ellezelles, Hainaut; 9%

A modern Belgian classic from the range produced at Légendes's smaller brewery, this strong, dry stout dominated by roasted malt is probably unspiced yet incorporates billowing spicy aromas.

HOP RUITER

Scheldebrouwerij, Meer, Antwerp; 8%

This Dutch-spirited brewery is parked next to a beer hypermarket and distribution centre on the Belgian side of the border. This hybrid *tripel*-cum-double IPA is the best in the range thanks to complex hopping.

JAN DE LICHTE

Glazen Toren, Erpe-Mere, Flemish Brabant; 7.5%

One of the most accomplished newer small breweries in Flanders that concentrates on making fulsome takes on classic beer styles, like this stronger, more citrus, doughier take on a Belgian wheat beer.

KAPITTEL PRIOR

Van Eecke, Watou, West Flanders; 9%

Watou's smaller brewery is also the Leroy family's smaller one. Deep, dark, pear-dropped Prior is the second strongest in the Kapittel range. At its best from a 75cl bottle that has been cellared for a decade.

KRIEK MARIAGE PARFAIT

Boon, Lembeek, Flemish Brabant; 8%

The honorary professor of lambic culture and the story of beer, Frank Boon produces this top-of-the-range cherry lambic by adding his best cherries to his best lambic casks and then waiting until its time has come.

KRIEKENLAMBIK

Girardin, Sint Ulriks-Kapelle, Flemish Brabant; 5%

The raw draught cherry lambic produced on this old Payottenland farm is still found at local bars like De Rare Vos in Schepdaal, baffling beer lovers with its absurd classical beauty.

LUPULUS

Les 3 Fourquets, Bovigny, Luxembourg; 8.5%

One of a host of well-run small craft-orientated breweries in Wallonia making a range of hop-forward Lupulus beers, among which this original blond version is arguably the best.

MALHEUR BIÈRE BRUT

Malheur, Buggenhout, East Flanders;11%

Applying similar techniques to making beer that the wine growers around Épernay employ in producing their local plonk creates this golden malt wine that manages to be light, ultra-spritzy and heady.

MANO NEGRA

Alvinne, Moen, West Flanders; 10%

Strong black ale, nearest to an Imperial stout, sometimes pepped up by spirits-cask exposure. The most consistent beer from a brewery dominated by experimentation.

ORVAL

Orval, Villers-devant-Orval, Luxembourg; 6.2%

Once unique and still rare, presented in a beautiful bottle, this pungent Trappist brew from deep in the Ardennes is the result of dry-hopping a well-made pale ale and refermenting it with *Brettanomyces*.

CAN'T-MISS BREWERIES

BLAUGIES

Blaugies, Hainaut

Family-run farmhouse brewery creating a unique range of beers to their personal preference. The star is yeasty buckwheat **Saison d'Epeautre** (6%); dry blond **La Bière Darbyste** (5.8%) is more elusive; heavy, earthy **La Moneuse** (8%) is a *saison* of sorts; while US collaboration **La Vermontoise** (6%) is a mid-Atlantic *saison*–IPA combo.

DE RANKE

Dottignies, Hainaut

Great beer designers revered by other brewers for bringing hops to Belgian ales and reviving *versnijsbier*, or "cut" beer, blended from lambics and ale. Summery pale ale **XX Bitter** (6%) is crammed with hops, delicately; **Guldenberg** (8%) succeeds in up-hopping a *tripel*; equally potent **Noir de Dottignies** (8.5%) defies easy styling; while **Cuvée de Ranke** (7%) ladles heavy lambic overtones onto sound pale ale.

DOCHTER VAN DE KORENAAR

Baarle-Hertog, Antwerp

On the Dutch border in many different ways, capturing the new Dutch spirit with a Belgian twist in internationally modern **Belle Fleur IPA** (6%); newer doubled-up **Extase** (8.5%); dry, vanilla stout **Charbon** (7%); and pan-Belgian amber-brown **Embrasse** (9%). Oak-aged and spirits-cask versions also appear.

DOLLE

Esen, West Flanders

Pioneering revivalists in the 1980s now producing singular beers like the perfectly complex, sharp, dark and messy keeper **Oerbier** (9%); best fresh, golden hoppy blond **Arabier** (8%); lush light amber Easter brew **Boskeun** (10%); and heavy, succulent Christmas stunner **Stille Nacht** (12%). Special reserve editions matured in spirits casks crop up, too.

DRIE FONTEINEN

Beersel, Flemish Brabant

Passion-fuelled producers of classic Payottenland lambics. **Lambik** (5%) and **Faro** (5.5%) are only found on draught regularly at the café–restaurant in Beersel and at the nearby, brewery-run Lambikodroom. The authentic cherry beers, **Oude Kriek** (5%) and original **Schaerbeekse Kriek** (6%), along with their gueuzes, travel the world in bottles.

CAN'T-MISS BREWERIES

DUPONT

Tourpes, Hainaut

Squeaky-clean, eco-enthusiastic brewery in an idyllic farm setting. Responsible in part via importation for the US beer revolution, with beers such as the authentic light *saison* **Biolégère** (3.5%); the pioneering, genre-defining **Saison Dupont** (6.5%); the strong blond, faintly rustic, cleverly balanced **Moinette Blond** (8.5%); and the outstanding, dry-hopped Christmas-beer-turned-mainstay **Avec les Bons Voeux de la Brasserie Dupont** (9.5%).

RULLES

Rulles, Luxembourg

Village visionary from La Gaume, making near-perfect local beers that travel the world on merit. Fragrantly hopped **Estivale** (5.2%) lights up the summer; the practice-perfect **Blonde** (7%) is possibly the best in Belgium; as is the **Triple** (8.4%). **Stout Rullquin** (7%) is what happens to their brown ale when spiked with 10% of Tilquin lambic.

DE LA SENNE

Brussels

Attitudinally inventive, challengingly straightforward multi-talented brewers who lead a generation. Ever-so-simple **Taras Boulba** (4.5%) is their hoppy light ale; **Stouterik** (4.5%) is the multi-award-winning, standard light stout; **Jambe-de-Bois** (8%) is the cosy triple with a complicated aftertaste; and the 100% *Brettanomyces*-fermented **Bruxellensis** (6.5%) pushes all the buttons put there by ancient Orval.

ST. BERNARDUS

Watou, West Flanders

Originally created to make beers for Trappist Westvleteren Brewery, now expanded to serve the world. Their **Wit** (5.5%) is most expressive of the Belgian style; **Prior 8** (8%) is brown, fruity, complex and good-looking; **Abt 12** (10%) is the heavyweight, fruity, bittersweet, self-styled *quadrupel*; and **Christmas Ale** (10%) is the dark and spicy winter warmer.

STRUISE

Oostvleteren, West Flanders

Determinedly boundary-pushing show-offs with a lot to show off about. Famed for long-aged, strong and soured heavy beers like heavy, dark **Pannepot** (10%), the lighter-hued and aged winter ale **Tsjeeses** (10%), an absurdly strong Imperial stout **Black Albert** (13%) and more recently for the cask-aged **Ypres** (7%). Ageing in reused casks is common.

OUDBEITJE

Hanssens Artisanaal, Dworp, Flemish Brabant; 6%

The lambic world's only authentic strawberry lambic loses the fruit's flavours within weeks, but retains a haunting and unmistakable aroma that cuts across the natural sourness of the lambic underlay.

OUDE KRIEK

Oud Beersel, Beersel, Flemish Brabant; 6.5%

Created largely from bespoke brews made at Boon (*see* page 42) and steeped to a unique recipe, this darker-than-average, earthy and rustic bottled cherry lambic is one of the classics of the style.

OUDE LAMBIEK

De Cam, Gooik, Flemish Brabant; 5%

This small *gueuze* blender and lambic steeper matures other brewers' lambics to create beers of distinctly different character. Bottling at the end of maturation creates this ultra-dry single-cask lambic.

PETRUS AGED PALE

De Brabandere, Bavikhove, West Flanders; 7.3%

Arguably crude but unquestionably important, this was the first oak-aged mixer beer to be allowed out on its own, having been formerly used only in the creation of lesser blends.

PILS

Strubbe, Ichtegem, West Flanders; 5%

Founded in 1830, the same year as Belgium itself, this sixth-generation small family business creates almost every style of beer in Belgium, including perhaps the country's hoppiest and tastiest blond lager.

PORTER

Viven, Sijsele, West Flanders; 7%

Commissioning their beers from the Proef brewery at Lochristi and seeking unashamedly international flavour profiles, this drinks distributor has the best range of Belgian-made US-style beers, including this hoppy stout porter.

QUETSCHE

Tilquin, Bierghes, Wallonian Brabant; 6.4%

The lambic world's new star has pushed the envelope wisely with this clever and delicious, sharp-edged yet sumptuous plum lambic. Expect variants using other plum varieties.

ROCHEFORT 10

Abbaye Notre Dame de Saint-Rémy, Rochefort, Namur; 11.3%

One of three beers made in a classic copper-kettled brewhouse beneath a crucifix. A many-layered, heady, dried-fruit and caramelled elixir, demanding room-temperature service.

BREWERIES TO WATCH

BRUSSELS

Beer Project, Brussels

Brewing mostly at Anders in Limburg, to create modern Belgian takes on IPA **Delta** (6.5%), black IPA **Dark Sister** (6.5%) and strong *hefeweizen* **Grosse Bertha** (7%).

BZART

Niel-bij-As, Limburg

Beer club experimentalists maturing mostly Oud Beersel brews on Champagne yeast for their **Kriekenlambiek** (8%), **Session Triple** (6.3%) and **Geuze Cuvée** (8%).

DE LEITE

Ruddervoorde, West Flanders

Jobbing new waver now developing prowess with new brews such as lactic **Fils à Papa** (6.5%), herbal **Enfant Terrible d'Hiver** (8.2%) and vinous **Cuvée Mam'zelle** (8.5%).

DE PLUKKER

Poperinge, West Flanders

Hop-farm brewery using local varieties in regular pale **Keikoppenbier** (6.1%) and annual specials **Single Green Hop** (5.5%) and **All Inclusive IPA** (8%).

EN STOEMELINGS

Brussels

Shoestring adventurers creating off-centre ales like **Noirølles** (5%) porter and unclassifiable pale **Curieuse Neus** (7%).

HOF TEN DORMAAL

Tildonk, Flemish Brabant

Hit-and-miss creators of myriad one-off, barrel-aged **BA Project** creations based on solid dark **Donker** or **Blond** ales (10–12%).

LIENNE

Lierneux, Liège

Husband and wife team gaining confidence and skills, best demonstrated in delicate hoppy **Grandgousier** (5%), **Noire** (5.5%) porter and heavier **Brune** (8%).

VERZET

Anzegem, West Flanders

Three young friends making waves with variants of oak-aged **Oud Bruin** (6%), **Golden Tricky IPA** (7.5%) and stronger **Rebel Local** (8.5%).

VLIEGENDE PAARD

Nomadic, West Flanders

Award-winning contracting brewer creating beers under the **Préaris** label, including the single-hopped **Session Ale** (4.5–5%), **Quadrupel** (10%) and variously barrel-aged **Grand Cru** (10%), mostly at the Proef brewery.

SAISON

Cazeau, Templeuve, Hainaut; 5%

Better known for its Tournay brands
of more classical Wallonian beer styles,
this twice-revived brewery also makes
this spritzy summer variant on a *saison*,
with added elderflower.

SAISONNEKE

Belgoo, Sint-Pieters-Leeuw, Flemish
Brabant; 4.4%

The lightest, simplest and catchiest
beer from a talented Payottenland
ale brewery that had been practising
elsewhere for some years.

SCOTCH

Silly, Silly, Hainaut; 8%

This long-established Wallonian
village brewery derives its most
interesting beer from a pre-1914
version of a Scotch ale or wee heavy.
It is sometimes enhanced by whisky-
cask-ageing, but is always dark, sweet,
rich and playful.

SPECIAL

De Ryck, Herzele, East Flanders; 5.5%

This small-town family brewery, more
famous for its Arend brands, also makes
this masterpiece of sophisticated
innocence, the supreme example of the
easy-drinking *special* or *spéciale* style
of pale ale.

STRAFFE HENDRIK
HERITAGE

Halve Maan, Brugge, West Flanders;
11%

The gradual regrowth of the Vanneste
family's brewery in Bruges has now
expanded to include some exceptional
beers, such as this strong black ale that
is developed in oak for a year before
being bottled.

TRIPEL KLOK

Boelens, Belsele, East Flanders; 8.5%

A brewery in a drinks merchant's
premises that began by making
honeyed beers and has gone on to
create this exceptional and ever-
evolving interpretation of a *tripel*,
with not a bee in sight.

STYLE SPOTLIGHT

GUEUZE – THE WORLD'S MOST UNLIKELY HERITAGE BEER

First, mash a grain bill designed for wheat beer; then brew with old hops that have lost aroma and bitterness but retained preservative qualities; next, cool and inoculate with wild yeasts overnight in a shallow metal cooler; and in the morning filter it into oak barrels or tuns and let sit for six months to three years. Decant and blend, bottle and wait.

An *oude* or *vieille geuze* or *gueuze* should shock the nose with its strong aromas of old books, musty leather or a hay barn in late summer, then confuse the palate with its spritzy mouthfeel and tart, invasive edges set off against a base redolent of grain. Approach its sharper forms as if they were a sparkling wine in a beery cloak and ignore your immediate reaction. Hold back judgement for your next encounter, too, as it can sometimes take years to properly understand an unlikely type of beer fermented only by wild yeast that happens across its path.

The best proponents of this brewing art form are all from Brussels and the surrounding region, the Payottenland. Cantillon with their light citrus **Gueuze** and best blend **Lou Pepe**; Drie Fonteinen with **Oude Geuze** and long-cellared **Vintage**; Boon (*see* page 42) with **Oude Geuze** and his upscale **Mariage Parfait**; Girardin's **Gueuze 1882** when sporting a black label; Lindemans light and lemony **Oude Geuze Cuvée René**; and four non-brewing blenders – Tilquin with bottled **Oude Geuze à l'Ancienne** and draught **Gueuze** lambic; De Cam with **Oude Geuze**; Oud Beersel for their **Oude Geuze**; and Hanssens Artisanaal **Oude Geuze**.

TROUBADOUR MAGMA

The Musketeers, Ursel, East Flanders; 9%

One of the longer-standing teams of beer designers acquired their own brewery recently to make this, their triple-strong, Czech-hopped IPA, among others.

VALEIR EXTRA

Contreras, Gavere, East Flanders; 6.5%

Hard-working but fairly conservative small family brewery in the Schelde valley making a typically Flemish Valeir range, extra to which is this standout, cleverly hopped, Belgian-influenced IPA.

VICARIS GENERAAL

Dilewyns, Dendermonde, East Flanders; 8.5%

In 2010, the four Dilewyns sisters were gifted a state-of-the art brewery by their father, where among other Vicaris beers they make this hefty, rich and fruity red-brown ale, dedicated to their grandma.

VICHTENAAR

Verhaeghe, Vichte, West Flanders; 5.1%

Better known for their Duchesse de Bourgogne, the Verhaeghe brothers' lighter, less-well-travelled, oak-aged brown ale is sharper and probably truer to the old local Kortrijk styles.

WESTVLETEREN BLOND

Sint-Sixtusabdij, Westveleteren, West Flanders; 5.8%

A rustic pale ale that is the simplest and best-made beer from this Trappist brewery, which bears its mostly unwelcome and partly unearned adulation with dignity. Best when drunk fresh at the on-site abbey café.

WITKAP PATER STIMULO

Slaghmuylder, Ninove, East Flanders; 6%

A close look at this old family brewery reveals most of its range to be off-centre, none more so than this yeasty, grassy, slightly citrus blond ale, best in the bottle or else locally on draught.

GERMANY

There is probably no country as universally synonymous with beer as Germany. The latter part of the 20th century was not, however, kind to the birthplace of lager and Oktoberfest, as a lessening appetite for beer coupled with some industry consolidation resulted in declining brewery numbers and tougher times for those that remained. Thankfully, that situation has now changed and German breweries are not only once again growing in size and quantity, but also expressing renewed creativity in both the creation of new beers and the revival of old, almost forgotten styles.

7:45 ESCALATION

CREW Republic, Unterscheißheim, Munich, Bavaria; 8.3%

Of the regular beers from this 2011 *kraft* pioneer, the most challenging to Bavarian brewing orthodoxy is this powerful and strong IPA, resinous with US hops yet managing reasonable balance despite its bitterness. Sacrilegious but arty.

1838ER

Ferdinand Schumacher, Düsseldorf, North Rhine-Westphalia; 5%

Created for the brewery's 175th anniversary in 2013 as an up-market *altbier* with more aroma and fruitier hopping, this proved popular enough

to stay in the range. Whether other new takes follow remains to be seen.

ABRAXXXAS

Freigeist Bierkultur, nomadic; 6%

A "free spirit" operation that since 2010 has been reviving defunct styles and pushing others to extremes, as with this smoky, pepped-up take on the north German, light and lactic style of wheat beer called *lichtenhainer*.

ALT

Im Füchschen, Düsseldorf, North Rhine-Westphalia; 4.5%

One of the four classic *altbier* brewers that can be found in the old city, or Altstadt. Perhaps the most aromatic, but also earthier than others of its ilk, it is best sampled in its heavily food-slanted taphouse.

ALT

Zum Schlüssel, Düsseldorf, North Rhine-Westphalia; 5%

Another of the four historic brewers that preserve the *altbier* tradition in Düsseldorf's Altstadt, where gravity-feed, same-day-service casks dispense a precise, light-copper-hued beer with a bit of caramelly sweetness.

ASAM BOCK

Weltenburger Kloster, Kelheim, Bavaria; 6.9%

A frequently prize-winning *doppelbock*, all the more surprising for having to punch well above its weight. Sweet and intense, but filled with endless nuances of flavour, from a former monastery on the banks of the Danube.

AUFSESSER DUNKEL

Rothenbach, Aufseß, Bavaria; 4.7%

Not the punchiest beer from this village *brauereigasthof*, or guesthouse brewery, but an alluring, dryish, oddly maroon-coloured, roasty-toasty quaffer that sets you up for the rest of the range.

BAMBERGER HERREN PILS

Keesmann, Bamberg, Bavaria; 4.6%

One of the lightest-coloured lagers in the world, more *helles* than pilsner with its delicate, floral, grassy and innocent-

ICONIC BREWERY

G SCHNEIDER & SOHN

Kelheim, Bavaria

The family brewery that re-invigorated Bavarian white beer back in 1872, recreating a style that predated the *Reinheitsgebot*. From the complex and spicy **Mein Original** (5.4%), also known as Tap 7 or, more colloquially, simply Schneider Weisse, they pushed forward to luscious, spicy wheat *doppelbock* **Mein Aventinus** (Tap 6; 8.2%) and on to the absurdly but deliciously intense **Aventinus Eisbock** (12%). A collaboration with the Brooklyn Brewery (*see* page 208) yielded the fresh, aromatically hopped **Meine Hopfenweisse** (Tap 5; 8.2%), which has gone on to become a style unto itself (*see* page 17).

ICONIC BREWERIES

HELLER-BRÄU TRUM (SCHLENKERLA)

Bamberg, Bavaria

The family brewery responsible for the global fame of Bamberg brewing, the survival of smoked beers and their modern-day renaissance. The **Aecht Schlenkerla Rauchbier** range includes the unmistakable if indelicate smoke-sweated brown **Märzen** (5.1%); barbecued, sweet-cured autumnal **Urbock** (6.5%); heavyweight and heady, local Easter treat **Fastenbier** (5.5%); and winter's oak-smoked **Eiche Doppelbock** (8%), an exquisite strong lager that legitimizes smoked malt at the highest level of brewing achievement.

UERIGE

Düsseldorf, North Rhineland-Westphalia

The brewery at the heart of Düsseldorf's Altstadt that creates the epitome of the local lagered ale known simply as *alt*. The uncarbonated, auburn and bready **Uerige Alt** (4.7%) served in its taphouse is now captured in the spritzier, bottled **Nicht Filtriert** (4.7%). Brewed only for the city's annual carnival special, the availability of the stronger **Sticke** (6%) is now prolonged by bottling. In recent years it has been joined by *alt*–*bock* fusion beer **Doppelsticke** (8.5%) as, swan-like, the style begins to spread its wings.

looking countenance. Always more delicious when drunk at the brewery's handsome taphouse.

BERLINER KINDL WEISSE

Schultheiss [Oetker], Berlin; 3%

The Berlin-style wheat beer that survived the era of standardization by losing character while heading mainstream is (very) slowly regaining its light, hazy, lactic, thirst-defeating individuality.

BLACK IPA

Heidenpeters, Berlin; 5.6%

From a small brewery located in the cellar of the German capital's Markthalle Neun, this occasional release boasts a plummy nose with blackberry tones and similarly fruity body, with date and light citrus notes alongside a moderate bitterness.

BOCK

Kneitinger, Regensburg, Bavaria; 6.8%

One of the south's best bocks, deep ruby brown and full of Vienna malt that comes through at every stage from the aroma to the toffee-sweet follow-through, so much so that the hopping is barely noticeable.

BOSCH BRAUNBIER

Bosch, Bad Laasphe, North Rhineland-Westphalia; 5%

A beer not necessarily loved by the new beer cognoscenti, this simple, workaday, resinous and nutty brown offering is in an old local style from a brewery with heart as well as technical excellence.

CURATOR DOPPELBOCK

Ettaler, Ettal, Bavaria; 9%

A modern brewery and distillery based in and part of a Benedictine monastery near Oberammergau, creating numerous beers of superior quality and character, including this deep, heavy, multi-toned dark lager intended for nights of quiet contemplation.

DER DUNKLE REH-BOCK

Reh, Lohndorf, Bavaria; 7.1%

An interesting dark *bock*, with both sweet and dry aspects, the former hitting maple-syrup notes and the latter in a surprisingly harsh finish, due we think to being Franconian rather than flawed.

DIPLOM PILS

Waldhaus, Waldhaus, Baden-Württemburg; 4.9%

What some might consider a fairy-tale German pils – light, crisp, floral, beautiful in the glass and profoundly quaffable. It really does exist, but you will have to take a walk in the southern Black Forest.

DOPPEL-ALT

Giesinger, Munich, Bavaria; 7%

For time out from *helles* in a beer garden, try this modern southern interpretation of a northern

hausbrauerei and its cheekily contrived, potent take on an *altbier*, amber with notes of toast and dried fruit.

DUNKEL

Kreuzberger Kloster, Bischofsheim an der Rhön, Bavaria; 5.4%

Light golden-brown *dunkel*, made within the grounds of an inhabited Franciscan abbey. Slightly stronger than many, allowing a more intense light caramel flavour to pervade.

DUNKEL NATURTRÜB

Schöre, Tettnang, Baden-Württemburg; 4.8%

Locally famed guesthouse brewery in hop country, which cracks out some classic brews on a small scale, like this well-constructed, dark, traditional *Münchener* that barely needs its local hops.

DUNKLES

Goldener Engel, Ingelheim, Rhineland-Palatinate; 4.8%

After spending a lot of money constructing and beautifying their exceptional modern brewpub, the Winkelser family made it a worthy destination by creating this clean, tar-laced, black *dunkel* with a lingering finish.

DUNKLES KELLERBRÄU

Seinsheimer, Seinsheim, Bavaria; 4.9%

Technically just outside Oberfranken, but spiritually at its heart, the flagship

CAN'T-MISS BREWERIES

AYINGER

Aying, Bavaria

Unusual for being independent and family owned yet relatively well known internationally. The brewery's range is broad, if traditional, led on the global stage by the molasses-accented, gently bitter **Celebrator Doppelbock** (6.7%). Stellar wheat beers include the blond **Bräuweisse** (5.1%) and amber, yeasty and equally exemplary **Ur-Weisse** (5.8%), while the centenary of the brewery in 1978 is still celebrated in the form of the firmly malty **Jahrhundert Bier** (5.5%).

BAYERISCHE STAATSBRAUEREI WEIHENSTEPHAN

Freising, Bavaria

Regardless of whether this Bavarian state-owned brewery truly is the world's oldest in continuous production, it unquestionably makes some of the nation's finest session beers, like mousse-topped, cloudy blond, banana-laced **Hefeweissbier** (5.4%) and its auburn equivalent **Hefeweissbier Dunkel** (5.3%). It can also go serious with the intensely focused and amplified dark *weizenbock* **Korbinian** (7.4%) or its equally ornate golden dance partner **Vitus** (7.7%), making this a reference brewery for any wheat beer producer.

CAMBA BAVARIA

Truchtlaching, Bavaria

Almost iconic for its insistent infusion of the IPA concept into the long-

established Bavarian beer culture, with beers like the gently questioning **German IPA** (6.5%), the stronger, assertive and slightly cocky double IPA **Ei Pi Ai** (8%) and just plain ballsy "Imperial black IPA" **Black Shark** (8.5%). It is, however, with the placing of a tropical-fruity hop in an otherwise traditionally banana-ish wheat beer to make **Nelson Sauvin Weissbier** (5.2%) that the wickedness of their inventive streak is best revealed.

GÄNSTALLER

Hallerndorf, Bavaria

Arguably modern German brewing's best brewing talent. Good enough to pioneer Mandarina Bavaria hops in a striking **Kellerbier** (5.3%) and craft a stellar **Zwickelpils** (5%) that is head and shoulders above the sea of others sharing the same moniker, but also comfortable with big beers such as chewy, rich wheat bouillon **Weizenator** (8.1%) and the ground-breaking 10 layers of smoked-powered nuance in **Affumicator** (9.6%).

of this small-town brewery is a ruddy-brown *kellerbier* with great balance that finds room for a barnyardy aroma and apple-pie notes within a sound mainstream *dunkel*.

EXPORT HEFE WEIZEN

Wolferstetter, Vilshofen, Bavaria; 5.5%

A full-on yet nicely balanced cloudy wheat beer, dominated by neither clove nor banana but led by a bready and fresh grain character. Made by a well-established and sound local brewery.

FASSBIER

Krug Geisfeld, Geisfeld, Bavaria; 4.9%

The name means "draught beer", which is how it is at its best, preferably drawn by gravity. Golden amber in colour, it is rustic, herbal-hoppy and oddly caramelized, far from a *helles* but neither *dunkel* nor Vienna.

FESTBIER DUNKEL

Stern-Bräu Scheubel, Schlüsselfeld, Bavaria; 5.5%

Increasingly in regular, year-round production, this quite delicately smoked dark lager, from a Franconian "farm brewery in a village" with strong rural values, is certainly deserving of more widespread recognition.

GÖRCHLA

Höhn, Memmelsdorf, Bavaria; 4.9%

Classically Franconian in its way, this light, hazy, dryish and earthy *landbier* is the effective centrepiece of a small village brewery that has developed into a polished, traditional guesthouse and local restaurant.

HAUSBRÄU

Kommunbrauhaus Seßlacher, Seßlach, Bavaria; 4.1%

A sort of *dunkel landbier* brewed in the spirit of *zoigl* (*see* page 63), if not the method. Herbal and earthy with enough sweetness to appeal to the mainstream drinker, this is a beer for quaffing rather than sipping.

HEFE-PILS

Winkler, Velburg/Lengenfeld, Bavaria; 4.7%

With an obvious name for a *zwickelbier*-cum-*kellerbier*, this delivers exactly what the name suggests – slight haziness, with grassy, earthy edges to its sweet floral maltiness and a satisfying hop bite in the finish.

HELIOS

Braustelle, Cologne, North Rhine-Westphalia; 4.8%

This pub brewery has since 2001 been pushing envelopes and changing perceptions, but its best beer is a blond lagered ale in the local style, a *kölsch* that, for now at least, will not speak its name.

HOCHFÜRST PILSENER

Hacklberg, Passau, Bavaria; 5%

A crisp, light and hoppy well-made blond lager that retains its bitterness throughout. Dominant in its home town, located next to the Austrian border in the far southwest, but still known elsewhere.

HOPFENPFLÜCKER PILS

Pyraser, Thalmässing, Bavaria; 5%

What could very well be Germany's best intensely hoppy beer is an annual indulgence, packed as it is with freshly harvested green hops and many-layered. It is produced by a brewery that makes a wide range of other fine beers year round.

HOPFENSTOPFER INCREDIBLE PALE ALE

Häffner, Bad Rappenau; Baden-Württemburg; 6.1%

One of the regulars from this otherwise conventional brewery's "hop shot" range, which appears in myriad forms through the year, highlighting the use of style-specific hop experiments, in this case Taurus, Saphir, Nelson Sauvin and Cascade.

INSELHOPF

Feierling, Freiburg, Baden-Württemberg; 5.2%

The main and often only beer from this *hausbrauerei* and *biergarten* that brought new life to the site of the family's former brewery. Freshly hoppy, solidly malty, light and hazy, it is among the country's best *zwickelpils*.

KELLER BIER

St Georgen, Buttenheim, Bavaria; 4.9%

The house brew of an elegant village brewery, beers from which travel more often and to greater distances than do most. Bready and nutty malt flavours are consistent, but its fairly assertive hop streak sometimes vanishes on leaving Franconia.

KELLERBIER

Eichhorn, Dörfleins, Bavaria; 5%

Another of those Franconian *kellerbiers* that are best when drunk on the premises – a short bus ride out of Bamberg – but are quietly impressive in a grassy, yeasty, not-quite-defined sort of way in the bottle, too.

KELLERBIER

Griess, Geisfeld, Bavaria; 5.1%

The most distinctive of the beers made at this small family concern in the Franconian brewery belt east of Bamberg. Citrus leanings in the nose and body, and a tad herbal and yeasty, yet quite refreshing and hard to dislike.

KELLERBIER

Lieberth, Hallerndorf, Bavaria; 4.8%

From a small Franconian brewery that also makes a couple of neat blond lagers comes this one-of-a-kind house brew, pinging dried-fruit, herbal and citrus lightning forks into a breadily toned beer.

CAN'T-MISS BREWERIES

KLOSTERBRAUEREI ANDECHS

Andechs, Bavaria

A Benedictine monastery with one of the most picturesque *biergartens* in Bavaria and a wide assortment of excellent beers with which to enjoy its Alpine views. **Spezial Hell** (5.9%) is an easy-to-overlook refresher with emphasis on a luscious yet dry maltiness, while **Doppelbock Dunkel** (7%) is the showstopper with dense maltiness and a drying, warming finish. On the wheat beer side, **Weissbier Dunkel** (5%) adds appley and tropical-fruit notes to the expected aromas and flavours, while the **Weissbier Hell** (5.5%) tends toward the crisp and yeasty aspect.

RIEGELE

Augsburg, Bavaria

Augsburg's brewers have long played second fiddle to their colleagues in Munich, but this fifth-generation family brewer has no equal there.

With beers like blond **Feines Ur-Hell** (4.7%), it acts the local brewer, and with top heavyweight **Speziator** (7.5%) *doppelbock* it joins other leading Bavarians, while the chocolaty **Robust Porter** (5%) makes it a modernist and the **Biermanufaktur** range of specialties, including the intense, triple yeast-fermented **Magnus 16** (12%) and the fruit-forward **Simco 3** (5%), plus other unconventional, potent and barrel-aged offerings, defines it is an exponent of modern *kraft*.

SCHÖNRAM

Petting, Bavaria

The first long-established Bavaria family brewery to project itself into the era of craft beer, covering both traditional German styles and "new era" ales. Its across-the-board high quality Schönramer range is diverse enough to include fresh hop showboat **Grünhopfen Pils** (5%); both basic and barrel-aged versions of **Imperial Stout** (9.5%); hop-edged but classic **Dunkel** (5%); and the best-in-class, crisp light *helles*, **Surtaler Schankbier** (3.5%).

BREWERIES TO WATCH

BRAUKOLLECTIV

nomadic

Four young brewers cracking out beers at a couple of local breweries, highlighted by the Chinook, Cascade and Columbus hop-fuelled **Jacques West Coast IPA** (7.9%) and **Horst California Brown Ale** (6.2), which finds common ground for US and German hops.

BUDDELSHIP

Hamburg

Clear vision, an artistic eye and the ability to articulate in words and deeds has meant that even the dull Hamburg beer scene has been impacted by beers as diverse as session IPA **Deichbrise** (3.9%), schwarzbier **Kohlentrimmer** (5.3%) and Imperial stout **Doktor Schabel** (8%).

KELLERBIER

Roppelt, Stiebarlimbach, Bavaria; 4.9%

This classic Franconian house beer from near Forchheim is impossible to classify, but has citrus character throughout, with a hazy golden appearance that nudges amateurish yet ends up superbly complete on draught, albeit less so in the bottle.

KNUTTENFORZ SCHWARZBIER

Lüdde, Quedlinburg, Saxony-Anhalt; 4.9%

Deep brown with a tan head, the brewery takes the roasted malt route to building a schwarzbier, with hoppiness in relatively little evidence. This off-centre pub-based brewery also makes its own low-alcohol malzbier.

KÖLSCH

Gaffel Becker & Co, Cologne, North Rhineland-Westphalia; 4.8%

Oft-maligned for the sin of being both well marketed and widely available – even in cans, no less – this is probably the driest, arguably the hoppiest of its kind, with a quenchingly bitter finish.

KÖLSCH

Päffgen, Cologne, North Rhineland-Westphalia; 4.8%

From perhaps the most dedicated of the city's remaining kölsch brewers, this straw-blond beer boasts a full and aromatic hoppiness that is fresh and floral without being overly bitter.

KRÄUSEN-PILS

Elzacher Löwenbräu, Elzach,
Baden-Württemberg; 4.9%

Beautifully balanced unfiltered pils
from a small-scale family brewery in
the Black Forest brewing a good range
of other styles besides. Starts softly
with a floral Tettnang hop character
and builds to a long, balanced finish.

KYRITZER MORD
UND TOTSCHLAG

Klosterbrauerei Neuzelle, Neuzelle,
Brandenburg; 7.2%

An adventurous and almost *bock*-
like take on coal-black *schwarzbier*,
roasted to the extreme without acridity,
arguably begging the designation of a
doppelschwarz style.

LAGER BIER

Greifenklau, Bamberg, Bavaria; 4.9%

The best of the range from Bamberg's
least immediately impressive, greyish
taphouse is this solid, no-nonsense
helles, forgoing subtlety, gimmickry
or anything distinctive, yet a beer one
could stick to all night.

LAGERBIER HELL

Augustiner-Bräu, Munich, Bavaria;
5.2%

Of the six big Munich breweries
dominating the city and its
Oktoberfest, this is the only true
independent and its light, crisp but
smooth and fulsome blond lager is the
quintessential *Münchener helles*.

LOFFELDER DUNKEL

Staffelberg-Bräu, Loffeld, Bavaria;
5.2%

There is a wisp of smokiness and
decidedly savoury character to this dark
lager brewed just north of Bamberg,
with sweet grain, tobacco and roasted-
chestnut notes combining in the body
and an off-dry finish.

MAI-UR-BOCK

Einbecker, Einbeck, Lower Saxony;
6.5%

The paler (*heller*), springtime offering
from the brewery most associated
with the stronger north German lager
tradition. Gold of hue with a honey-ish,
toffee maltiness that plays host to
rising and drying hoppiness.

MEMMELSDORF
STÖFFLA

Drei Kronen, Memmelsdorf, Bavaria;
4.9%

A seasonal beer evolved into a regular
offering, this deep amber *rauchbier* has
a smoky aroma and smoked caramel
body, sweet upfront but slowly drying
to a wood-smoke finish.

MÖNCHSAMBACHER WEINACHTS-BOCK

Zehendner, Mönchsambach, Bavaria; 7%

Rightly famed for its *kellerbier*, this village brewery, located west of Bamberg, also makes this indulgently fulsome golden Christmas *bock* with bready, floral maltiness and touches of spice without spicing.

MÜHLEN KÖLSCH

Malzmühle Schwartz, Cologne, North Rhineland-Westphalia; 4.8%

Considered by many to be the definitive *kölsch*, this clever blond lagered ale has a rustic, gently fruity maltiness and mellow hop character. Best enjoyed in situ at the brewery's genial beer hall.

NANKENDORFER LANDBIER

Schroll, Nankendorf, Bavaria; 5.2%

Golden brown in colour, this has an earthiness to its aroma that translates well into the body, which is possessed of a richness beyond its alcohol content. Sweetish and caramel–chocolaty with a gentle nuttiness in the finish.

OKTOBERFESTBIER

Hofbräu München, Munich, Bavaria; 6.3%

The notion that there are two sorts of Oktoberfest *märzen* – a traditional, toastier one and a modern, sweetly malty one – is supported by this marvel of balance with a floral nose, sweet honeyed start and mildly bitter finish.

ORIGINAL LEIPZIGER GOSE

Bayerischer Bahnhof, Leipzig, Saxony, 4.5–4.6%

One of the early revivals of a style of beer originally from the north but popular in the city before 1919, based on wheat but dried by salting, although not really salty; tangy, a bit tart and spiced with coriander.

ORIGINAL RITTERGUTS GOSE

nomadic; 4.7%

Far from being *Reinheitsgebot*-compatible yet claimed by its commissioners to have been in production since 1824. Brewed for some years in Chemnitz. Global imitators of the style have tended to ape its malty, sourish and lightly spiced character ahead of its Leipziger counterpart.

PILS

Bischofshof, Regensburg, Bavaria; 4.7%

A typical Bavarian pils boasting perfumey aromas of noble hops and pilsner malt, looking polished with a chef's-hat mousse, promising and delivering a crisp, clean and deceptively direct blond lager.

PILSISSIMUS

Forschungsbrauerei, Perlach, Munich, Bavaria; 5.5%

An unusually fruity, aromatically hoppy blond lager from an early-20th-century family brewery on Munich's outskirts.

BREWERIES TO WATCH

HANSCRAFT & CO

nomadic

One of the more energetic groups of beer marketers, punching out impressive brews like **Single Hop Kellerpils** (4.9%) and IPA **Backbone Splitter** (6.6%), but with style and marketing high on the list of priorities.

INSEL-BRAUEREI

Rambin auf Rügen, Mecklenburg-Vorpommern

As close to Copenhagen as it is to Hamburg, this island brewery displays more Scandinavian creativity than German traditionalism in beers such as the off-dry, mocha-ish **Baltic Dubbel** (8.5%) and the lactic, sweet-and-sour **Seepferd Wildsauer** (6%).

KEHRWIEDER

Hamburg

Running before they can walk, perhaps, but thus far yet to stumble badly, with red ale **Hamburger Rot** (5%), **Rogger**

Roggen IPA (6.5%) rye IPA and **Kogge** (6.9%) Baltic porter. Hamburg's second scene-stirrer.

SCHNEEEULE

Berlin

Set up in 2016, this staunch and yeast-obsessed brewer is focused on perfecting traditional north German light and sour beers, beginning with the dry and enticingly subtle *Berliner weisse* **Marlene** (3%) and its elderflower-flavoured sibling **Otto** (3%).

STONE

Berlin

A European base for the US producer of Arrogant Bastard (*see* page 200), testing the *wasser* with a UK-style "strong ale" **Little Bastard** (4.7%), honestly named **Berliner Weisse Prototype** (4.7%) and jet-black **Imperial Belgian IPA** (10.1%).

Very gentle carbonation and Bohemian in its rather rounded mouthfeel, if not in its hopping.

PINKUS PILS

Pinkus Müller, Münster, North Rhine-Westphalia; 5.2%

From a brewery that tried its hand at everything comes a great organic, or "bio", beer with grassy and bready edges, though lacking the sharp hop presence of a northern pils.

POTSDAMMER WEISSE

Forsthaus Templin, Potsdam, Brandenburg; 3%

A cheekily named light, lactic, lemony *Berliner weisse* that some consider is too tart and even one dimensional, but we consider challenging to orthodoxy.

RAUCHBIER LAGER

Spezial, Bamberg, Bavaria; 4.7%

Unavailable outside of a 15-kilometre (9-mile) radius of the brewery – or so it is claimed – this is a masterpiece of smoky nuance and understated maltiness, delivering whiffs of sweet, caramelly smoke rather than a trip to the smokehouse.

RÄUCHERLA

Hummel, Merkendorf/Memmelsdorf, Bavaria; 5.5%

The darker, more frequently made, smokier *rauchbier* from this Franconian village brewery. Its name references "incense smoke", but after the aroma of a granary fire passes, a well-balanced smoked *märzen* follows.

SCHLOTFEGERLA

Weyermann, Bamberg, Bavaria; 5.2%

Germany's most famous malting facility has a tiny brewhouse for the creation of sample brews, among which the regular is this dark, sweetly bitter and earthy *rauchbier*, the smokiness of which is designed to showcase their smoked malt.

SCHWARZBIER

Eisgrub-Bräu, Mainz, Rhineland-Palatinate; 4.9%

A jet-black *schwarzbier* with more dark chocolate flavours than most, the malt residing principally on the nose rather than in the body. As with many of this eastern German style, it tastes thinner that its colour implies.

SCHWARZBIER

Altstadthof, Nürnberg, Bavaria; 4.8%

More a dark Bavarian *dunkel* than an eastern-style *schwarzbier*, with more sweet caramel maltiness than coal-dusty roast, from a large and popular Nürnberg brewpub.

STETTFELDER PILS

Adler, Stettfeld, Bavaria; 5%

The most striking beer from a solid brewery near Bamberg, illustrating the southern tradition of pale pilseners with a solid hop character, but accompanied by a crisp and hoppy edge.

STYLE SPOTLIGHT

ZOIGL – MORE A WAY OF LIVING THAN A BEER STYLE

It may be argued, particularly by those who consider that a beer style must be fermented by yeast from a specific range, that *zoigl* should not be regarded as one. We disagree. The tradition of the *kommunbrauhaus*, or communal brewery, is probably as old as commercial brewing itself. Shared town breweries existed in Bohemia by the 11th century and have brewing rights in Bavaria that pre-date the *Reinheitsgebot*.

The principle is that a group of local people or a town council fund a brewhouse where citizens brew to create wort that, after cooling overnight in a *kühlschiff* – a large, shallow, open vat – is taken away to be fermented and lagered by one or more stakeholders in different ways, who eventually sell their finished beer from their *zoiglstube*, usually a bar or small restaurant that is an extension of a home and traditionally identified by a hanging six-pointed *zoigl* star.

These beers vary according to the brewery, the brewer, the batch and who conditions it, but typically lie somewhere between an earthy infant lambic and a herbal *kellerbier*.

The tradition survives in the Oberpfalz region of eastern Bavaria – in Eslarn, where **Beim Ströhern** serves its eponymous rustic, hazy orange, multi-dimensional light brew; in Falkenberg, where the brewhouse makes golden, grassier and lemony beers like **Kramer-Wolf** and the darker, clearer, sweeter **Schwoazhansl**; in Mitterteich's brewhouse where a tranche of beers is crafted, among which the best is the cidery-tart, yeasty yet honeyed **Oppl**; in Neuhaus an der Waldnaab, where the brewhouse serves seven *zoiglstuben*; and in the most active brewery at Windischeschenbach, which yields a range from soft, full, more "normal" **Weisser Schwann** to earthier, nuttier **Posterer**.

STRALSUNDER TRADITIONSBOCK

Störtebeker, Stralsund, Mecklenburg-Vorpommern; 6.5%

A dark and heavily roasty *bock*-meets-Baltic-porter from a Baltic Sea coast brewery that has revived a huge range of beers, with this being the pre-eminent head-turner.

UNGESPUNDET HEFETRÜB

Mahrs, Bamberg, Bavaria; 5.2%

From a brewery that is a favourite among beer-savvy Bamberg tourists, this lightly carbonated, yeasty lager is grassy and grainy in equal degrees, and most of all refreshing. Now bottled, but best enjoyed at the brewery.

UNGESPUNDETES LAGERBIER

Wagner-Bräu, Kemmern, Bavaria; 4.5%

The gravity-poured beer from the brewery tap is a rich and herbaceous

take on the more cellar-aged style of blond lager, its gently rising bitterness culminating in an appetizing finish.

VETTER'S WEIHNACHTSBOCK

Alt Heidelberger, Heidelberg, Baden-Württemberg; 6.2%

Brewed each year for Christmas, this relatively understated, caramel-malty, amber *bock* is typical of the excellent seasonal offerings from this popular *häusbrauerei*, better known for its barley wine.

VOLLBIER HELL

Heckel, Waischenfeld, Bavaria; 5.5%

Vollbier translates metaphorically as "house brew" and this herbal, grassy, hazy, tangy-edged and delightfully disjointed copper-blond lager is typical of the local talent for the imprecise. Unusual for Franconia in that it can crop up in far-flung places.

WEIHERER RAUCH

Kundmüller, Viereth-Trunstadt, Bavaria; 5.3%

Deep gold in colour, with a sweet and relatively soft smokiness to the aroma. That reserve is also evident in the body, which neither whispers nor screams its balanced, smoky maltiness and gradually drying caramel sweetness.

WEIZEN-BOCK

Jacob, Bodenwöhr, Bavaria; 6.5%

Part of the winter offering from this busy, small-scale family brewer of wheat beer specialties. The liquid equivalent of partly burned toast spread with banana paste.

WEIZEN-BOCK

Karg, Murnau, Bavaria; 7%

An accomplished beer from a wheat beer specialist that is like a classically proportioned Bavarian *weizen*, only bigger. To banana and clove characteristics add overripe peaches in the aroma and a dab of caramel toffee in the body.

WEIZENBOCK

Gutmann, Titting, Bavaria; 7.2%

Arguably the best and certainly the most intense of the range offered by this wheat beer specialist, emphasizing the house flavour characteristics of banana and sweet fruit set against a full, malty backbone.

WEIZLA DUNKEL

Fässla, Bamberg, Bavaria; 5%

All the beers from this atmospheric *hausbrauerei* (and hotel) are to a greater or lesser degree classics of their kind, but this fruity, aromatic, banana–malt dark wheat beer stands out for being the best from Bamberg.

WITZGALL-BIER

Witzgall, Schlammersdorf, Bavaria; 5.2%

By whichever name it is marketed – Lagerbier, Landbier or Kellerbier – this straw-golden local beer, with its faintly citrus-zingy hop bite, is held by

many to epitomize Franconian brewing – laissez-faire on style, precise on delivery. This is best enjoyed as fresh as possible.

WÖLLNITZER WEISSBIER

Talschänke, Jena, Thuringia; 4.2%

Of a style that combines smoked malt, wheat and lactic fermentation, known as *lichtenhainer*, this sole product of a 1997 guesthouse brewery is tart, cloudy, a bit smoky, citric and just rustic enough. Truly a beer of myth and legend.

ZWICKELBIER

Lübeck Brauberger, Lübeck, Schleswig-Holstein; 4.8%

One of the few north German gravity-feed cask beers, delicately hopped, possibly containing some wheat. Highly quaffable at the brewery taphouse, if less impressive in the bottle.

AUSTRIA

Austria, having long resided in Germany's sizeable shadow and despite laying claim to some historic brewing advances (*see* Schwechater, page 68), is now well ahead of its much larger neighbour in terms of craft brewing development, while still supporting the country's many traditional breweries.

BOCKBIER

Augustiner, Kloster Mülln, Salzburg; 6.5%

Seasonal brew from the monastery-owned brewery with Austria's largest beer halls just outside Salzburg's city centre. Bold and somewhat bready in the nose, it's a stronger version of the *märzen* that is available all year.

BONIFATIUS BARRIQUE

Handbrauerei Forstner, Kalsdorf bei Graz, Styria; 9.5%

Belgian-style strong ale from one of Austria's smallest breweries, aged in red wine barrels that add intense raspberry notes, plus hints of almonds and kiwi fruit. Sweet on the palate, dry and bitter in the aftertaste.

CARINTHIPA

Loncium, Kötschach-Mauthen, Carinthia; 5.6%

Orange-coloured ale with fruity aromas (mango and grapefruit), relatively highly carbonated, medium body and moderately bitter from start to finish.

EISBOCK

Rieder, Ried im Innkreis, Upper Austria; 10.3%

From a storeyed brewery, this is a concentrated (through freezing) version of their 6.5% *weizenbock*. The warming result has aromas of almonds and roses,

and finishes with a long-lasting banana-
and nut-like aftertaste.

FLANDERS RED

Brauwerk, Vienna; 7.2%

Ruby red with aromas of sour cherries
and red wine, and refreshing acidity in the
body that helps hide the beer's strength.

GOLD FASSL PILS

Ottakringer, Vienna; 4.6%

Grassy aromas of Tettnang hops
characterize this classic German-style
pilsner, brewed at Vienna's largest
brewery. Straw in colour, the medium-
weight body is crisp and refreshing with
a dry finish.

GOLDBRÄU

Stiegl, Salzburg; 4.9%

Mildly hopped, medium-bodied golden
lager with a grainy malt aroma from
Salzburg's most famous brewery, which
still operates in 19th-century buildings.

GÖSSER DUNKLES ZWICKL

Falkenstein, Lienz, Tyrol; 5.7%

Nut-brown unfiltered lager with a
caramelly aroma and some sweetness,
balanced by a hint of roastiness and a
generous hoppiness in the surprisingly
dry finish.

GRANITBOCK ICE

Hofstetten, St Martin im Mühlkreis,
Upper Austria; 11.5%

The strongest lager in Peter Krammer's
Granitbier series, this *eisbock* features
the caramelly, smoky and burned taste
of the base beer, plus notes of dried
plum, chocolate and coffee.

GREGORIUS

Engelszell, Engelhartszell, Upper Austria;
9.7%

Austria's first Trappist beer is usually
bottled very fresh, tasting sweet
and unbalanced when young, but

CAN'T-MISS BREWERY
● ●

1516

Vienna

Close to 20 years in, this is still the only US-style brewpub in Austria. It
rolls out new beers on a regular basis, including at least one highly aromatic
yet refreshing **Wit Series** (~4.8%) in the summer, often using different
citrus fruits, and a chilli-spiced and chocolate-flavoured **Tovarich Sanchez
Bourbon Cask Matured Imperial stout** (9.7%) in winter, in addition to
their full-bodied and citrusy regular **Victory Hop Devil IPA** (7%), brewed
in cooperation with Victory Brewing of Pennsylvania since 2004.

ICONIC BREWERY

SCHWECHATER [HEINEKEN]

Schwechat, Vienna

Vienna-style lagers – and, in fact, industrial-scale lager brewing – were invented at this brewery by Anton Dreher in 1841, but all buildings from that time are gone. Now part of the Heineken empire, it is responsible for beers such as the golden **Schwechater Bier** (5%) with a nutty, mildly bitter taste; the straw-coloured, very hazy **Zwickl** (5.4%) with a herbal hoppiness, a creamy body and a distinctively bitter finish; and the recently revived, reddish-amber **Wiener Lager** (5.5%) with a cake-like aroma.

developing complexity after a year or more. The evolution brings a plum-like fruity aroma, with the sweetness balanced by a chocolaty bitterness.

HADMAR

Weitra, Weitra, Lower Austria; 5.2%

Vienna-style lagers were revived in 1994 in Austria's oldest brewing town – dating from 1321 – with this dark amber, roasty and full-bodied yet well-hopped organic beer.

HOPFENSPIEL

Trumer, Josef Sigl, Obertrum, Salzburg; 2.9%

A hop-dominated, light version of the pils style that Trumer is famous for, with a trio of hops adding enough flavour for the beer to taste more full bodied than one would expect.

HUBER BRÄU SPEZIAL

Familienbrauerei Huber, St Johann, Tyrol; 5.4%

Golden *helles*-style lager with a full white head, aromas of malt and Tettnang hops, high carbonation, medium to full body with an almost creamy mouthfeel and a dry, bitter finish.

MÄRZEN

Murauer, Murau, Styria; 5.2%

In Austria, *märzen* is typically lighter both in colour and alcohol than the German versions. This example from Styria is golden, highly carbonated and combines full body and a nutty, medium bitterness.

BREWERIES TO WATCH

BREW AGE

nomadic

Four itinerant brewers from Vienna who brew award-winning ales such as the fruity (dried plums, raisins, blackberries, walnuts) barley wine, **Nussknacker** (10%) and the resinous, citrusy and off-dry **Affenkönig Imperial IPA** (8.2%) at different small breweries.

COLLABS

nomadic

Originally meant to supply the Hawidere pub in Vienna but now brewing in Austria and England, responsible for the extremely hoppy **Domrep Pils** (5.2%), the acidic, sorrel-flavoured *Berliner weisse* **Sauer! Lump!** (3%) and the vinous **Burgen** (5.6%).

CRAFT COUNTRY

Hall, Tyrol

Small brewery started in 2015 and brewing a series of bold ales such as the coconut-ish **Miyamato Japanese Pale Ale** (5.5%), alongside their standard **da'Hoam** pale lager (5%).

NEXT LEVEL

nomadic

Founded in late 2015, this Vienna-based company has put out rather extreme beers like the **Bitter Freak** (7.5%), which claims to have 200 IBUs, and the herbal-aromatic **Lemon Thyme** (4.9%), a *gose* with a distinct acidity, a sweet body that underlines the taste of thyme and a dry, very salty finish.

MORCHL

Hirter, Micheldorf, Carinthia; 5%

Chestnut-brown lager with a caramelly aroma and some residual sweetness that combines well with roasted nuttiness and hoppy bitterness. A style-defining beer for Austrian dark lagers.

NO. 4 BELLE SAISON

Schleppe, Klagenfurt, Carinthia; 5.4%

Light gold, fruity and rose-like, this is the fourth in a series of ales from the centuries-old Schleppe brewery that has been resized to brew small batches of craft beer.

OND BEVOG

Bad Radkersburg, Styria; 6.3%

Robust smoked porter with a distinct smoke aroma and a full, roasty body from a rapidly growing micro on the Styrian–Slovenian border.

ROGGEN BIO BIER

Schremser, Schrems, Lower Austria; 5.2%

Orange-coloured, unfiltered organic rye ale, aromatically grainy and doughy, with a full yet refreshing body carrying rye-bread notes and gentle bitterness.

SAMICHLAUS BARRIQUE

Schloss Eggenberg, Vorchdorf, Upper Austria; 14%

Most recent addition to the range originally brewed by Hürliman in Zurich, once the world's strongest beer. Mahogany coloured with subtle carbonation, sweet, ripe fruit, warming and a mere hint of the wooden casks.

SAPHIR PILS

Zwettler, Zwettl, Lower Austria; 5.3%

While the Zwettler brewery usually favours local ingredients, they employ the citrusy German Saphir hops for this straw-coloured, spritzy and moderately bitter German-style pilsner.

SCHWARZBIER

Wieselburger, Wieselburg, Lower Austria; 4.8%

Black in colour, caramelly and roasty in the nose, but bitter with just a hint of sweetness on the palate. Packaged in flip-top bottles that the brewery reserves for its speciality brews.

DIE SCHWARZE KUH

Gusswerk, Hof bei Salzburg, Salzburg; 9.2%

Deep black with a slightly sweet, fruity malt character, this organic Imperial stout shows a hearty bitterness with notes of coffee and hops in a beer that has good balance and a long-lasting, roasty finish.

SILBERPFEIL

Raschhofer, Altheim, Upper Austria; 5.3%

Once known for their inexpensive lager, in recent years this brewery has added a range of more interesting beers to their repertoire including this pale ale with a fruity, grapefruit-like aroma and a moderate bitterness.

URTYP

Zipfer, Zipf, Upper Austria; 5.4%

One of Austria's bestselling premium lagers, brewed with whole hops. Although rice was dropped from the grain bill in 2016, this straw-coloured beer is still spritzy and crisp, with a slightly herbal bitterness at the start, a medium to full body and a dry finish.

WEISSE HELL

(Baumgartner, Schärding, Upper Austria; 5.4%

Golden *hefeweizen* from a town that belonged to Bavaria until 1779, with just the right amount of banana, vanilla and clove aromas, a faintly sweet body, lively carbonation and a medium bitterness in the finish.

SWITZERLAND

Having got off to a slow start in craft brewing, Switzerland now counts among the global leaders in terms of breweries per number of residents, although the national practice of licensing those who are little more than home-brewers skews the numbers somewhat. Still, the growth and improvement of Swiss beer in general begs exploration today.

523 INDIA PALE ALE

523, Köniz, Bern; 7.2%

Does just what it promises on the label, which is a straightforward, clean, quaffable and fragrant IPA, brewed by a tiny operation in the suburbs of Bern that is also notable for its constant stream of one-off beers.

L'AMBRÉE

Jorat, Vuillens, Vaud; 6%

The standout brew of an otherwise fairly pedestrian brewery; a smooth, balanced, subtly smoked amber ale, marrying caramelly malt, beech smoke and meaty notes.

BÄRNER JUNKER

Felsenau, Bern; 5.2%

A good example of a Swiss take on pilsner, especially in its unpasteurized draught form – flowery, fragrant and with a crisp final bitterness underpinning an almost honey-ish malt base.

BIÈRE DE TABLE

Virage, Plan-les-Ouates, Geneva; 3%

A fine example of the low-gravity ales that are growing in popularity among Swiss craft breweries. The recipe for this shape-shifting beast changes with every new brew, but the beer remains dry, quenching and fruity.

GALLUS 612

Schützengarten, St Gallen; 5.6%

Originally brewed for the city's 1400th anniversary, this is a juniper-infused, light brown, dry, spicy and moderately fruity ale, the brewery's first foray beyond Germanic orthodoxy.

MERCURY SAISON

Blackwell, Burgdorf, Bern; 4.2%

One of the core beers in Blackwell's prolific range of seasonals, collaborations and one-offs, dubbed a "*saison de table*" and brewed with rye to a dry and quaffable character.

OROINCENSO

Officina della Birra, Bioggio, Ticino; 8%

Initially a Christmas seasonal, an ale that has become pretty much the flagship of this pioneering brewery established in 1998. Dark and dry, it showcases beautifully a healthy dose of chestnut honey, including its bitter edge.

PACIFIC PIONEER PORTER

Sudwerk, Pfäffikon, Zurich; 6%

Very smooth, chocolaty and medium-bodied, this is a stylish interpretation of porter by a brewery whose range focuses on British and US beer styles.

PALE ALE

Müller, Baden, Aargau; 5.9%

A creditably spicy, orangey, caramel-edged take on British-style pale ale brewed by a family brewery otherwise known for its conservative lagers. It is mostly available in cans across German-speaking Switzerland.

PILGRIM TRIPLE BLONDE

Kloster Fischingen, Fischingen, Thurgau; 10%

A dangerously quaffable, lingering and warming abbey-style *tripel* that pushes all the right spicy–peachy–orangey buttons, brewed at Switzerland's lone brewery located on monastic premises at the St Iddazell Abbey.

SCHWARZER KRISTALL

Locher, Appenzell, Appenzell Innerrhoden; 6.3%

Impressively smooth, rounded, roasty and rich, this creamy black beer comes with a hint of smokiness, leaving it somewhere between a *schwarzbier* and a Baltic porter.

SKINNY DIPPER

Storm & Anchor, nomadic; 6.1%

Brewed at Doppelleu by itinerant brewer Tom Strickler, this IPA showcases his sizeable talent for creating hop-accented, US-style beers with rich peach, watermelon and bitter-orange notes.

TEMPÊTE

Docteur Gab's, Savigny, Vaud; 8%

From a pioneering craft brewery founded in 2001, this is a typical example of a Swiss take on a *tripel* that errs on the dry, quaffable side of the style.

CAN'T-MISS BREWERIES

BIER FACTORY

Rapperswil-Jona, St Gallen

Possibly the first craft brewery to venture off the Germanic beaten path in eastern Switzerland, it has seen its range thoroughly overhauled for the better following the arrival of Katie Pietsch at the brewing helm. Grassy, slightly citrusy, dry **Rappi Gold** (4.8%) is their golden ale in response to local pale lagers, **Blackbier** (5%) is a smooth, dry stout with chocolaty notes, while **Oh IPA** (6.7%) is a powerfully fragrant, fruity ale in the US style.

DES FRANCHES-MONTAGNES (BFM)

Saignelégier, Jura

Craft brewing pioneer founded in 1997 and widely credited with single-handedly putting Switzerland on the world beer map. Its flagship label is **Abbaye de Saint Bon-Chien** (11%), a tart, dark-red, fruity, oak-aged beer also available in a variety of usually singular "Grand Cru" versions. **Cuvée Alex Le Rouge** (10.3%) is an idiosyncratic spicy "Imperial Jurassian stout", while dry, bitter, fragrant, sage-infused **La Meule** (6%) is the most distinctive in BFM's core range.

TROIS DAMES

Sainte-Croix, Vaud

Raphaël Mettler was the first to brew authentically British-style beers in Switzerland and his citrusy, peppery, earthy but smooth **India Pale Ale** (6.5%) has been an eye-opener for many a Swiss drinker. Smooth, rounded, fruity, rich **La Pasionaria** (9%) was the first double IPA released in quantity in Switzerland, while old brown **Grande Dame** (7%), a blend of strong stout and spontaneously fermented apricots, has paved the way for what is now a whole programme of wild fermentations and barrel-ageing worth watching.

BREWERY TO WATCH

LA NÉBULEUSE

Renens, Vaud

Youthful and not afraid of growth, this potent brewery is responsible for **Stirling** (5.3%), a fragrant, citrusy, dry steam beer; **Embuscade** (6.7%), an IPA bursting with orange and grapefruit notes; and the vanilla- and bourbon-infused porter **Malt Capone** (7%).

GREAT BRITAIN

With the march of craft beer in full swing, British beer orthodoxy, in large part inspired by the work of the Campaign for Real Ale (CAMRA), has had a difficult time accepting the new world of brewing, even as it has thrived and wildly expanded within the country's borders. A massive expansion of the market led by a rather remarkable growth in the number of new breweries, however, has the potential to drag British beer well into the 21st century, kicking and screaming or not.

ENGLAND

6X

Wadworth, Devizes, Wiltshire; 4.1%, cask

An amber bitter with treacly malt, rounded fruit and a slightly nutty almond note in a herbal coating finish, this isn't as ubiquitous as it once was, but is still a solid ale from an important Victorian survivor.

1872 PORTER

Elland, Elland, West Yorkshire; 6.5%

This much-lauded erstwhile Champion Beer of Britain is a meaty, toasty liquorice-tinged mouthful based on a historic recipe, from a brewery merged from two predecessors in 2002.

AGELESS

Redwillow, Macclesfield, Cheshire; 7.2%

Grapefruit, burned toast, sesame oil, lavender and pineapple waft through this, one of the UK's best modern IPAs, which comes from a former home-brewer who turned pro in 2010.

AUDIT ALE

Westerham, Westerham, Kent; 6.2%

One of a growing number of conventionally brewed beers that have been treated to remove gluten imperceptibly, this recreation of a pre-Second World War strong ale is rich and vinous, with the bitter orange tang of locally grown hops.

AXE EDGE

Buxton, Buxton, Derbyshire; 6.8%

There are numerous beers worth trying from this Peak District producer, but among the standouts is this smooth, zesty IPA with tangerine, passion-fruit and mango notes, and a comfortably bitter finish.

BABY-FACED ASSASSIN

Roosters, Knaresborough, North Yorkshire; 6.1%

Modern IPA from a brewery that championed New World hops in the 1990s. Vividly flavoured but delicate, with hints of fresh mango and papaya, and an emerging peppery bitterness on the finish.

BAD KITTY

Brass Castle, Malton, North Yorkshire; 5.5%

Full-bodied, creamy and complex vanilla porter finishing with gentle rooty hops and roastiness, from a brewery

ICONIC BREWERY

FULLER'S, SMITH & TURNER

London

Long-standing independent family-led brewery on a wisteria-clad Chiswick riverside site with evidence of brewing from the 16th century. Well known for exemplary cask beers like style-defining marmalade-tinged **ESB** (5.5%), but gaining new respect for historical revivals, wood-aged beers and bottle-conditioned specialities such as biscuity, slightly smoky amber ale **1845** (6.3%) and outstanding annually released barley wine **Vintage Ale** (8.5%), which becomes magnificently complex and port-like with age. Gentle yet crisp **Chiswick Bitter** (3.5%), sadly now only an occasional special, and medium-bodied but assertively roasty **London Porter** (5.4%) are also highly rated.

ICONIC BREWERY

THORNBRIDGE

Bakewell, Derbyshire

Hailed by many as Britain's leading 21st-century brewery, set up with the help of Kelham Island's Dave Wickett (*see* page 84) at the eponymous Peak District stately home and since expanded to nearby Bakewell. Flagship is the resinous but approachable **Jaipur IPA** (5.9%), one of Britain's first in the new transatlantic style, while the rest of an imaginative and consistently impressive range includes the intense and fragrant double IPA **Halcyon** (7.4%), toasty Vienna lager **Kill Your Darlings** (5%) and unique dark, sweet and spicy honey beer **Bracia** (10%).

that started in a garage in 2011 and deservedly expanded six months later.

BARNSLEY BITTER

Acorn, Barnsley, South Yorkshire; 3.8%, cask

Flowery, fruity and resinously dry local favourite, resurrected with the original yeast following the demise of the old Barnsley brewery by an outfit that has also ventured into contemporary single-hop pale ales.

BEARDED LADY

Magic Rock, Huddersfield, West Yorkshire; 10.5%

One of Britain's most successful and respected new US-influenced craft brewers makes a range of punchy beers, of which this charred ooze of an Imperial stout is arguably the standout.

BEAST

Exmoor, Wiveliscombe, Somerset; 6.6%

Deeply grainy and coffee-ish dark brown beer with chocolate and fruit on the finish, from a brewery established in 1990 on the site of the historic Hancocks brewery.

BEDE'S CHALICE

Durham, Bowburn, County Durham; 9%

Big, sweetish, orange-liqueur-tinged *tripel*, rich in creamy fruit and herbal hops, from an older micro that has long been a reliable source of strong bottle-conditioned ales inspired by its home city's ecclesiastical heritage.

BIG BEN

Thwaites, Blackburn, Lancashire; 5.8%

US-style brown ale with a fusion of fruit and herbal hops and chewy malt, from a 210-year-old brewery that in 2015 unexpectedly downsized to "craft" scale, farming out its cask-conditioned beers to Marston's (*see* page 84).

BISHOPS FAREWELL

Oakham, Peterborough, Cambridgeshire; 4.6%, cask

Soft strawberry lime and passion fruit sustain over a firm cereal base in this hoppy but not too bitter golden ale from an early UK adopter of New World hops, founded in Rutland in 1996.

BLACK ADDER

Mauldons, Sudbury, Suffolk; 5.3%

From a historic brewery reinvented in 1981, this slightly tarry and tart stout has elements of cocoa, black coffee and cola, with almond-like bitterness on a smooth finish.

BLACK DOG FREDDY

Beckstones, Millom, Cumbria; 3.9%, cask

Multi-award-winning dark mild with caramel and blackberry flavours and a notably bitterish roast note, from a small brewery in good walking country founded by an ex-InBev drayman.

BLUEBIRD BITTER

Coniston, Coniston, Cumbria; 3.6%, cask

Popular and influential lime- and ginger-tinged golden bitter, from a modest plant behind the Black Bull pub. Also worth trying in its US-hopped and bottle-conditioned versions.

BODGER'S BARLEY WINE

Chiltern, Aylesbury, Buckinghamshire; 8.5%

Gracefully ageing, smooth, substantial and spicily honeyed chestnut-coloured ale with salted-olive notes, from a well-established farmhouse brewery.

BRIGSTOW BITTER

Arbor, Bristol; 4.3%, cask

Now one of the oldest of Bristol's new wave of breweries and noted for fresh contemporary styles, but also for this delightfully grainy, honeyed and orange-tinged bitter using English hops.

CHARRINGTONS IPA

Heritage, Burton upon Trent, Staffordshire; 4.5%, cask

Heritage London pale ale with a fine blend of toffee, toast, nuts and a very dry bitter finish, resurrected by legendary ex-Bass brewer Steve Wellington with its original yeast at the National Brewery Centre.

COHORT

Summer Wine, Holmfirth, West Yorkshire; 7.5%

"Double black Belgian rye IPA" from a determinedly modern operation, with herbs, pineapple and citrus successfully layered over a base of dry chocolate and soothing caramel.

COOLSHIP

Elgood's, Wisbech, Cambridgeshire; 6%

A remarkably successful, spontaneously fermented lambic-style beer from an old family-owned brewery, made in a long-disused coolship, with sherry-like tones, tart jam and biscuit sweetness and a mild lactic sourness.

CUMBRIAN FIVE HOP

Hawkshead, Staveley, Cumbria; 5%, cask

Notes of floral peach and sweet onion lead this firmly bitter but refreshing, contemporary pale ale from a brewery that began in a Lake District barn, but soon expanded on the success of numerous beers of similar quality.

DARK RUBY

Sarah Hughes, Dudley, West Midlands; 6%, cask

Benchmark strong Black Country mild from a brewery revived in 1987 when the current owner rediscovered his grandmother's recipes, with notes of brown toast, caramel, port and cherries, and a decidedly dry finish.

DOROTHY GOODBODY'S WHOLESOME STOUT

Wye Valley, Stoke Lacy, Herefordshire; 4.6%

Excellent creamy and medium-bodied stout with a notably dry and ashy Irish-inspired roast-barley bite, long a mainstay of this reliable rural small brewery in hop country.

DOUBLE MAXIM

Maxim, Houghton-le-Spring, Tyne and Wear; 4.7%

Distinctive heritage brown ale in the dry northeastern style, with citrus, caramel and raspberry notes, and a bitter, slightly resinous finish.

DOUBLE MOMENTUM

Hopshackle, Market Deeping, Lincolnshire; 7%

Exemplary double IPA from an often-overlooked, ahead-of-its time brewer, with honey, pollen and roses on a firm malt palate and an assertive yet controlled, peppery-bitter finish.

FLAGSHIP

Hook Norton, Hook Norton, Oxfordshire; 5.3%

A rare, revived strongish IPA with English hops from a village-based, Victorian-era brewery that is still partly steam-powered, with notes of spring meadows, orange, honey and plum, and a chewy lettuce finish.

GADDS' FAITHFUL DOGBOLTER

Ramsgate, Broadstairs, Kent; 5.6%, cask

Mildly roasty porter with orange-marmalade and liquorice tones, this was the celebrated mainstay of the Firkin brewpub chain during the 1980s, resurrected by brewer Eddie Gadd at his brewery on the Isle of Thanet.

CAN'T-MISS BREWERIES

ADNAMS

Southwold, Suffolk

Long-established, family-dominated independent brewery and wine importer in a particularly pretty Suffolk seaside town. Revered for benchmark cask ales like **Southwold Bitter** (3.7%, cask), with complex marmalade and peppery flavours, and recently revived and rich, classic bottled barley wine **Tally-Ho** (7.2%), which improves with ageing. Successfully cultivating a contemporary edge under the Jack Brand label with beers such as earthy but tropical-fruit-tinged **Innovation IPA** (6.7%).

BURNING SKY

Firle, East Sussex

Eagerly anticipated solo project from one of Britain's most influential brewers, Mark Tranter, from a rural setting on the South Downs. Hit the ground running in 2013 with a succession of outstanding, often seasonally influenced beers, including the fruity, grassy and refreshing **Saison à la Provision** (6.5%); a vividly flavoured **Devil's Rest IPA** (7%), with melon, mint and tobacco notes; and the grape-ish, oaky, lightly phenolic barrel-aged dark **Monolith** (8%).

HARVEY'S

Lewes, East Sussex

Revered independent brewery on the south coast, best known for its old-fashioned, dryish, beautifully balanced and slightly toffee-accented **Sussex**

Best Bitter (4%) and, internationally, for the benchmark grainy, leathery, slightly sour and long-ageing **Imperial Extra Double Stout** (9%). Numerous cask and bottled specialities, often in endangered styles, include an indulgently sweet and complex **Christmas Ale** (7.5%).

THE KERNEL

London

Perhaps the most influential and respected of the new wave London breweries and the inadvertent founder of the Bermondsey "beer mile". Equally adept at artisanal **Pale Ale** (~5.5%) made with ever-changing hops – the Mosaic and Simcoe versions have been particularly fragrant, fresh and balanced – and strong heritage stouts and porters such as the complex, velvety and tobacco-tinged **Export Stout London 1890** (7.2%). In contrast, **Table Beer** (3.3%) is a cheerfully light and citric refresher.

CAN'T-MISS BREWERIES

MARBLE

Manchester

The brewery that arguably kicked off Manchester's current brewing renaissance, founded in 1998 in the Marble Arch heritage pub just north of the city centre, though since relocated to a bigger site nearby. **Chocolate Marble** (5.5%, cask) is a strong mild with berry notes and a rich, indeed chocolaty finish, while creamy, delicately flowery **Manchester Bitter** (4.2%, cask) was inspired by Boddingtons at its best. Among highly recommended specials are complex but beautifully integrated **Earl Grey IPA** (6.8%), originally a collaboration with Dutch brewer Emelisse (*see* pages 115 and 119), and deep, plum-cake-tinged Imperial stout **Decadence** (8.7%).

SIREN

Finchampstead, Berkshire

Probably the UK's most consistently high-achieving new-style craft brewery, founded by a Home Counties home-brewer in 2012. Red ale **Liquid**

Mistress (5.8%) expertly blends chewy, toasty, cherry-like malt with spicy hops, while smoky, coconut-tinged and indulgent sweet stout **Broken Dream** (6%) is also available in wood-aged versions. **Calypso** (4%) succeeds in laying peach and lychee hop notes over a refreshingly lemony *Berliner weisse* base.

ST AUSTELL

St Austell, Cornwall

The last-surviving Victorian independent in Cornwall, deploying a canny contemporary sensibility by supplementing its regular cask bitters with beers like **Proper Job** (4.5%, cask), a flavourful strawberry- and citrus-tinged IPA, and richly biscuit-malty, lightly fruity **Admiral's Ale** (5%), brewed from a malt specially kilned to the brewery's specifications. New stout **Mena Dhu** (4.5%) deploys a dose of smoked malt in a lightly sweet, liquoricey and easy-drinking brew.

GAMMA RAY

Beavertown, London; 5.4%

Vivid but balanced pale ale bursting with flavours of pineapple, lemon marmalade and grapefruit, this is deservedly one of the most successful new London beers, from an ambitious outfit that has pioneered the use of cans in the UK market.

GOOD KING HENRY SPECIAL RESERVE

Old Chimneys, Market Weston, Suffolk; 11%

Sought-after but rare, oaked Imperial stout from a tiny farm brewery, with a heady whisky–sherry–blackcurrant aroma and candied fruit, marzipan and oaky tannins in the body.

HARVEST ALE

J W Lees, Middleton Junction, Manchester; 11.5%

Seasonal barley wine using the harvest's ingredients to give a nutty, sherried and slightly salty, olive-imbued complexity to an ale that often benefits from a degree of ageing.

INDIA PALE ALE

Harbour, Kirland, Cornwall; 5%

Resinous and grapefruity, but comparatively restrained transatlantic-style IPA with subtle tropical-fruit and apricot notes from an impressive US-influenced set-up launched in rural Cornwall by a former Sharp's brewer.

INDIA PALE ALE

Shepherd Neame, Faversham, Kent; 6.1%

Revival of a 19th-century recipe from the archives of what is probably Britain's oldest brewery, situated in hop country on the north Kent coast. Characterized by nutty malt, orange cream and earthy resins, with seedy aromas.

JJJ IPA

Moor, Bristol; 9%

One of the UK's best double IPAs, from one of its persistently ground-breaking brewers, heading up the rapidly emerging Bristol beer scene with increasing aplomb. Citrus and hay aromas, biscuity, white wine and coconut flavours and a long tannic, peppery finish.

LONDON KEEPER

Truman's, London; 8%

Brown sugar, toasted coconut, tart rosehip and a gently roasty finish mark out this complex export porter, revived from an 1880 recipe using US hops. Still maturing splendidly.

LONDON PORTER

Meantime [Asahi], London; 6.5%

Reliably fine and complex 19th-century-inspired porter, with sappy blackcurrant and chocolate-mousse flavours and earthy hoppiness, from London's second-biggest and second-oldest brewery.

LURCHER STOUT

Green Jack, Lowestoft, Suffolk; 4.8%

Soft, chocolaty and very sessionable stout with a taste of spicy black grape, from Britain's most easterly brewery, whose founder has brewed locally since 1993.

MAD GOOSE

Purity, Great Alne, Warwickshire; 4.2%, cask

Arguably the tastiest choice from a reliable and popular producer of clean-tasting and consistent session ales, filled with hoppy perfume and orchard-fruit aromas over generous maltiness in a satisfying golden ale.

MARY JANE

Ilkley, Ilkley, West Yorkshire; 3.5%, cask

Lots to admire at this rapidly expanding brewery located on the edge of the Yorkshire Dales, but this cheerful and supremely quaffable pale ale with gentle citric and earthy bitterness makes a great go-to beer.

MIDNIGHT BELL

Leeds, Leeds, West Yorkshire; 4.8%, cask

Lightly treacly, vermouth-tinged but very approachable strong mild, the calling card of a highly professional and ambitious 2007 set-up, now filling a niche in the city where Tetley was king until closed by Carlsberg.

MILK SHAKE STOUT

Wiper & True, Bristol; 5%

Lactose-dosed, not at all oversweet, fruity–vanilla sweet stout that is a fine example of a revived local speciality and the flagship of acclaimed brewers who acquired their own premises in 2015.

MOROCCO ALE

Daleside, Harrogate, North Yorkshire; 5.5%

Unusual spiced ale slightly reminiscent of red vermouth, with flavours of ginger and cough drops supported by rich cakey malt, based on a recipe allegedly brought back from Morocco by a Crusader.

MUD CITY STOUT

Sadler's, Lye, West Midlands; 6%

Chocolate liqueur, coconut, dark malt and a relatively bitter finish characterize this strong stout flavoured with cocoa and vanilla, brewed by an operation revived by a new generation of Sadlers in 2004.

MUTINY

Stringers, Ulverston, Cumbria; 9.3%

Slightly yeasty pear notes add interest to this Imperial stout, rich with dark chocolate and cakey malt, and capable of bottle-ageing, from a small brewery on the edge of the Lake District.

NINKASI

Wild, Evercreech, Somerset; 9%

Spicy, fruity and extraordinarily complex big blond ale tinged with vanilla, fenugreek and tropical fruit, made with local apples and wild and Champagne yeasts by a confidently innovative 2012 farmhouse-based team.

NORWEGIAN FARMHOUSE STRONG ALE

Poppyland, Cromer, Norfolk; 7.4%

A near-still rye bread-, eucalyptus- and treacle-tinged brew made with authentic Norwegian *kveik* yeast by a tiny and highly experimental seaside brewery, worth looking out.

OLD FORD EXPORT STOUT

Redchurch, Bethnal Green, London; 7.5%

Arguably the best of a strong range of older English beer styles from this bottle-conditioned specialist, dark as Hades and rammed with burned malt, coffee and bitter chocolate character.

OLD NO. 6

Joule's, Market Drayton, Shropshire; 4.8%, cask

Historic dark amber winter brew, with flavours of toffee, burned vine fruit and chocolate, and building bitterness in the finish, from a once-revered local name closed by Bass and resurrected in 2010.

OLD PECULIER

Theakston, Masham, North Yorkshire; 5.6%

Named after the medieval privileges exercised through a so-called "peculiar" (or "peculier") court such as Masham, this rich and famous old ale turns remarkably dry after a complex and sweetish, molasses-accented start.

OLD THUMPER

Ringwood [Marston's], Ringwood, Hampshire; 5.6%, cask

A substantial, reddish-brown bitter, with blackcurrant and almond flavours and a nutty, resinous finish, this is the signature beer of a brewery founded by late craft brewing pioneer Peter Austin.

OLD TOM

Robinsons, Stockport, Cheshire; 8.5%

Classic barley wine from an 1899 recipe illustrated with a cat's face, tasting of rum, chocolate and red wine with a rounded spirity finish turning dry and tannic. The flavoured brand extensions are best avoided.

OMERTA

Fixed Wheel, Blackheath, West Midlands; 7.5%

Gentler take on an Imperial stout from a 2014 Black Country start-up created by cycling enthusiasts. Its grainy, chewy body has hints of ash and rum over sweet chocolate.

ORACLE

Salopian, Hadnall, Shropshire; 4%, cask

Dry, creamy golden ale with tantalizing tropical-fruit and grapefruit notes and an oily, spicy but not too bitter finish, from a brewery already ahead of its time when founded in 1995, now gaining overdue respect.

BREWERIES TO WATCH

BULLFINCH

London

Former sound engineer Ryan McLean branched out in 2014 to produce beers such as fruity and moreishly drying **Born to be Mild** (3.3%), and the refreshingly lemon-tinged and spicy **Milou** (6%) *saison*.

CHORLTON

Manchester

Specialist in tart German styles and *Brettanomyces* fermentation, best known for the surprisingly successful hop-forward take on a *Berliner weisse* **Amarillo Sour** (5.4%), while **Citra Brett Pale** (4.5%) does what it says on the can, and rather well.

CLOUDWATER

Manchester

Manchester's most ambitious new brewery offering charming seasonally rotating **Session IPAs** (~4.8%) and well-hopped lagers, plus a varied series of **DIPAs**, each highly anticipated.

ORIGINAL

Dark Star, Partridge Green, West Sussex; 5%, cask

Toasty and autumnal tart dark ale recreating the first "microbrew" to win Champion Beer of Britain in 1987, from a renowned brewery that began in Brighton's Evening Star pub, also famed for hoppy brews.

OSCAR WILDE

Mighty Oak, Maldon, Essex; 3.7%, cask

Rare and impressive southern mild from a brewery founded in 1996 by an ex-Ind Coope brewer, with a full malty caramel palate, some blackcurrant fruit, a touch of roast and bracing hops around the edges.

PALE RIDER

Kelham Island, Sheffield, South Yorkshire; 5.2%, cask

Lively golden ale brimming with lychee, pineapple and citrus, and a prickly finish, the best-known beer from a revered pub brewery founded by the late Dave Wickett, one of the architects of the British beer revolution.

PEDIGREE

Marston's, Burton upon Trent, Staffordshire; 4.5%, cask

The only beer still fermented using Burton Unions at the last-surviving historic, non-multinational brewery in England's brewing capital, this is a toffee-ish pale ale with gently spicy–orange hoppiness, apple notes and a delicately drying finish.

PENNY LANE PALE

Mad Hatter, Liverpool, Merseyside; 3.9%

Fine modern-style pale ale that is the brewery's flagship brand, with orange and mango aromas and peppery bitterness within a sweetish body.

THE PORTER

Anspach & Hobday, London; 6.7%

A home-brew competition victory with this luscious, complex, tangy fruit and chocolate porter prompted Paul Anspach and Jack Hobday to turn commercial as one of the highlights of London's Bermondsey "beer mile".

REPUBLIKA

Windsor & Eton, Windsor, Berkshire; 4.8%

Impressively authentic Bohemian-style pilsner with flowery, grassy notes and a firmly bitter edge, created with Czech assistance by ex-Courage brewers in the shadow of the famous royal castle by the Thames.

RUBY MILD

Rudgate, Tockwith, North Yorkshire; 4.4%, cask

Firm grainy malt, brown sugar, dark fruit and quite a bracing hoppy, chalky finish on an award-winning dark mild from a brewery founded in 1992 that does well at both traditional and contemporary styles.

BREWERIES TO WATCH

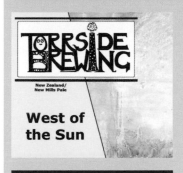

New Zealand/
New Mills Pale

West of the Sun

SACRE BREW

Wolverhampton, West Midlands

New York City native Gwen Sanchirico conjures highly inventive beers including semi-regular rye *saison* **Man on the Oss** (4.7%), and Belgian-style golden ale **Dracunculus** (4.8%).

TORRSIDE

New Mills, Derbyshire

Brewery commanding immediate attention on its late 2015 launch with beers like the accomplished session IPA **West of the Sun** (4.5%), with white grape and floral notes, and **Sto Lat** (2.8%), a rare British *grodziskie*.

SAISON RHUBARB AND GINGER

Partizan, London; 3.9%

One of numerous often-changing Belgian-inspired beers, this elegant and refreshing brew skilfully integrates subtle ginger and rhubarb flavours and fruity yeast notes with a light lactic edge.

SBA

Donnington, Stow-on-the-Wold, Gloucestershire; 4.4%, cask

Smooth, dry premium bitter tinged with caramel, fruit and sometimes buttery tones, from a small, picturesque Cotswold independent with its own trout lake.

SINGLE HOP

Mallinsons, Huddersfield, West Yorkshire; 3.9%, cask

Series of fine, clean golden ales showcasing various hops that have steadily enhanced the reputation of this notably small outfit. The Galaxy-hopped version is grassy and citric.

SNECK LIFTER

Jennings [Marston's], Cockermouth, Cumbria; 5.1%, cask

Signature dark ale, rich with flavours of treacle toffee, burned toast and tangy orange peel, from a classic Victorian small town brewery on the northwestern edge of the Lake District.

SNOW TOP

Old Dairy, Tenterden, Kent; 6%, cask

Cakey, creamy and chocolaty award-winning winter special dark ale lifted by quite a dose of spicy and fruity hops, from an unassuming but reliable farm-based brewery opened in 2010.

SONOMA PALE ALE

Track, Manchester; 3.8%

Session pale ale from a railway arch behind Manchester Piccadilly Station occupied by an ex-Camden Town brewer late in 2014, with focused floral, fruit-salad and citrus aromas and flavours, most courtesy of Mosaic hops.

SOUR GRAPES

Lovibonds, Henley-on-Thames, Oxfordshire; 5.4%

Wine-barrel-aged sour beer that began as a mistake but went on to win a medal in international competitions; zesty, tartly fruity and floral, with a balanced lactic character.

STOUT

Titanic, Stoke-on-Trent, Staffordshire; 4.5%

Intense, roast- and mocha-tinged stout successfully developed as alternative to the Irish variety by a consistently high-achieving brewery in the home city of the captain of the SS *Titanic*.

STRANNIK

Northern Monk, Leeds, West Yorkshire; 9%

Assertively rich, near-black Imperial stout with marzipan, port and sherry flavours, and a roasty rosehip-tart finish, from a youthful and inventive team with great promise.

STRONG SUFFOLK

Greene King, Bury St Edmunds, Suffolk; 6%

Unique blend of Old 5X, a strong, vinous and slightly sour stock ale aged in oak vats, and a malty, sweetish Burton ale, neither of which is regularly available separately. The best-kept secret from Britain's biggest non-multinational brewer.

SUBLIME CHAOS

Anarchy, Morpeth, Northumberland; 7%

Punchy coffee stout with blackcurrant, liquorice, honey and fruity New Zealand hop notes, and a surprisingly gentle, chocolaty finish, from what is one of northeast England's most acclaimed contemporary breweries.

SUMMER LIGHTNING

Hop Back, Downton, Wiltshire; 5%, cask

This lovely golden ale, from a former brewpub, galvanized British brewing in the 1990s by successfully taking a swipe at the premium lager market. Still a zesty, perfumed delight, with a long finish for the style.

T.E.A.

Hogs Back, Tongham, Surrey; 4.2%, cask

Popular and very English bitter from a farmhouse brewery perched atop a chalk ridge, with notes of plum, autumn fruit and tobacco, and earthy hops on a mellow, sweetish finish.

THREEONESIX

Grain, Harleston, Norfolk; 3.9%, cask

Excellent low-strength refresher, parchment pale but gloriously fruity, brewed from pilsner malt and Amarillo hops at a farm brewery opened in the Waveney Valley in 2006.

TRINITY

Redemption, London; 3%, cask

Citrus and rose notes and lightly bitter resins over a decent malty body characterize this masterclass of a low-gravity, high-flavour light ale, made from three malts and three hops by one of the earliest (2010) and still one of the best of London's new wave.

STYLE SPOTLIGHT

CASK BITTER AND MILD

Britain remains the only country where draught beer that continues fermenting in its cask has survived as a mainstream commercial format. Known as cask-conditioned or sometimes "real" ale, the beer is served without additional gas pressure, straight from the cask or via a handpump. Its quality relies on competent and conscientious retailers, and not all are up to the challenge.

A variety of economic and cultural factors contributed to cask's survival in Britain, along with the fact that the subtle flavours and aromas of the low-strength session bitters and milds that increasingly dominated British drinking habits after the First World War were enhanced by cask-conditioning, but obliterated by kegging.

When the industry attempted to dump this format in the late 1960s, a consumer movement led by the Campaign for Real Ale (CAMRA) arose to resist it. Even in today's market of diverse and distinctive beers, there remains something special about a top-quality cask bitter or mild in peak condition, gently carbonated and cellar cool.

To fully appreciate this, try **Holden's Golden Glow**, sweetish and light-coloured with subtle hopping; **Black Sheep Bitter**, a blackcurrant-tinged classic; or the lightly peppery and resinous **Butcombe Bitter**. An unapologetically old-school, chalky-dry pint with a gingery note is **Timothy Taylor's Landlord**.

Mild is an object lesson in how to squeeze maximum flavour from a low-strength beer, evident in the lightly tart, chocolaty **Hobsons Champion Mild**, or subtly nutty amber-coloured **Banks's Original**. Other beers particularly recommended in cask are highlighted elsewhere in this section.

TRIPLE CHOCOHOLIC

Saltaire, Shipley, West Yorkshire; 4.8%, cask

Accomplished stout featuring chocolate malt, chocolate syrup and cocoa nibs (hence the name), but supported by nutty malt and tart citric fruit.

UNFILTERED HELLS

Camden Town [AB InBev], London; 4.6%

Flagship of a craft brewer plucked up by AB InBev in 2015 for its solid street cred. The hazy version of this London lager has plenty of juicy malt, crisp polleny hops and a slightly citrus finish.

VINTAGE

Bristol Beer Factory, Bristol; 6.6%

Annually produced old ale usually blended from oak-aged beers, with rich malt, cherry and tobacco notes. One of many strong options from a Bristol stalwart based on the historic Ashton Gate brewery site.

WHERRY

Woodforde's, Woodbastwick, Norfolk; 3.8%, cask

Popular, cheerfully light, slightly astringent but satisfying blackcurrant-tinged golden bitter, called after a traditional style of sailing boat.

WORKIE TICKET

Mordue, North Shields, Tyne and Wear; 4.5%, cask

Deliciously autumnal malt-forward dark bitter with a waft of blackberry fruit, named with a local dialect term for a troublemaker.

WORTHINGTON'S WHITE SHIELD

Molson Coors UK, Burton upon Trent, Staffordshire; 5.6%

Historic bottle-conditioned pale ale with a taste of fresh apricot jam, nutty grainy maltiness and quite a pursing hop note at the finish. Cellar-worthy despite its low strength. One of the UK's most authentic heritage ales.

XB

Batemans, Wainfleet, Lincolnshire; 3.7%, cask

Chewy best bitter with hints of russet apples and almonds, from a picturesque family-owned brewer that excels at traditional bitters, milds and other quaffable styles.

XXXX

Hydes, Salford, Manchester; 6.8%

Notes of mint toffee, whisky and brown sugar characterize this spicy seasonal barley wine from a brewer once known as the most conservative in the UK, with some recipes unchanged for 50 years, yet now refreshed.

YORKSHIRE STINGO

Samuel Smith, Tadcaster, North Yorkshire; 8–9%

Oak-aged, bottle-conditioned old ale packed with flavours of nutty malt, spiced toffee and red fruit, this is a standout entry in a range of bottled specialities from Yorkshire's oldest and most eccentric brewery.

YOUNG'S WINTER WARMER

Charles Wells [Marston's], Bedford, Bedfordshire; 5%, cask

With its rich malted-milk body layered with coffee, liquorice and cola, this seasonal is arguably the best cask beer from Charles Wells, which absorbed the brands of former London stalwart Young's in 2006 before itself being purchased by Marston's in mid-2017.

ISLE OF MAN

BITTER

Okells, Kewaigue; 3.7%, cask

Classic amber bitter with a twist of
Muscat-like fruitiness from New World
hops over a soft but dry, biscuity
base, from the only surviving historic
independent brewery located on the
Isle of Man.

NORTHERN IRELAND

BREWERY TO WATCH

BOUNDARY

Belfast

Proving that Ireland's burgeoning
craft beer scene knows no borders,
Boundary's beers include a fragrant
American Pale Ale (3.5%) and a
more obviously **Irish Export Stout**
(7%), plus Belgian styles and mixed-
fermentation brews.

BALTIC PORTER

Farmageddon, Comber, Co Down;
10.8%, bottle

The most ambitious brew so far from
a young co-operative based near
Newtownards and typical of new beer
in the north. Pushes the coffee a bit, along
with the definition of Irish porter, but
warming and mellow with huge presence.

BELFAST ALE

Whitewater, Newry, Co Down; 4.5%, cask

Delightful reddish amber ale, substantial
and distinctive with crisp malt and mineral
tones, from the province of County Down's
second-largest and oldest brewery,
producing quality ale since 1996.

SCOTLAND

5AM SAINT

BrewDog, Ellon, Aberdeenshire; 5%

The UK's most successful brewery in a century, influential and rapidly expanding, producing a huge range that includes this reliable, flavourful and quaffable red ale with elements of pine, lemon tea and biscuit malt.

80/-

Belhaven [Greene King], Dunbar, East Lothian; 4.2%, cask

Once dubbed "the Burgundy of Scotland", this rare surviving traditional "80 shilling" ale is richly malty but dry, suffused with nutty notes and a light touch of sulphur.

80/-

Stewart, Loanhead, Edinburgh; 4.4%, cask

Spot-on traditional Scottish session ale, lusciously malty and comforting with tobacco and dark fruit flavours, from one of the few new Scottish breweries conserving such retro styles.

BEARFACE LAGER

Drygate [C&C], Glasgow; 4.4%

Fruity, hazy, hop-forward but balanced and crisp contemporary lager from inventive craft brewery and taproom outside the gates of Glasgow's historic

ICONIC BREWERY

TRAQUAIR HOUSE

Innerleithen, Scottish Borders

The oldest-inhabited stately home in Scotland, where the late laird revived the 16th-century brewhouse in the grounds in 1965 to create what was in effect the UK's first microbrewery. Signature revivalist **Traquair House Ale** (7.2%) is a dark delight of rich malt with tart-fruit and vermouth tones, while **Jacobite Ale** (8%) is sweetish, complex and liquoriced, its name reflecting the family's historic loyalties.

Tennent's lager brewery, a joint venture with Williams Brothers.

BROCKVILLE DARK

Tryst, Falkirk; 3.8%, cask

Chocolaty, husky, roasty and slightly briny Scottish mild from a reliable producer named after Falkirk's historic cattle market, offering several other imaginative choices.

DARK ISLAND RESERVE

Orkney [Sinclair], Quoyloo, Orkney; 10%

This well-established northern island brewery supercharges its Dark Island ale to create this fruity, peaty whisky-barrel-aged delight, with rich, smooth sultana and chocolate-cake malt, rosehip tartness and a faint whiff of seaweed.

FRAOCH

Williams Brothers, Alloa, Clackmannanshire; 5%

The beer that changed perceptions of Scottish brewing in 1992, using local heather to create lavender and ginger-like notes over tartly fruity malt in this light amber ale.

HOPCLASSIC BELGIAN IPA

Six° North, Stonehaven, Aberdeenshire; 6.6%

An IPA fermented with Belgian yeast, yielding notes of ripe apricot pastry and raspberry, and a bittering but persistently fruity finish, from a brewery so named because it is six degrees of latitude north of Brussels.

JARL

Fyne, Cairndow, Argyll and Bute; 3.8%, cask

One of the UK's most flavourful contemporary golden ales, boasting zesty lychee and kiwi fruit supported by crisp malt, from a farm-based brewery overlooking Loch Fyne.

OLA DUBH 18

Harviestoun, Alva, Clackmannanshire; 8%

One of Scotland's oldest craft breweries ages already notable oaked porter Old Engine Oil in ex-whisky barrels to create this complex, spicy, malty delight, labelled according to the age of the previous Highland Park whisky contents.

ORKNEY BLAST

Swannay, by Evie, Orkney; 6%

Fruit salad, peach and grapefruit dominate this nectarish strong pale ale with a peppery-sulphur note, from a small but reliable operation also known as the Highland Brewery.

ROGUE WAVE

Cromarty, Cromarty, Highland; 5.7%

Cheerful contemporary pale ale with flavours of lime, raspberry jam, elderflower and cracked pepper, and a bitter quinine quality, from a family-run brewery in a far-flung coastal location northeast of Inverness.

CAN'T-MISS BREWERY

TEMPEST

Tweedbank, Scottish Borders

Always interesting, this multiple award-winning team progressed to greatness via garage brewing in New Zealand and a gastro-brewpub in the Scottish Lowlands to a new 30-hectolitre brewhouse that opened in 2015. The stalwart is tropical-fruity pale ale **Long White Cloud** (5.6%); the charmer is more piney but balanced IPA **Brave New World** (7%); the masterpiece is beautifully balanced mocha porter **Red Eye Flight** (7.4%); and the explorer is burned, short of smoky, Imperial stout-cum-wee heavy **Old Parochial** (10%).

WALES

DARK MATTER

Vale of Glamorgan, Barry, Vale of Glamorgan; 4.4%, cask

Award-winning dark brown porter with rich layers of chocolate, blackcurrant and roasted malt tones from a 2005 brewery with a growing reputation and food-friendly leanings.

OCHR DYWYLL Y MÔS/DARK SIDE OF THE MOOSE

Mŵs Piws/Purple Moose, Porthmadog, Gwynedd; 4.6%, cask

Unusually hoppy dark ale with citrus and pineapple notes set over a coffee and cola body, from a small brewery on the coastal strip of the Snowdonia National Park.

BREWERIES TO WATCH

HOPCRAFT

Pontyclun, Mid-Glamorgan

A gathering collective of South Wales talent is now boosting a project creating hoppy beers like Citra-hopped cask pale **Citraic** (5.2%), black IPA **Devilfish Ink** (5.8%) and versions of toffee–grapefruit brown ale **Diggin' up the King** (4.6–5.4%).

LINES

Caerphilly

Experimental brewer focused on eco-friendly production and developing six "lines" of beer, impressing early with light ale **Munich Table Beer** (2.8%), **Farmhouse IPA** (6.1%) and Imperial stout **Primary Brett** (9.5%).

RAMNESIA STRONG ALE

Penlon Cottage, New Quay, Ceredigion; 5.6%

Complex, nutty and plummy strong ale with a mellow stab of hops in the finish from a brewery that began on a farm in 2004 and is noted for an eclectic bottled range.

SA

Brains, Cardiff; 4.2%, cask

This curious mid-gold bitter, dry and seedy with autumn fruit and a gooseberry-tart finish, is arguably the most distinctive regular from one of only two surviving old-established Welsh independents, soon to move to a new site.

CAN'T-MISS BREWERY

TINY REBEL

Newport

Youthful craft brewery rocketing to prominence since 2012 with bold and flavourful beers like the raspberryish red ale **Cwtch** (4.6%), Champion Beer of Britain in 2015; **Dirty Stop Out** (5%), a complex but well-integrated oatmeal stout with a dash of smoked malt; and the floral and fruity flagship ale **FUBAR** (4.4%). The brewery also has a pair of fine pubs in Cardiff and Newport.

REPUBLIC OF IRELAND

While many, indeed perhaps most, beer drinkers still think of stout when the term Irish is mentioned, Ireland's brewers have in recent years made great strides in brewing all manner of styles, including many new variants of porter and stout.

BLACK LIGHTNING

9 White Deer, Ballyvourney, Co Cork; 6.5%

The most hop-forward of Ireland's regular black IPAs, making great use of Simcoe hops for flavours of orange candy and lemon peel, plus a balancing dry, roasted finish.

BLACK ROCK

Dungarvan, Dungarvan, Co Waterford; 4.3%

Though it was first brewed as recently as 2010, this dry stout is as classic as they come with all the signature roasted flavours of the style, plus an added fruity complexity from its bottle-conditioning.

BLOND

White Gypsy, Templemore, Co Tipperary; 4%

A light take on a Bavarian *weissbier*, pale and hazy yellow with a highly refreshing crispness and gentle celery hop flavours. Perfect easy-going, summertime fare.

BLUE JUMPER

Western Herd, Kilmaley, Co Clare; 6.2%

An IPA to remind you why you first fell in love with the style, this offers the classic US combination of palate-scrubbing grapefruit bitterness and rich warming toffee set on a rounded, filling body.

CARRAIG DUBH

West Kerry, Ballyferriter, Co Kerry; 6%

A big porter from West Kerry, one of the country's smallest breweries, delivering luscious rich chocolate with a fun, fresh herbal character resulting from the unorthodox use of German hop varieties.

CASTAWAY

YellowBelly, Wexford, Co Wexford; 4.2%

At a time when breweries everywhere seem to be turning out *Berliner weisse*, this one really grabs the attention, with a strong, refreshing tartness balanced by massively juicy, and real, passion-fruit. No half measures here.

COALFACE

Carrig, Drumshanbo, Co Leitrim; 5.5%

Fruit-forward black IPAs are rare, but this fits the bill. The hops bring zesty citrus notes, enhanced by a sweet

chocolate flavour from the dark malt, resulting in the unusual marriage of warming satisfaction and refreshment.

CONNEMARA PALE

Independent, Carraroe, Co Galway; 6%

Loaded with more pine-and-citrus US hops than most Irish IPAs, this is dominated by a dry and sharp bitterness. The addition of rye to the grain bill adds an extra vegetal spice.

FRANCIS' BIG BANGIN' IPA

Rye River, Celbridge, Co Kildare; 7.1%

Despite the jokey name, this is a seriously good multi-award-winning US-style IPA, part of the brewery's McGargles range; pale gold, light-bodied and popping with citrus bitterness, tropical fruit and a slight savoury complexity.

GRAFFITI

Trouble, Kill, Co Kildare; 3.6%

The campaign for hop-forward low-strength beer in Ireland was hard fought and Graffiti was one of the first. It remains one of the best examples, with big pine and grapefruit notes in a smart little package.

GUINNESS FOREIGN EXTRA

Diageo, Dublin; 7.5%

A classic since records began, with vital statistics essentially unchanged since the 1820s. Balancing dry roast against smooth treacle and seasoned with a signature lactic sharpness, this stout is complex yet accessible.

HEAT SINK

Metalman, Waterford, Co Waterford; 4.9%

A playful take on Irish porter, incorporating smoked malt and cayenne pepper. The smoke is little more than seasoning, while the chilli starts mild but builds pleasantly on the chocolate malt flavour as it goes.

IRISH PALE ALE

Galway Hooker, Oranmore, Co Galway; 4.3%

Ireland's original hop-forward pale ale, taking its cue from Sierra Nevada (*see page 206*). You get a taste of traditional Irish crystal malt biscuit with the bright, fresh grapefruit notes of US hops.

KENTUCKY COMMON

Wicklow Wolf, Bray, Co Wicklow; 4.8%

It is unclear why Wicklow Wolf picked this obscure southern US style, but it's great that they did. Jet black in colour, it mixes the light caramel of brown ale with the refreshing dry roast of porter.

LAGER

Boyne Brewhouse, Drogheda, Co Meath; 4.8%

A lightly carbonated lager in the *Dortmunder* style, this full-bodied beer is given a bold fresh-mown-grass flavour from the Saaz hops used.

O'HARA'S LEANN FOLLÁIN

Carlow, Bagenalstown, Co Carlow; 6%

"Revered" is not too strong a word for how this export-strength beer is treated by Irish stout connoisseurs. The texture is weighty and warming, while the generous hopping gives it an invigorating old-fashioned bitterness.

PORTER

J W Sweetman, Dublin; 4.8%

A simple name belies an immensely complex beer, mixing rich chocolate, bright floral perfume and sharper tar and tobacco. Despite all this, it never tastes busy, staying smooth and satisfying to drink.

THE PREACHER

O Brother, Kilcoole, Co Wicklow; 4.6%

Badged as a session IPA by the brewery, this delivers an authentically US taste experience. Pine and lemon peel are delivered by the West Coast hops, with the Wicklow water giving it a chalky mineral base.

RAIN CZECH

Rascals, Rathcoole, Co Dublin; 5%

Jaw-dropping pilsner is rare outside of central Europe, but Rascals have managed to score one for Ireland with this summer seasonal loaded with Saaz hops for a sumptuous and soft damp-grass flavour.

SHANCO DUBH

Brehon, Carrickmacross, Co Monaghan; 7.7%

A bruiser of a strong porter, packing in all the signature flavours – bitter coffee, high-cocoa dark chocolate and unctuous caramel. This uncompromising jet-black beer rewards slow sipping and savouring.

SHERKIN LASS

West Cork, Baltimore, Co Cork; 4.4%

Originally a cask exclusive, though now available in bottles, this makes superb use of the natural conditioning process to create a soft effervescence with bright apricot notes. Best enjoyed at the source – Casey's Hotel in Baltimore.

SPAILPÍN SAISON

Killarney, Killarney, Co Kerry; 5.5%

A perfect rendition of Belgian saison, lightly crisp with a refreshing pepperiness. The name, pronounced "SPAL-peen", is the Irish-language equivalent of saisonnaires, the farmhands who gave saison its name.

SPRING BOCK

St Mel's, Longford, Co Longford; 5.6%

An authentic-tasting German-style lager, rich gold in colour with a full body and a flavour that perfectly integrates smooth honey malt with the peppery greenness of German hops.

WESTERN WARRIOR

Black Donkey, Ballinlough, Co Roscommon; 4.6%

This farmhouse brewery has a saison as its flagship beer and this lager is brewed to an identical recipe, but with a different yeast. The result is crisp and clean with a wheaty cereal wholesomeness.

WESTPORT EXTRA

Mescan, Westport, Co Mayo; 9.3%

The brewery is a little bit of Belgium in rural west Ireland, and this is its strongest beer to date, broadly a supercharged tripel that is dark gold in colour with enticing spices and tropical fruit.

WORLD'S END

Blacks, Kinsale, Co Cork; 8.5%

An Imperial stout for the winter months, this adds cocoa and vanilla pods to a smooth and rounded base. Sweet without being cloying, it makes for a superb dessert beer.

WRASSLERS XXXX

Porterhouse, Dublin; 5%

The biggest and boldest of Ireland's drinking stouts, holding a full hand of Galena hops for a bitter green punch on top of the leather-and-tobacco rich roast malt. Best when on draught, though a slightly different bottled edition is available.

BREWERIES TO WATCH

HOPE

Dublin

So far just limited-edition brews from head brewer Mark Nixon – ex of Trouble Brewing (*see* page 96) – but watch this space.

WHITE HAG

Ballymote, Co Sligo

Revolutionizing with US-inspired styles like session IPA **Little Fawn** (4.2%) and Imperial oatmeal stout **Black Boar** (10.2%), plus Irish *gruit* ale **Beann Gulban** (7.5%).

CAN'T-MISS BREWERIES

EIGHT DEGREES

Mitchelstown, Co Cork

Their mastery of hop-forward styles is beyond dispute, with **Full Irish IPA** (6%) expertly blending the citrus and tropical sides of the hop flavour equation. **Big River IPA** (5.3%) celebrates the brewers' Antipodean roots, piling in Australian hops for fresh and refreshing juicy melon and guava elements alongside assertive pine and herbs, while **Amber Ella** (5.8%) offers a chewy biscuit malt base and notes of peach, plum and tangerine. Watch also for frequent specials and one-offs.

GALWAY BAY

Galway, Co Galway

Highlights of this prolific brewery's range include the multi-award-winning **Of Foam and Fury** (8.5%), a perfect rendering of American double IPA; classic porter **Stormy Port** (4.8%); and a more recent addition to the line-up, **Harvest Altar** (5.6%), a sumptuously

smooth autumnal brown ale. For something different, there is **Heathen** (3%), Ireland's only black *Berliner weisse* – a refreshingly tart palate-scrubber.

KINNEGAR

Rathmullan, Co Donegal

A tiny farmhouse brewery (rhymes with "vinegar") with big plans. **Rustbucket** (5.1%) rye ale is universally adored for its combination of peppery, grassy rye flavours with mouth-watering New World hop bitterness. A rarer black IPA version, **Black Bucket** (6.5%), adds liquorice and espresso notes to this, while the brewery explores the sour side of the spectrum with beers such as **Sour Grapes** (5%), lightly acidic and softly fruity, like a fine Sauvignon Blanc.

FRANCE

The French have always enjoyed beer, and indeed pre-First World War, France was awash in breweries, several thousand of them. The 20th century proved almost fatal to French brewing, however, and even at the start of this century one would have been hard pressed to predict the boom in *les bières artisanales* that has occurred since. The culture is still in its infancy, but having seen the rise of many hundred breweries across every *département* in the land, an observer would be equally imprudent to doubt that at least flashes of greatness shall surely follow.

3 MONTS

St-Sylvestre, St-Sylvestre-Cappel, Nord; 8.5%

From what was once viewed as the producer of many of France's finest ales, this flagship *bière de garde* is soft and slightly appley in aroma, full-bodied with dried-fruit and slight vinous flavours, finishing off-dry and warming.

ALPINE

Galibier, Valloire, Savoie; 4.8%

From the highest-altitude brewery in France comes this US-style pale ale with the hop emphasis on aroma rather than bitterness, hints of white wine in the aroma and tropical-fruit flavours defining its dry and lingering nature.

AMÈRE NOIRE

L'Agrivoise, Saint Agrève, Ardèche; 6.5%

A black IPA from a brewery noted for its well-hopped ales, this has an aroma of well-kilned malt and singed wood mixed with liquorice and pine, and a powerful, grassy bitterness that finishes quite dry.

BARBE BLEUE

Mélusine, Chambretaud, Vendée; 7%

A dark brown ale seasoned with aniseed and alchemilla, the latter a herb sometimes used in tea. Almost stout-like, it has a roasty, vanilla-ish aroma and flavours of coffee and liquorice with hints of banana.

BARRICADE RAMPONNEAU

La Canaille, Sail-sous-Couzan, Loire; 6%

From a brewery housed in a former mineral water plant comes this brown ale made with smoked malt and hot peppers, resulting in a nuanced smokiness, roasted maltiness and a note of spicy heat that balances everything out.

BIÈRE DE BRIE BLANCHE

Rabourdin, Courpalay, Seine-et-Marne; 4.5%

Named after the region renowned for its famed cheese, this farmhouse brewery beer demonstrates wonderfully the French take on the Belgian-style wheat beer, with exquisite balance between malt, hops and spice, and a slight sweetness in the aftertaste.

BIÈRE DE GARDE

ArtMalté, Annecy, Haute-Savoie; 6.5%

The product of a young female brewer respectful of traditional styles, this *bière de garde* is fermented with a *saison* yeast and maturated for eight weeks, delivering peppery flavours with fudge and coffee notes in the finish.

BIÈRE DES SANS CULOTTES

La Choulette, Hordain, Nord; 7%

So called in recognition of the heroes of the French Revolution, this golden *bière de garde* has a yeasty, spicy aroma with tones of honey and fruit, and a caramelly malt body layered with notes of brown spice and dried fruit.

BITTER

Joli Rouge, Canals, Tarn-et-Garonne; 5.5%

Hopped with an Alsatian hop called Barbe Rouge, this malt-driven French interpretation of the English bitter has a citrusy nose with hints of berries and a quenching body with grassy bitterness.

BM SIGNATURE

Rouget de Lisle, Bletterans, Jura; 11%

A barrel-aged Imperial stout that has cherries added three months prior to bottling, giving it a vinous character and flavours of chocolate and cherry. From a pioneering brewery that boasts one of the top brewery barrel rooms in France.

BORIS GOUDENOV

Corrézienne, Curemonte, Corrèze; 10.5%

An Imperial stout with a powerful toasted malt aroma boasting notes of dried fruits, with a full and balanced body offering elements of coffee, wood, dark chocolate and candied fruit balanced by floral hoppiness.

CABÉO'LUNE

de la Pleine Lune, Chabeuil, Drôme; 5.2%

Brewed entirely from barley grown and malted locally, this light bitter has an aroma that emphasizes the grains used, along with light citrusy notes and a body that does the same but becomes bitter as it progresses.

ICONIC BREWERY

THIRIEZ

Esquelbecq, Nord

For 20 years a leader in French *bière artisanale*, this brewery near Cassel is best known for its Kent Bramling Cross-hopped *saison* **Etoile du Nord** (5.5%). Other noteworthy beers include the red wine barrel-conditioned, Flemish-style **Vieille Brune** (5.8%); a revivalist French "table beer" created with the US brewery Jester King **Petite Princesse** (2.9%); **Dalva** (8.5%), a complex and nuanced double IPA with tropical-fruit and nutty notes; and **Ambrée d'Esquelbecq** (5.8%), a *bière de garde* boasting a fine balance between hops and caramelly malt.

CERVOISE LANCELOT

Lancelot, Le Roc-Saint-André, Morbihan; 6%

First brewed in 1990, this light amber ale is said to be in an ancient Gauloise style, seasoned with seven herbs, one of which is hops, to create a spicy–herbal palate with a honey-ish aroma and toasted-malt backdrop.

CHARLY'S BEER

Gilbert's, Rabastens, Tarn; 9.1%

A wonderful barley wine with aromas of candy cane and candied fruit, and a balanced and mouth-coating body with candied-orange and tangerine notes, powerful bitterness and caramelly malt, all leading to a long and hoppy finish.

LA CHIMÈRE DE CENDRE

L'Antre de l'Échoppe, Narbonne, Aude; 4.8%

An atypical stout in the French style, with powerful roasted malt aromas and flavours, some ashy dryness and complex hoppiness from Alsatian Triskel, Strisselspalt and Aramis hops.

CUVÉE DES JONQUILLES

Au Baron, Gussignies, Nord; 7%

From a brewery–restaurant on the Belgian border comes this *bière de garde* that blurs the line between its style and *saison*, with a refreshing, sparkling character, balanced bitterness and dry finish.

Bière de Lorraine
façon XVIII ᵉᵐᵉ siècle

DUCHESSE DE LORRAINE

Les Brasseurs de Lorraine, Pont-à-Mousson, Meurthe-et-Moselle; 5.5%

A mahogany ale made with smoked malt and sassafras, with a fruity and spicy aroma, a slight sourness and oaky aspects to the body and a bright, refreshing effervescence.

EAU DE PIERRE

Entre 2 Mondes, Mouthier-Haute-Pierre, Doubs; 6.2%

A copper ale made from seven malts, hazy with a grassy nose, rich body and floral, well-balanced flavour leading to a more bitter finish with spicy notes.

L'EXILÉE

L'Excuse, Mauzevin, Hautes-Pyrénées; 6.5%

From a youthful and promising brewery, this amber ale is seasoned with cardamom and star anise for an aroma and flavour that are spicy but well balanced with malt and hops, having a firm but gentle bitterness and dry finish.

EXTRA STOUT

Les 3 Loups, Trélou-sur-Marne, Aisne; 6.9%

A deceptively approachable strong stout with a powerful aroma of chocolate and roasted malt and a creamy body balancing bitterness with hints of cocoa and spice.

FLEUR DE MONTREUIL

La Montreuilloise, Montreuil, Paris; 5–5.5%

A summer beer produced by a cooperative teaching brewery that emphasizes a local, organic approach. Flavoured with elderflowers, this is a biscuity ale with slight acidity and fruity, blackcurrant notes.

FRAMBRUNETTE

La Barbaude, Nîmes, Gard; 5.4–5.7%

Infused with local strawberries, this stout boasts an aroma that is unsurprisingly like gourmet chocolate-covered strawberries, although the body tends more to chocolate and floral blackberry flavours with a bitter finish.

GAILLARDE BRUNE

La Gaillarde, Gignac, Hérault; 9%

A strong and deep brown ale aged on oak chips, this has a chocolaty, spicy dried-fruit aroma and a taste to match, with dark fruits dominant and mocha, spicy vanilla and liquorice in support.

CAN'T-MISS BREWERIES

● ● ● ● ● ● ● ● ● ● ● ●

LA DÉBAUCHE

Angoulême, Charente

The brewery that has become a reference point for others wishing to create strong dark ales or barrel-aged beers in France, characterized by **Nevermore** (9.5%), an intense and full-bodied Imperial stout with strong notes of chocolate and vanilla, and **Cognac Barrel** (9.5%), a self-describing ale boasting flavours of candied fruit and raisins. More experimental beers include **Amorena** (14%), an Imperial stout flavoured with almond paste and Amarena cherries and then barrel-conditioned on a bed of either cherries or raspberries.

DES GARRIGUES

Sommières, Gard

Pioneer of ultra-hoppy beers in the land of wine, boasting brands like **La Frappadingue** (7.5%), with powerful bitterness and citrus notes on a caramelly malt base, and **P'tite Frapp'** (3.8%), a light but still amply hopped variation. Other beers include the seasonal barley wine **Sacré Grôle** (12.6%); **La Ribouldingue** (4.5%), a wheat ale seasoned with local herbs; **La Belle en Goguette** (6%), a spicy wheat pale ale; and **La Bière du Coing** (5.5%), a tangy seasonal ale flavoured with quince.

GOSE'ILLA

Sulauze, Miramas, Bouches-du-Rhône; 5%

From a farmhouse brewery with a biodynamic approach to farming and brewing comes this refreshing take on the *gose* style, complete with minerally aromas and a suitably tart and refreshing character.

GRÄTZER

du Haut Buëch, Lus-la-Croix-Haute, Drôme; 3.4%

A specialist in obscure beer styles, brewer David Desmars enjoys developing wheat beers in particular, as with this hazy, light gold *grätzer* with smoked-meat aromas and a dry, highly effervescent and tangy character.

HOME OUTLAND

Fontenay-sous-Bois, Paris; 5.4%

Brewed on the outskirts of Paris, this US-style pale ale is bright gold with an aroma of lemon, mandarin and hints of cooked fruit and a dry, firm bitterness in the body.

HOUBLONNÉE À CRU

de la Plaine, Marseille, Bouches-du-Rhône; 5.5%

An organic pale ale dry-hopped to a full and floral aroma of white flowers and peach, with a refreshing and herbal bitterness holding flavours of tropical fruit and wild flowers.

INDAR JOKO

Etxeko Bob's Beer, Hasparren, Pyrénées-Atlantiques; 4.5%

A deep black dry stout in the Irish style produced by an English brewer in the Basque part of France, with notes of coffee and a gentle bitterness leading to a quaffably dry finish.

INSOMNUIT

La Rente Rouge, Chargey-lès-Gray, Haute-Saône; 7%

An annual release aged six months in Nuits-St-Georges wine barrels, emerging with a predictably winey character, an earthy, tobacco-ish aroma and notes of red fruit and oak in the creamy and rich body.

IPA

Parisis, Épinay-sous-Sénart, Essonne; 6.2%

A US-style IPA brewed in the Île-de-France region near Paris, this has an intense aroma of citrus, peach and honey and a rich malty–grainy flavour, with significant bitterness and hints of honey. The lingering finish is dry and fruity–bitter.

CAN'T-MISS BREWERIES
● ● ● ● ● ● ● ● ● ● ● ● ● ●

DU MONT SALÈVE

Neydens, Haute-Savoie

An impressive range of styles and sometimes audacious experiments are turned out by this brewery near the Swiss border. **Tsarine** (13%) is a powerful Imperial stout with espresso notes and a spicy bitterness in the finish; **Mademoiselle Aramis** (6%) is an IPA that highlights the Alsatian hop of its name alongside orange, pineapple and peach tones; **Tourbée** (5.5%) is a quaffable smoked malt ale with flavours of dark fruit and liquorice; and **Berliner Weisse** (3.3%) is tangy, wheaty and lemony.

SAINT GERMAIN

Aix-Noulette, Pas-de-Calais

A countryside brewery near Arras emphasizing the use of local hops and barley in their "Page 24"-labelled beers, such as **Réserve Hildegarde Blonde** (5.9%), a hoppy blond with sublime balance. Other terroir-focused efforts include **La Rhub'IPA** (6.9%), using local rhubarb to produce a floral, tangy and fruity flavour, while among the more limited-run brands are **Imperial Stout Whisky Barrel** (9.5%), boasting hoppiness in harmony with whisky and wood notes, and **Sour Ale** (4.9%), which displays a keen acidity on a sweet citrus-accented malty base.

CAN'T-MISS BREWERY

● ● ● ● ● ● ● ● ● ● ● ● ● ● ● ●

DE LA VALLÉE DU GIFFRE

Verchaix, Haute-Savoie

A young brewery with a wide range of styles and ongoing experiments. Their smoked malt beer, **La Petite Fumée** (4.8%), offers strong elements of roast and chimney, while the soft double IPA **Alt Sept 65** (8.3%) brings forth a resinous and lasting bitterness, and **La Rioule** (5.8%) is a single-hopped IPA that changes hop regularly – the version made with Alsatian Mistral hops was breathtaking. Also of note is the highly aromatic **Du Bout du Monde** (4.7%), a *saison* refermented with *Brettanomyces*.

IPA CITRA GALACTIQUE

du Grand Paris, St Denis, Seine-Saint-Denis; 6.5%

The result of a "union Franco–Américaine", this is a startling expression of the Citra hop, with a big mix of citrus, pine and tropical fruit on the nose and a dry and bitter body with lasting fruitiness.

JENLAIN AMBRÉE

Duyck, Jenlain, Nord; 7.5%

Widely regarded as an iconic *bière de garde*, this copper ale has a caramel and toasted bread body with earthy bitterness and gentle nutty tones. So successful in the 1990s that the brand changed from the family name Duyck to Jenlain.

KERZU

An Alarc'h, La Feuillée, Finistère; 7%

A seasonal Breton Imperial stout – the name means December in the Breton language – that is thick, rich, creamy and somewhat sweet, with notes of strong coffee and smoky wood.

MONGY TRIPLE

Cambier, Croix, Nord; 8%

From the brewery's line dedicated to the northern French engineer Alfred Mongy, this complex *tripel* has a fruity, spicy grain nose and a near-perfect balance of crisp maltiness, grassy bitterness and spicy fruitiness with just a hint of juniper.

NOIRE

Ninkasi, Tarare, Rhône; 6.6%

A revival of a 19th-century city beer style known as noire de Lyon, this sweet dark ale is similar to a porter, with caramel, coffee, fig, chocolate and toasted breadcrumb aromas and flavours, and a light bitterness.

PLANCHE ODE À LA VIE

La Franche, La Ferté, Jura; 7%

This hazy copper-gold ale is aged in barrels that were previously used for Jura's famous *vin jaune*, emerging with a powerfully vinous aroma and a tart and spicy body filled with yellow fruit, white wine and walnut.

RODÉO +

Bendorf, Strasbourg, Bas-Rhin; 10%

Made with apricot juice and aged in oak barrels for three months, this malty *tripel*-style ale combines the taste of apricot nectar with a light bitterness and leafy and fruity flavours from the local Triskel hops, finishing with a gentle sweetness.

SALAMANDRA

de l'Être, Paris, Paris; 6.5%

Located near the Gare de l'Est, this brewery brings "green" brewing to the French capital with, among other brands, this aromatically fruity, organic malt *saison* with spicy notes in the nose, a firm maltiness and drying bitterness on the finish.

SANGUINE

Iron, Montauban, Tarn-et-Garonne; 4.5–5%

From one of France's youngest and most promising brewers, David Garrigues, comes this hibiscus-flavoured wheat beer with an intense red hue, slightly lactic aromas of red berry and citrus and a tart, fruity and floral body.

BREWERY TO WATCH

PERLE

Strasbourg, Bas-Rhin

After years of brewing abroad, Christian Artzner returned to France to revive the 19th-century Perle brand with beers like the herbaceous, Strisselspalt-hopped **Perle Blonde** (5.4%) alongside grape ale **La Perle dans les Vignes** (7.7%) and the US-style **IPA** (6.6%).

SEIGLÉE

La Caussenarde, Saint-Beaulize, Aveyron; 6%

A unique ale made from barley both grown and malted on the farm where it is brewed, grainy with considerable spiciness, fruity notes and a long and lingering hop bitterness.

SYLVIE'CIOUS

Le Paradis, Blaiville-sur-l'Eau, Meurthe-et-Moselle; 5.5%

A "session-strength" version of the brewery's P'tite Sylvie IPA, this has a fragrant and fruity citrus aroma and sweetish, malty front that starts fruity but dries to a refreshing, hoppy finish.

TRIPLE

d'Orgemont, Sommepy-Tahure, Marne; 8.5%

In a brewery located not far from the Champagne capital of Reims, a different sort of golden elixir is produced, strongly Belgian influenced with spicy, peppery tones on a toasty, yellow, fruity malt base.

TROBAIRITZ

de Quercorb, Puivert, Aude; 6%

Brewed in the foothills of the Pyrenees, this *saison*-style blond ale boasts an appealing grassy aroma and a pale malt-driven palate with notes of citrus fruit and spice and a refreshing, herbal hop finish.

VOLCELEST ÉLEVÉE EN BARRIQUE

de la Vallée de Chevreuse, Bonnelles, Yvelines; 9.5%

Aged three months in French oak, this Imperial stout is aromatic with chocolate and blackberry notes and boasts fruity chocolate flavours in the body, but finishes dry and reminiscent of a spiced coffee.

LUXEMBOURG

In contrast to its more prolific neighbours, craft beer culture is developing slowly in the "lux" portion of the Benelux, but some small progress is nonetheless being made

BLACK WIDOW

Stuff, Steinsel; 6.5%

Created by two young brewers with arguably the country's first real new wave craft brewery, this lightweight, very drinkable porter has blackcurrant notes and hints of bitter chocolate and dried fruit that veer it toward a black IPA.

IPA

Simon, Wiltz; 5%

The first attempt by a Luxembourg "major" at something approaching craft is a quaffable, gently bitter and citrusy pale ale that is deliberately restrained to break a nation gently into a global phenomenon for which it may not quite be ready.

SATELLITE

Grand, Luxembourg City; 4.9%

Previously known as Capital City, the expat Kiwi owner was brewing at Simon (*see* left), but is switching to his own installation in 2017 to create his easy-drinking range, which includes this hoppy, fruity and citrusy golden-blond session IPA.

THE NETHERLANDS

Arguably no European beer scene has improved as remarkably over the past 10–15 years as has that of the Netherlands. From what was once a landscape dominated utterly by a small cabal of mighty breweries has emerged one of the Continent's most vibrant and creative craft beer markets.

58 HANDLANGER

Kompaan, The Hague, South Holland; 8.2%

An ultra-dry, slightly grassy triple-hopped golden-blond Imperial IPA with a fresh hop taste, medium bitter finish and an easy, quaffable drinking quality belying its strength.

400 VOLT VANILLE

Eindhoven, Eindhoven, North Brabant; 10%

This heavyweight Imperial stout has the inky black, viscous appearance of crude oil and is infused with Madagascar bourbon vanilla, which gives a sweet edge to balance the strong alcohol and bitter finish.

1818

Maallust, Veenhuizen, Drenthe; 10%

Sold as a limited edition in 75cl bottles, this full-bodied almost stout-like winter barley wine has hints of raisin, cocoa, aniseed and banana that keep the waves of warming alcohol in check.

AMSTERDAM PALE ALE

Amsterdam Brewboys, nomadic; 5.2%

Despite the geographically precise name, these brewers use various locations to brew hop-forward beers such as this crisp, floral and fruity US-hopped amber pale ale, which is dry-hopped to give a lingering bitter finish.

ARMADA

Pelgrim, Rotterdam, South Holland;
11%

Based in Rotterdam's historic
Delfshaven district, this brewer makes
consistently reliable ales that include
this complex, full-bodied Imperial stout
with notes of dried fruit, chocolate and
cocoa and a bitter finish. Also sold in
barrel-aged versions.

BEA

Kaapse, Rotterdam, South Holland;
6.5%

Four-hopped and double dry-hopped
for extra aroma and bitterness, this
full-bodied black rye IPA is a melting
pot with hints of cocoa, coffee, roasted
malt and citrus fruit, and a strongly
bitter finish.

BIG BLACK BEAVER

Pontus, nomadic; 7.6%

This Amsterdam-based brewer
creates beers with an assured touch
at De Naeckte Brouwers in nearby
Amstelveen (see page 117), in this
case a richly rounded export stout with
alcohol to the fore balanced by sweeter
chocolate/cocoa notes.

BLACK BIRD

Brouwpact, nomadic; 7.4%

The brewer Brouwpact uses brewery-
for-hire Loonbrouwerij in Cothen to
make beers such as this balanced,
dark and bitter black IPA, with rich
roasted-malt and coffee flavours giving
it porter-ish qualities.

BROEDERLIEFDE

De Moersleutel, Heiloo, North Holland;
8%

New arrivals on the Dutch beer scene
have made an instant impression with
their early offerings, including this
delightfully rich, bitter and superbly
balanced golden-blond double IPA.

BRONSTIG

Eem, Amersfoort, Utrecht; 6.5%

A superior example of an autumnal
Dutch bock, this chestnut-brown ale
has a bittersweet balance of caramel
and burned malt boosted by light
Centennial hopping. This formerly
nomadic brewer established his own
self-built brewery in 2017.

BRUTUS

Maximus, Utrecht; 6%

A superb and deeply appealing, rich,
fruity–hoppy US-style amber lager that

is practically an IPA, with malty notes upfront and an intensely bitter finish, brewed with European hops for a nod toward subtlety.

CALF

LOC, Tilburg, North Brabant; 9.5%

A malty and bitter Imperial milk porter with added everything – espresso beans lending an intense coffee flavour, and Madagascar vanilla pods and cocoa nibs providing depth and sweetness to balance the bitter finish.

CEAUX CANE

Ceaux, nomadic; 10.5%

Created by an Utrecht-based brewer using various locations, "Cocaine" is a warming, strong amber Imperial IPA with added sugar cane and smoked peppers to create a lightly bittersweet and very smoky brew, not unlike a German *rauchbier* on steroids.

DE RUMOERIGE ROODBORST

Bird, nomadic; 5.8%

A bright and crisp, copper-coloured US-style amber ale containing malted rye with hints of tropical fruits and a little caramel balancing the light bitterness. Brewed at Jopen (*see* page 116) by this Amsterdam-based outfit.

DIRTY KATARINA

Two Chefs, Amsterdam, North Holland; 10.5%

Two formerly nomadic brewers now have their own installation with which

to make their range of impressive beers, including this strong, rounded and bitter-finishing Imperial stout that hides its strength well.

DOERAK

Van Moll, Eindhoven, North Brabant; 6.5%

A city-centre brewpub making a wide variety of usually excellent beers, including this assertive, full-bodied, golden-blond IPA that balances a basket of tropical- and citrus-fruit flavours with a bitter finish.

EN GARDE!

Oersoep, Nijmegen, Gelderland; 6.5%

This lovely, light, dry, refreshing and (variously) single-hopped and fruity *saison* comes from a brewery known for using innovative fermentation to make a reliably great range of cutting-edge beers.

EXTRA STOUT

Praght, Dronten, Flevoland; 8%

Also seen as Stout Weesje Extra Stout, this lovely dark ale has background raspberry aromas, bittersweet chocolate and roasted malt in the body and a dry bitter finish.

GAJES

Bruut, nomadic; 8%

Brewed at Praght by two Amsterdam-based friends, this golden-blond abbey-style *tripel* has fruity notes and a floral perfumed sweetness balanced by gentle bitterness, and is one of the finer Dutch examples of its class.

GREEN CAP

Butcher's Tears, Amsterdam, North Holland; 6%

Brewed by a Swedish expat, this bitter and flowery golden-blond pale ale has a smooth, dry finish and restrained earthiness from the use of Eastern European rather than trendier US hops.

HEER VAN GRAMSBERGEN

Mommeriete, Gramsbergen, Overijssel; 12%

A beer that has evolved over time from a barley wine into a full-bodied dark Imperial stout, with dominant notes of roasted malt, coffee and chocolate, and background hints of vanilla.

HOP ART

VandeStreek, nomadic; 5%

These two talented Utrecht-based brothers brew their beers mainly at nearby De Leckere, including this lightly citrusy, dry and refreshing blond session-style IPA.

HOPFEN WEISSE

Oldskool, nomadic; 8.2%

An Eindhoven-based brewer making beers at various locations in German and British styles, including this hoppy amber *dunkelweizen* with strong and sweetish banana overtones kept in check by bitter single-hopping in changing varieties.

ICONIC BREWERY

DE MOLEN

Bodegraven, South Holland

A powerhouse brewery that effectively began the Dutch craft beer revolution and remains one of its leading pioneers. Known for its hundreds of experimental special releases as well as hard-hitting Imperial stouts, the permanent range includes a full-bodied amber IPA **Vuur & Vlam** (6.2%); the balanced and easily accessible **Hel & Verdoemenis** (10%) Imperial stout; a more complex Imperial porter **Tsarina Esra** (11%), which is even better in its oak-aged Reserva form; and the rich, chewy and powerful **Bommen & Granaten** (15.2%) barley wine.

HOUTGERIJPTE ROOK DUBBELBOCK

Duits & Lauret, Everdingen, Utrecht; 7.5%

This subtly smoked, wood-aged dark *bock* has hints of dried fruit and a dryly bitter finish, plus peaty notes throughout, like a diluted Islay malt. One for fireside chats on long winter evenings.

IMPERIAL OATMEAL STOUT

Oproer, Utrecht; 9.5%

From a brewery created by the merger of Ruig and Rooie Dop, this rich bittersweet stout is a heady mix of roasted-malt, chocolate, oats and prune flavours that give way to a light bitterness in the finish.

IPA

Lowlander, nomadic; 6%

This Amsterdam-based brewer makes beers at Jopen (*see* page 116), using his roots designing botanicals at a gin distillery to create unusually spiced ales, such as this refreshingly citrusy, hoppy and bitter amber IPA with notes of coriander, white tea and spice.

IPA

Troost, Amsterdam, North Holland; 6.5%

This dry, bitter and fruity US-hopped golden-amber ale has improved greatly since its 2013 launch, and comes from a growing empire of brewpubs that currently numbers two in Amsterdam with a planned third in Utrecht.

JOLLY ROGER

Raven Bone Hill, nomadic; 6.6%

Three brewers based in Maassluis but making beers at Ramses in North Brabant, including this eminently quaffable black IPA-meets-porter, with notes of coffee and chocolate and a touch of chilli and vanilla.

KOUD VUUR

Bax, Groningen; 6.3%

A fruity, bitter, dry-edged and impenetrably black smoked porter given depth and a sweet edge by malted oats, with plentiful hints of bonfire, but remaining balanced and subtle enough not to frighten the smoke-averse.

LA TRAPPE QUADRUPEL

Koningshoeven, Berkel-Enschot, North Brabant; 10%

This amber barley wine has banana esters that are characteristic of this Trappist abbey's output, but avoids sweetness and improves with cellaring, as does its deeper and richer Oak Aged sister.

MESTREECHS AAJT

Gulpener, Gulpen, Limburg; 3.5%

A sweet-and-sour, wood-aged ale in the style of a Belgian old brown with a richness belying its slight strength. Mainly available only in the Maastricht area, although an unsweetened and stronger version is sold in the USA.

CAN'T-MISS BREWERIES

● ●

BRONCKHORSTER

Rha, Gelderland

Formerly known as Rodenburg, this expat British brewer creates his beers with across-the-board assuredness. Standouts include the beautifully rounded and fruity smoked *altbier* **ALTernative** 6.5%); **Hoptimist** (9.5%), a spicy, fruity and seductive double IPA; the characterful and dark **Nightporter** (8%), with bitter hints of coffee and dark chocolate; and Nightporter's richer, darker, spicier and altogether bossier Imperial, evening-ending sister **Midnight Porter** (11%).

HET UILTJE

Haarlem, North Holland

This young brewer with a growing international reputation makes experimental, occasionally uncompromising, but usually great beers, including the fruity, quaffable summer session IPA **FF Lekker Met Je Bek In Het Zonnetje** (3.6%); the easy-drinking black IPA **Bosuil** (6%),

which balances hoppy bitterness with coffee and cocoa tones; the fresh and outstandingly bitter, five-hopped and dry-hopped **Big Fat 5 Double IPA** (8%); and the barrel-aged, take-no-prisoners heavyweight Imperial stout **Meneer de Uil** (~12%).

KEES

Middelburg, Zeeland

The brewer responsible for building Emelisse's (see page 119) global reputation, now making great beer in various styles at his own self-titled brewery. Standouts include refreshing golden-blond **Pale ale Citra** (4.6%), with grassy hop notes; fruity, bitter and full-bodied **Farmhouse IPA** (6.5%); rich, malty **Export Porter 1750** (10.5%) that packs a punch and tastes barrel-aged but isn't; and the whisky malt **Peated Imperial Stout** (11%), the smokiness of which is balanced by dark chocolate and prune sweetness.

RAMSES

Wagenberg, North Brabant

The eponymous brewer uses his experience in US brewing to create a range of consistently great single-hopped ales, usually with dry-hopping involved. Examples include the dark, fruity and attractive **Mamba Porter** (6.2%) using Galena hops; dark amber, Centennial-infused **Den Dorstige Tijger** (6%) IPA with fruity aspects and an intensely bitter finish; and cocoa-tinged **Shire Stout** (8.9%), which adds British Pilgrim hops and is sometimes sold as the wood-aged **Met Hout**.

MILK STOUT

Prael, Amsterdam, North Holland; 4 9%

This delightful black milk stout has cocoa overtones, a burned caramel edge, hints of coconut macaroon and a sharpness coming from the added lactose to bring balance to all the sweetish elements.

MOOIE NEL IPA

Jopen, Haarlem, North Holland; 6.5%

This slightly hazy, golden-blond and award-winning ale is aromatic, fruity and full-bodied with a subtle bitter finish. Sold internationally as North Sea IPA, it is considered by some as the flagship "Dutch IPA".

MORSPORTER

Leidsch, Leiden, South Holland; 6.1%

With chocolaty cocoa and coffee notes to the fore, backed by raisins, dark fruit and a bitter finish, this highly accomplished, pitch-black porter is named after an old city gate dating from 1669.

NIEUW LIGT GRAND CRU

Hemel, Nijmegen, Gelderland; 12%

This cellared version of the already excellent Nieuw Ligt, from a craft pioneer with 30 years of history, is a warming and rounded barley wine with a bitter astringency that balances both alcohol and sweetness.

NOT TOTALLY BLACK IPA

Hilldevils, nomadic; 6.7%

A dry black IPA with roasted malt in the nose and a tart fruity finish, created by brewers from the North Brabant village of Wouwse Plantage who make beers at the Pimplemeesch brewery in Chaam.

QUADRUPEL POORTER

Kleiburg, Amsterdam, North Holland; 10.7%

This intense and lovely deep black porter offers a witches' brew of chocolate, coffee and raisins, and comes from talented formerly nomadic newcomers with their own brewery since early 2017.

ROOK IN DE KACHEL

Gulzige Gans, Coevorden, Drenthe; 10%

From a very small house brewery, this rich, strong and hazy dark amber winter ale uses smoked malt to create a sharp, peaty, smoky bitterness that perfectly balances the nutty notes and the sugary sweetness.

SAENSE KRACHT

Breugem, Zaandijk, North Holland; 11%

A dark ruby, full-bodied, rich and sweetish but well-balanced barley wine with a mildly bitter finish. Its occasional limited-edition sister, Saense Kracht Houtgerijpt, is aged with aromatic South American Palo Santo wood.

SAISON

Schans, Uithoorn, North Holland; 7%

An enigmatic brewer whose beers are sometimes hard to find but always worth the effort, including this delightful, golden-blond farmhouse *saison* that balances banana, peach and touches of clove with a bitter, almost peppery finish.

SCHÔON MÈDJE

KraftBier, Tilburg, North Brabant; 6.2%

An aromatic, hazy, golden-blond "white IPA" wheat ale that uses both German and US hops to create a blend of citrusy and herbal flavours with a strongly bitter finish.

SHAKTI

Walhalla, nomadic; 8.8%

A new Amsterdam-based brewer making beer at various locations. The label range is still developing but includes this dryly bitter, golden double IPA, with a floral and fruity mixed bag of aromas coming from a cocktail of US hops.

SHIPA

De Naeckte, Amstelveen, North Holland; 6.8%

Ever-changing hop varieties result in minor taste fluctuations in this golden-blond single-hopped IPA, but the quality is seldom less than great and is occasionally spectacular, as in the case of the Sorachi Ace version.

SMOKEY THE BARRACUDA

Kromme Haring, Utrecht; 7.5%

This lovely rich and rounded smoked porter balances earthy peat, tar and liquorice notes with a slight chocolate sweetness. Brewed by a formerly nomadic American–Dutch team now at their own brewpub.

SOOTY OTTER

Neobosski, nomadic; 8.5%

Made by a pair of Utrecht-based brewers at nearby Loonbrouwerij, this tangy black IPA has hints of black treacle but avoids sweetness, while adding flavours of roasted malt and liquorice that edge it toward a stout or porter.

STORMBOCK

Texels, Oudeschild, North Holland; 10%

A heavy-hitting, ruby-brown winter barley wine from one of the country's largest craft breweries, with dark fruit, burned sugar and a slight but not intrusive caramel sweetness balanced by a lightly bittersweet finish.

BREWERIES TO WATCH

NEVEL

Nijmegen, Gelderland

Young brewers making low-alcohol experimental ales under the Katjelam brand such as the floral–spicy, slightly sour *saison* **Pepper Rebellion** (5.4%), the malty, chocolaty **London Porter** (4%) and the subtly sour **Bloei** (5%) *Berliner weisse*.

TOMMIE SJEF WILD ALES

Den Helder, North Holland

Outstanding young brewer cellar-ageing to produce sharp, tart ales such as the fruit-heavy **Cassis-Braam** (5%), *gueuze*-like **Cuvée** (5%) and citrusy blond **Sici** (5%).

STOUT + MOEDIG

7 Deugden, Amsterdam, North Holland; 7%

This dry and lightly bitter dark stout is made using three types of malt, and comes from a brewer known for adding unusual herbs, although in this case the adjunct is merely coffee.

STRUIS

I J [partnership with Duvel Moortgat], Amsterdam, North Holland; 9%

One of the early creations from Amsterdam's longest-running craft brewery, this pleasing, dark brown, full-bodied and lightly bittersweet English-style barley wine has notes of caramel and rich dark fruit with hints of chocolate.

TANKARD

Frontaal, Breda, North Brabant; 3.9%

This highly accomplished and quaffable light golden-blond US-style session ale uses four American hop varieties to create a strongly aromatic, hop-forward and bitter ale that doesn't taste as light as it is.

THAI THAI

Oedipus, Amsterdam, North Holland; 8%

From a quartet of brewers with a growing reputation for bold, experimental beers, such as this Belgian-style *tripel* given a Thai-spiced edge by added galangal, lemongrass, chilli and coriander, balanced by generous hopping.

US HEIT ELFSTEDENBIER

De Friese, Bolsward, Friesland; 8%

A dark, quaffable and strong Belgian brown ale with a bittersweet balance of malt, nuts and fruit and warming tones in the background, brewed for the winter months by an early pioneer of Dutch craft brewing.

VREDESGIJT

De Natte Gijt, Weert, Limburg; 6.8%

A hazy gold smoked rye IPA with a subtle smokiness that doesn't overpower fruity hoppy notes or the lingering bitter finish, created by two talented brewing brothers with a taste for hop-forward ales.

WATERGEUS

Vandenbroek, Midwolde, Groningen; 5–7%

This softly sour and refreshing blond *gueuze*-style beer is 100% spontaneously fermented with wild yeast, then oak-aged, adding a fruity counterpoint to the sourness. Hard to find, but highly recommended.

WHITE LABEL SERIES

Emelisse, Kamperland, Zeeland; ABV varies, usually 11%

An ever-changing range of usually barrel-aged Imperial stouts, seldom less than world class, created by a once-iconic brewery currently in a state of flux following the departure of its star brewers.

XTREME BALTIC COFFEE CHOCO MOCCA PORTER

Klein Duimpje, Hillegom, South Holland; 9%

The name signals a beer trying too hard to be all things at once, but this Baltic porter largely succeeds and is subtler than expected, despite having coffee and cocoa in abundance.

ZUNDERT

Kievit, Zundert, North Brabant; 0%

The single offering from the second Trappist brewery in the Netherlands is a richly rounded amber ale that has gained in confidence since its 2013 origins, with elements of toffee in the nose and taste, and a bittersweet balancing finish.

ZUSTER AGATHA

Muifel, Oss, North Brabant; 10%

This ruby-brown barley wine hints at being an abbey-style *quadrupel* with no ecclesiastical connections, and has background notes of sour cherry and dark fruit combined with a light bitterness to keep its caramel sweetness in check.

ZWARTE SNORRE

Berghoeve, Den Ham, Overijssel; 11%

This heavy-hitting darkly black Imperial stout with a handsomely dark brown foam is brewed with five malts to create an intriguingly complex blend of dark fruit and liquorice with a warming alcoholic glow in the finish.

ITALY

In its early days, the Italian craft beer scene was characterized by ornate bottles at elevated prices, sometimes dodgy consistency and a peculiar fascination with chestnut beers. As the first decade of the 21st century gave way to the second, however, Italian brewers uniformly upped their game, improving standards of quality, combining seasonings in the most sublime and imaginative ways and developing a beer style all their own, borrowed from the country's long history of wine production.

LA 5

L'Olmaia, Montepulciano, Tuscany; 5.5%

Moreno Ercolani is always in search of quaffability and this golden ale is testament to that quest, with a fragrant aroma and a light, malty sweetness well balanced by hops.

10 E LODE

Opperbacco, Notaresco, Abruzzo; 10%

Inspired by Belgian strong and dark ales, this is a powerful, lavish masterpiece, rich with vinous, spicy aromas and a smooth and balanced flavour completed by a warming, fruity–chocolaty finish.

A.KOLSCH

Borderline, Buttrio, Friuli-Venezia Giulia; 4.8%

From a publican-turned-brewer comes this successful take on a *kölsch*-style beer brewed with US hops. Fragrant, floral, bready and dry.

AMERICAN IPA

Canediguerra, Alessandria, Piedmont; 6.7%

Brewer Alessio Gatti worked for Toccalmatto (*see* page 128) and Brewfist (*see* page 127) before landing at Canediguerra, where his US-style IPA has an intriguing piney, balsamic note and a sharply citrusy, bitter finish.

AMERICAN MAGUT

Lambrate, Milan, Lombardy; 5%

The oldest brewpub in Milan has expanded its portfolio in recent years, including this pilsner dry-hopped with US hops for a citrus and mango nose, grain and white-bread body and dry and thirst-quenching character.

AREA 51

Free Lions, Viterbo, Lazio; 5.4%

A quaffable and sessionable US-style pale ale with a rich bouquet well balanced between tones of exotic fruit, malt and honey, a medium-weight body and a pleasant, bitter finish.

ARSA

Birranova, Triggianello, Apulia; 5.5%

An unusual smoked porter made from *grano arso*, the wheat left on the ground after the harvest and the burning of the stubble, and smoked malt from Bamberg, Germany. Toasted notes and hints of dried plums in a light body.

BABÉL

Foglie d'Erba, Forni di Sopra, Friuli-Venezia Giulia; 5%

A highly quaffable pale ale made with a blend of six different hops for a complex aroma of citrus, tropical fruit and resin – gentle rather than aggressive – and medium-weight, malty and sessionable body.

ICONIC BREWERIES

BALADIN

Piozzo, Cuneo, Piedmont

Teo Musso may be a brilliant self-promoter, but he is also a great visionary brewer, from **Nazionale** (6.5%), a quaffable all-Italian ale with a light aroma of coriander and bergamot, to the powerful dark **Leön** (9%), rich with flavours of dried fruit, toffee and liquorice. Then there are the experimental creations, such as **Xyauyù** (14%), a silky, intentionally oxidized beer with a complex bouquet of figs, sweet fortified wines and soy sauce, and **Lune** (11.5%), matured in white-wine barrels for a rich bouquet of walnuts, dried apricots and vanilla.

ITALIANO

Limido Comasco, Como, Lombardy

With his fragrant, herbal **Tipopils** (5.2%), Agostino Arioli created a benchmark in Italian craft beer and gave notice to the world that Italian beer was ready to be taken seriously. Arioli also loves to explore new frontiers in brewing, with beers like fruity and slightly vinous **Cassissona** (6.5%), made with cassis, **Scires** (7.5%) with Vignola cherries, perfectly balanced between sweetness and sourness, and **Inclusio Ultima** (7%), a softer version of Tipopils refermented in bottle with hops, part of a new project called Barbarrique.

BREWERIES TO WATCH

EBERS

Foggia, Puglia

Skills across a variety of styles are shown in beers like **Blanche** (5.3%), refreshing and elegant with citrus and coriander notes, and **Hopsfall** (7%), a black IPA with floral and resinous tones and a persistent bitterness.

HAMMER

Villa d'Adda, Lombardy

Menaresta alumnus Marco Valeriani indulges his love of hops with **Wave Runner** (6.5%), an IPA with exotic aromas and well-balanced bitterness, and **Black Queen** (7%), an earthy, grassy black IPA with a toasty finish.

HILLTOP

Bassano Romano, Lazio

Irish expat Conor Gallagher is one of Italy's most promising brewers, crafting beers like the toasty, brackish **Gallagher Stout** (5.5%) made with smoked seaweed, and the dry-finishing **Barry's Bitter** (4.2%).

VENTO FORTE

Bracciano, Lazio

Helmed by a surfer-brewer, this operation is garnering praise for beers like **Follower IPA** (7.1%), with a tropical-fruit aroma, hidden strength and dry, clean finish, and **Amber Oatmeal** (4.5%), floral and smooth with hints of white chocolate.

BB BOOM

Barley, Maracalagonis, Sardinia; 9%

The father of the Italian Grape Ale style, Nicola Perra, is still at work, his latest featuring Vermentino *mosto cotto*, or cooked must, resulting in a full-bodied, slightly sour and balanced ale with a floral, green-grape aroma.

CHOCOLATE PORTER

Perugia, Pontenuovo di Torgiano, Perugia, Umbria; 5%

An impressive brewery growing in quality year after year, as seen in this porter with a persuasive aroma of chocolate and roast, and a creamy and slightly bitter palate.

COFFEE BRETT IMPERIAL STOUT

Carrobiolo, Monza, Lombardy; 11%

Pietro Fontana is a talented brewer with no fear of experimentation, hence this beer as a meeting point between coffee and *Brettanomyces*, the former dominant but accompanied by an earthy wildness.

CORVINA

Mastino, San Martino Buon Albergo, Verona, Veneto; 10%

Corvina, one of the grapes used in Amarone wine, brings a vinous, wooden bouquet to this sour ale and accents of alcohol-soaked cherries to its flavour.

D-DAY

Decimoprimo, Trinitapoli, Puglia; 5.5%

A hoppy, elegant pale ale with a
subtle citrus and tangerine aroma
and an initially malty body that is
quickly overwhelmed by aromatic
bitterness from a combination of
British and US hops.

DUE DI PICCHE

Menaresta, Carate Brianza, Lombardy;
6.8%

A black IPA with a hoppy, toasty aroma
holding notes of burned caramel and
red fruit. The body is deceiving in its
ability to hide its strength, presenting
an approachably fruity and toasty body
before a pleasingly bitter finish.

DUNKEL

Batzen Bräu, Bolzano, Trentino-
South Tyrol; 4.9%

With rich toasted and caramel notes, a
rounded body and well-balanced finish,
this dark lager is the highlight of the
brewery's accomplished, German-
inspired portfolio.

FLEUR SOFRONIA

M-C77, Serrapetrona, Marche; 5%

From one of the most interesting young
microbreweries in Italy comes this
Belgian-style wheat beer flavoured
with hibiscus flowers for a pink hue,
an elegant, floral aroma and a touch
of acidity to keep it all refreshing.

GERICA

Birrone, Isola Vicentina, Veneto; 4.5%

From a brewery equally inspired by
German traditions and US hops comes
this "Cascadian lager", well balanced
between herbal and citrus aromas and
highly thirst-quenching in the body,
with a long and lingering, bitter finish.

HELLER BOCK

Elvo, Graglia, Piedmont; 7.2%

From one of Italy's finest lager
breweries, a classic German-style beer
well balanced between the sweet honey
and fruity malt in the body and a dry
finish that hides its strength well.

LATTE PIÙ

Retorto, Podenzano, Emilia-Romagna;
4.8%

The name pays tribute to Stanley
Kubrick's *A Clockwork Orange*, but the
effects of this "Milk Plus" Belgian-style
wheat beer are refreshing rather than
dangerous, with distinctive orange
notes and hints of coriander evident
in the finish.

CAN'T-MISS BREWERIES

32 VIA DEI BIRRAI

Pederobba, Veneto

Consistency is key to the success of this operation helmed by Belgian–Italian Fabiano Toffoli, who structures all his beers with optimal balance. **Oppale** (5.5%) is a hoppy ale with a distinctive herbal, fruity aroma and a round body, while **Curmi** (5.8%) is a refreshing floral and spiced *witbier* with a slight spike of acidity, and **Admiral** (6.3%) is a Scotch ale with toasted and caramel notes, smooth and persistent.

ALMOND '22

Loreto Aprutino, Pescara, Abruzzo

Jurij Ferri has a surgical hand with ingredients, creating beers that are well structured and original. **Blanche de Valerie** (4.5%) is a *witbier* spiced with black and pink pepper, floral and elegant with a slightly dry finish; **Pink IPA** (6%) is a personal interpretation of the style made with pink peppercorns for a delicate, tangerine-accented flavour; and **Maxima** (6.9%), brewed with acacia honey, is a strong ale with a warm aroma of biscuits and a light body.

LOVERBEER

Marentino, Piedmont

A true explorer of flavour, Valter Loverier loves to push the limit. His uniformly excellent beers include **BeerBera** (8%), spontaneously fermented with Barbera grapes to a vinous, fruity and wonderfully balanced body; **BeerBrugna** (6.2%), made with Damaschine plums and wild yeasts, fruity and citrusy with well-balanced acidity; and **Saison de l'Ouvrier** (5.8%), with a woody, vinous, red-fruit bouquet and a very dry body.

MONTEGIOCO

Montegioco, Piedmont

Riccardo Franzosi is a multi-tasking brewer known for his creative side, which brings us **Quarta Runa** (7%), a fruit beer made with Volpedo peaches that boasts an amazing bouquet of flowers, almonds and peach, the vinous and minerally **Tibir** (7.5%), with Timorasso grapes, and **La Mummia** (5.2%), a cask-aged blended ale with complex notes of wood, wine, citrus and honey in outstanding harmony.

MARRUCA

Amiata, Arcidosso, Tuscany; 6.5%

The Cerullo brothers are brewers strongly connected to their region, brewing with local chestnuts, saffron and, as with this ale, honey. Warming and full-bodied with tones of caramel, toffee and honey in the aftertaste.

MOLO

Ivan Borsato, Camalò, Treviso, Veneto; 5.5%

An unusual porter characterized by a small amount of port wine added for bottle fermentation, creating a silky, warming ale with round notes of coffee and bitter chocolate.

NADIR

Il Chiostro, Nocera Inferiore, Campania; 10%

Rested for two years in US oak, this silky, fruity and warming ale with a big aroma of tobacco, wood and red fruit is testament to Simone Della Porta's fruitful love affair with wood-ageing.

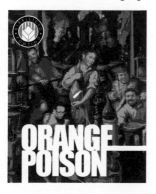

'NDO WAISS

Hibu, Burago di Molgora, Lombardy; 5.5%

A solid interpretation of the *weizen* style with honey and fruit on the nose and slightly spicy banana and candied apple in the body. Quaffable with a light bitterness drying out the finish.

NOBILE

dell'Eremo, Assisi, Umbria; 5%

A delicate, bready and herbal aroma introduces this highly sessionable golden ale, while a crispy, clean and quenching palate completes the picture.

NOCTURNA

Kamun, Pedrosa, Piedmont; 5.4%

An oatmeal stout brewed with a portion of smoked malt that stays apparent throughout but never grows overwhelming, with bitter chocolate and coffee notes in both the aroma and the smooth, persistent flavour.

ORANGE POISON

Pontino, Latina, Lazio; 7%

A very Italian take on a pumpkin ale, this adds almonds and three different kinds of pepper to the pumpkin for a complex bouquet of dry fruits, spices and pumpkin in the background.

PECORA NERA

Geco, Cornaredo, Lombardy; 4%

Seven different malts form the backbone of this milk stout with an appealing cappuccino-esque aroma and

STYLE SPOTLIGHT

THE WINE-INFLUENCED BEERS OF ITALY

The 2016 edition of the Italian national beer competition, Birra dell'Anno, saw the introduction of a category entitled, in English, Italian Grape Ale. This inclusion was an acknowledgement of a skill at which Italian brewers have been excelling for years, specifically the careful use of grape must in their beers.

In winemaking, must is the term used to denote freshly pressed grapes, which includes seeds, skins and some stems. From a brewing perspective, "must" can mean exactly that, or simply juice that is added during primary or secondary fermentation. Wine-influenced beer could also be said to include beers conditioned in wine barrels or aged on top of winemaking lees, which is to say the seeds and skins left behind after juice extraction. By whatever definition, it is a practice that Italian brewers are rapidly adopting as their calling card to the world.

Proponents skilled at this practice include LoverBeer, with **BeerBera** and **D'uvaBeer**; Montegioco, brewer of the excellent Barbera-barrel-aged **La Mummia**; Brùton, whose **Limes** is fermented with Verdicchio grape juice; the AB InBev-owned Birra del Borgo, with the multi-award-winning **Equilibrista**, made from 50% grape must; and Pasturana, whose **Filare!** is juiced with the white Piedmont grape Cortese di Gavi.

more coffee and cocoa elements in the smooth and highly approachable body.

PIAZZA DELLE ERBE

Ofelia, Sovizzo, Veneto; 4.9%

A spiced ale with readily apparent yet also balanced and clean notes of cardamom accenting a light, refreshing body, with a gentle touch of acidity grafted to its maltiness.

PIMPI

BAV, Martellago, Veneto, 7.2%

This wonderful pumpkin ale gets its unique flavour boost from fruit that is caramelized prior to brewing and just a pinch of coriander, resulting in a beer that is mildly pumpkin-y, round and very well balanced.

PUNKS DO IT BITTER

Elav, Comun Nuovo (Bergamo), Lombardy; 4.3%

The flagship brand of this fast-growing brewery is dry-hopped with Mosaic and Cascade hops for an intense citrus and grapefruit aroma, although the body remains light, dry and enjoyable with a thirst-quenching finish.

REALE

del Borgo [AB InBev], Borgorose, Lazio; 6.4%

Unchanged thus far by its acquisition, the del Borgo brewery continues to produce excellent beers like this original ale with a delicate grapefruit and orange aroma, a subtle hint of black pepper and great quaffability.

REGINA DEL MARE

del Forte, Pietrasanta, Tuscany; 8%

Belgian beer-inspired Francesco Mancini is the brewer of this rich dark ale with notes of caramel, candied orange and dried fruit on the nose and the palate, and a silky, clean and well-balanced character.

RODERSCH

Bi-Du, Olgiate Comasco, Lombardy; 5.1%

Brewer Beppe Vento has always prized drinkability in his beers, as witnessed by this *kölsch*-style beer with a light citrus and herbal aroma, dryly malty body and pleasant hoppy finish.

SALADA

Lariano, Sirone, Lombardy; 5%

Inspired by the *gose* style, this has pure Sicilian salt and some coriander in its recipe, giving it a refreshing and well-balanced flavour profile with a gentle, savoury note in the aftertaste.

SCARLIGA

Rurale, Desio, Lombardy; 8.5%

A powerful but well-balanced double IPA seasoned entirely with European hops for an intriguing aroma and a sneaky-strong body with a dryly hoppy, clean finish.

SLURP

Soralama', Vaie, Piedmont; 4.8%

A pilsner dry-hopped with US hops for a floral, citrusy aroma and a light, quenching body leaving an enjoyable and lingering bitterness; quite persistent and dry.

SPACEMAN INDIA PALE ALE

Brewfist, Codogno, Lombardy; 7%

A combination of Citra, Columbus and Simcoe hops gives this IPA a perfumed aroma of citrus and tropical fruit and a powerful mid-palate bitterness. A favourite among Italian hop fanatics.

STONER

Brùton, Lucca, Tuscany; 7.5%

An intensely fruity bouquet with notes of apricots and candy signals the arrival of this rounded and very well-balanced golden ale with fruity and honey tones on the palate.

SUN FLOWER

Valcavallina, Endine Gaiano, Lombardy; 4.3%

Delicate honey, citrus and exotic-fruit aromas introduce this light and highly aromatic golden ale, with the citrus and tropical fruit carrying through to the complex palate.

TEMPORIS

Croce di Malto, Trecate, Piedmont; 6.8%

A fascinating interpretation of *saison* style with a complex, expansive aroma that begins fruity and grows spicy, elegant and very well balanced on the palate, with a subtle spicy finish.

TERZO TEMPO

Argo, Lemignano di Collecchio, Emilia-Romagna; 4.4%

Perfectly balanced and thoroughly enjoyable, with a floral bouquet and a malty body, this cream ale is a much-appreciated rarity on the Italian craft beer scene.

TRE FONTANE

Abbazia Tre Fontane, Rome, Lazio; 8.5%

The one and only Italian Trappist brewery is located in Rome where the monks began brewing in 2015. Their *tripel* is made with eucalyptus, which gives it an elegant balsamic element in both aroma and taste.

TRIPLE

Maltus Faber, Genoa, Liguria; 8%

This classically styled *tripel* possesses an intensity and controlled strength that makes all the difference, with fruit and citrus notes apparent in the aroma and a slightly spicy, smooth and persistent palate.

TUPAMAROS

Ritual Lab, Formello, Lazio; 8%

Young but promising brewery making waves primarily due to this double IPA with an intense aroma of resin and grapefruit, powerful hoppiness and a punchy, bitter finish that mellows as it lingers.

L'ULTIMA LUNA

del Ducato, Soragna, Emilia-Romagna; 13%

A barley wine matured 18 months in Amarone barriques, this emerges with an aroma of vanilla, leather and cocoa, with a rich, sweet intensity and complexity in the body supported by soft tannins. One of many great beers from Giovanni Campari's brewery.

YELLOW DOCTOR

Black Barrels, Turin, Piedmont; 5.2%

Renzo Losi pioneered mixed fermentation in Italy with his Panil Barriquée, and now he is at work in Turin creating beers with tart complexity and light alcohol, like this refreshing, thyme-accented, slightly sour summer ale.

ZONA CESARINI

Toccalmatto, Fidenza, Emilia-Romagna; 6.6%

The flagship label of the brewery features a blend of hops from Japan, Australia, New Zealand and the USA, yielding an IPA with notes of tropical fruit, citrus and apricot that progress from nose to palate, ultimately finishing quite dry.

GREECE

Like much of the Balkans, Greece is still finding its feet where craft brewing is concerned, but a few lights are nevertheless beginning to shine, some even brightly.

ORA STOUT

Patraiki, Patras, Western Greece; 7%

There is a hint of Foreign Export Stout about this creamy and roasted Greek stout. Vanilla, mocha and chocolate notes make their mark alongside a peppery hoppiness. A complete and satisfying beer.

PILSNER

Nissos, Vagia, Tinos, Cyclades; 5%

Fifteen months after first being brewed, this crisp Czech-style beer won its first international medal. Flurries of soft lemon waft from its aroma, while the crisp body and bitter finish pair wonderfully with fried Greek food.

RED DONKEY

Santorini, Meso Gonia, Thira (Santorini); 5–5.2%

This island brewery produced the first Greek IPA in 2011, but its soft and sensuous red ale with a chewy mouthfeel, joined by caramel, vanilla and a dry, hop-fringed finish, is more memorable.

W DAY

Septem, Orologio, Euboea; 6%

Fragrant and fruity from Southern Hemisphere hops and bearing hints of banana and clove, this "wheat IPA" is a quaffable fusion of two styles with a slight sweetness in the finish, from one of the most adventurous new wave Greek breweries.

SPAIN & PORTUGAL

The adjoining nations of the Iberian peninsula began their journey to brewing respectability without any great brewing heritage to recreate. Spain got the jump on its neighbour with its culinary creativity influencing many of its better beers, following an Italian path to growing excellence, including early flaws and inconsistencies. Portugal, meanwhile, has taken longer to get going, but is now making steady strides towards joining Europe's family of brewing nations.

SPAIN

APOKALYPSE

Reptilian, El Vendrell, Catalonia; 11.5%

Black as night, this Imperial stout is dense and intensely toasty, with chocolate and coffee tones, warming strength and hints of vanilla, nut and grain. Also made in versions aged in Málaga, port and brandy barrels.

BLACKBLOCK

La Pirata, Súria, Catalonia; 11.2%

The brewery's second release set the course for this renowned brewery.

Dense and dark, with chocolate, brandy, nutty and dried-fruit notes, plus an impressive flavour balance of sweet and bitter. Also available in a bourbon-barrelled version.

CHOC INFESTED PORTER

Vic, Vic, Catalonia; 6%

This pitch-black porter has an attractive hoppy profile reminiscent of orange zest and strawberry, an intense toasty character, gently caramelly maltiness and a pleasing hint of cocoa in a creamy body.

CLAUDIA

BlackLab, Barcelona, Catalonia; 7%

The flagship of this brewpub by the city's seaside, this US-style IPA is aggressively hopped, as per its fresh, juicy, tropical-fruit and citrus aromas, but with a strong malty balance as well.

DOUBLE DRAGON II

Falken, nomadic; 10%

Known and revered for the retro video-game imagery of their beers, this dark brown wee heavy is intense yet also mellow, with a rich toffee and caramelly character holding notes of biscuit and ripe fruit leading to a warming finish.

EX 1 IPA SEVE-BORIS

Sevebräu, Villanueva de la Serena, Extremadura; 7%

Created in partnership with renowned master brewer Boris de Mesones, this intense ale delivers citrusy, grassy and piney aromas, with a nice caramel and nutty malt character for balance.

FRANCESKA

Art, Canovelles, Catalonia; 5.2%

From a brewery of great personality comes this "steam pilsner", made with Czech malts, Kiwi hops and Californian yeast for a mild citrus and tropical-fruit character, a light spiciness and crisp, quenching demeanour.

GALAXY FARM

Instituto de la Cerveza Artesana (ICA), Barcelona, Catalonia; 7.5%

A contemporary take on the *saison* style single-hopped with Galaxy. Fruity with aromas ranging from citrus to passion-fruit, and pleasantly peppery, yeasty and slightly musty.

GOMA 2

Caleya, Rioseco, Asturias; 6.3%

With the name of an industrial explosive, this IPA is designed to target its aim at the drinkers' taste buds with an explosion of tropical fruits, peach and citrus, all on a soft and malty base with refreshing bitterness.

GRECO

Domus, Toledo, Castilla-La Mancha; 8.2%

Evoking the marzipan for which Toledo is famous, this gently sweet ale spiced with almond, saffron, lemon and cinnamon has a herbal character throughout, with almond accents and a steadily growing hoppiness that finishes slightly bitter and vaguely nutty.

GREEN MADNESS

NaparBCN, Barcelona, Catalonia; 6%

Naparbier's brewpub was launched in 2016 and quickly became one of the reference breweries for the city. This hazy, heavily hopped IPA is full of juicy citrus flavours and aromas, with a residual malt presence.

HAPPY OTTER

Dougall's, Liérganes, Cantabria, 5.6%

Bright amber-gold with an intense and fresh hoppy aroma, this pale ale delivers all sorts of fruity notes from peach to grapefruit to tropical fruit, all with a firm and pleasant malt backbone to keep it quite quaffable.

HOPTIMISTA

Edge, Barcelona, Catalonia, 6.6%

This crystal-clear amber ale is very American in style, with citrus zest, grapefruit, pine and orange in the

aroma and a lightly caramelly body. Dry, medium-bodied and resinous.

HØRNY PILSNER

La Quince, nomadic; 5.2%

Best known for their innovative collaborations with some renowned national and European brewers, these brewing nomads offer a hoppy pilsner that is fresh and lively, with a tropical and citrus-fruit nose followed by a bitter, dry finish.

IMPARABLE

Basqueland, Hernani, Basque Country; 6.8%

An impressive recent arrival brings this hazy amber beer with a wide range of hoppy aromas from citrus to pine to mango, balanced with a moderately full maltiness producing an effect that is both sweet and bitter.

IPA ANIVERSARI

Montseny, Sant Miquel de Balenyà, Catalonia; 6.4%

Released on the brewery's fifth anniversary and brewed ever since, this amber IPA offers aromas of pine, grapefruit, dried apricot and grapes, with a biscuity, lightly caramelly malt base for balance.

JULIETT

L'Anjub, Flix, Catalonia; 6.2%

A long-time favourite among local drinkers, this strong stout is deep black with a roasty aroma combined with hints of prunes and liquorice and a coffee-ish body with dry, herbal notes from the northern Spanish hops used.

MORENETA BRUNE

Barna, nomadic; 5.5%

Designed to evoke the flavours of *rom cremat*, a Catalonian rum and coffee drink, this cinnamon-spiced *dubbel* has a roasty body with mocha and spice notes and a richness that belies its modest strength.

PORTER

Arriaca, Yunquera de Henares, Castilla-La Mancha; 5.9%

Black and intensely flavoured, this offers aromas of coffee, dark bitter chocolate and liquorice, along with a bit of dried fruitiness and boozy warmth despite its relatively low strength.

RINER

Guineu, Valls de Torroella, Barcelona, Catalonia; 2.5%

In existence since almost the start of Spanish craft brewing, this low-strength hoppy beer was a trailblazer with its zesty apricot and orange hoppiness, and delicately bready, yeasty body.

ROYAL PORTER

Nómada [Mahou San Miguel], nomadic; 10%

Now brewed on Mahou's pilot facility, this full-bodied and boozy, roasty ale offering chocolate, raisin, fig and vanilla notes is one of the reasons the larger brewery bought a 40% stake in the much younger company.

BREWERIES TO WATCH

GARAGE

Barcelona, Catalonia

A modern, exciting brewpub founded in 2015 that launched a new production brewery in 2017, meaning that the fruity session IPA **In Green We Trust** (4.7%) and the more assertive, citrusy IPA **Slinger** (5.8%) will reach a wider circle of palates.

JAKOBSLAND

Santiago de Compostela, Galicia

This newcomer Galician brewery is rapidly spreading through the Iberian Peninsula with its impressive hop-forward beers, such as the Citra-hop-fuelled **Dumbstruck** (6.3%) and the tropical-fruity double IPA **Fix for the Fits** (9%).

MAD

Madrid

The recent arrival of this brewpub was very good news for sometimes beer-challenged Madrid, thanks to their impressive early offerings like **Trigo Hoppy** (5.2%), a hopped-up wheat ale, and **Red** (7.1%), a caramelly, spicy strong ale.

SETEMBRE

Ales Agullons, Sant Joan de Mediona, Catalonia; 5.5%

The brewery's single-hopped pale ale blended with young lambic and aged for two years, half in oak, this earthy and woody ale has a mild hoppiness, notes of tart red fruits and a distinctive *Brettanomyces* mustiness.

SIDERALE

Cotoya, Santo Adriano, Asturias; 6.2%

Brewed once a year and typical of the brewery's fruit-infatuated approach, this pale ale is flavoured with cider apples to delight drinkers' palates with its sweet fruity character, mild tartness, tannins, malty base and dry, bitter finish.

WHITE IPA

BIIR, nomadic; 6.8%

These wandering brewers with a Belgian inclination made their debut with this hybrid ale offering rich, fruity aromas from its Australian and US hopping, and a nice spicy profile coming from the coriander and orange peel also used.

ZENDRA

Zeta, Alboraia, Valencian Community; 7.8%

From a brewery that has truly conquered local palates, this smoked rye *bock* is medium-bodied with spicy, caramelly malt complemented by herbal hoppiness and a lovely, lingering smoked malt aftertaste.

ZZ+ AMBER ALE

Naparbier, Noain, Navarra; 5.5%

The catalyst for the growth in popularity of hoppy ales in Spain. The caramelly and biscuity malt base gives structure to this hop-forward beer, with juicy aromas of orange and mango, resin and jam. Medium-bodied and lively.

PORTUGAL

BLIND DATE 2.0 IPA

Passarola, nomadic; 6.5%

A somewhat restrained IPA when compared with the explosion of fruit in the brewer's Chindogu IPA, with a piney, slightly caramelly nose and a resiny hop body that sits atop biscuity malt. Quaffably bitter without being overwhelming.

CREATURE IPA

Dois Corvos, Lisbon; 6.5%

One of the first hazy, "New England-style" IPAs brewed in Portugal, this has a fruity nose with ample pineapple and other topical-fruit tones, and a slightly less fruity body with grassy, piney notes and an off-dry finish.

BREWERY TO WATCH

AMNESIA

Oeiras, Lisbon

Started when the owner won a home-brewing competition with the prize of being able to brew at Mean Sardine (*see* below), this impressed immediately with its debut **Juniper Smokin'** (8.5%), a smoked ale with juniper, and the newer double IPA **Amnesia You Talkin' To Me?** (7%).

IMPERIAL STOUT BY PEDRO SOUSA

Post Scriptum, Trofa, Porto; 11.6%

From one of Portugal's most accomplished breweries, this massive beer drinks more like a medium-strong stout, with toffee and ample hop in the aroma and a dense body filled with flavours of coffee and toffee.

MALDITA WHEATWINE

Faustino, Aveiro; 8%

Copper-coloured, this has a strongly malt-forward aroma with a near-ideal combination of toffee and caramel malt leading to a surprisingly soft but well-rounded body with toffee-ish sweetness and herbal bitterness. Best of a very good range.

URRACA VENDAVAL

Oitava Colina, Lisbon; 6%

From the "eighth hill" (*oitava colina*) of Lisbon, this is a well-constructed and copper-hued IPA with a fresh, piney, citrusy aroma and earthy, fruity (citrus and pineapple, plus some other tropical fruit), grassy body carrying full bitterness.

VORAGEM

Mean Sardine, Ericeira, Mafra; 7%

From one of the country's up-and-coming star breweries, this black IPA has a resinous aroma with some alcohol and coffee notes and a citrusy, earthy body holding hints of grapefruit and pine to a lively, lingering finish.

SCANDINAVIA

DENMARK

There is no common ground in Danish brewing these days, with some breweries emerging from basement home-brewing operations, others part of slickly designed city centre brewpubs and, perhaps most famously, still others gaining fame through beers produced by breweries-for-hire both within and outside of the country. There is no questioning the success of this multi-pronged approach, however, as the country has become both Scandinavia's undisputed craft beer leader and a bold and confident innovator.

ALSTÆRK

Munkebo, Munkebo, Funen; 9.4 %

An impressive tribute to the strong Scotch ale known as wee heavy. Low in bitterness and high in the roasted maltiness from seven types of malt, this is full-bodied with notes of toffee and raisins.

BEER GEEK BRUNCH WEASEL

Mikkeller, nomadic; 10.9%

Ignore the gimmick of making the beer with kopi luwak coffee, the most expensive in the world, and focus instead on an impressive Imperial oatmeal stout with flavours of cold coffee, dark chocolate and red berries.

BLACK MONSTER

Aarhus, Aarhus, Jutland; 10%

A deep black, full-bodied and syrupy Imperial stout aged first in rum barrels, then in a steel tank with oak chips and finally dry-hopped. Expect roasted maltiness with dark-chocolate, oak, whisky and vanilla tones.

CARIBBEAN RUMSTOUT

Hornbeer, Kirke Hyllinge, Zealand; 10%

An award-winning beer and new beloved Danish standard. Notes of rum, vanilla and oak from the barrel-ageing are prominent, with roasted malt flavours and hints of smoke, espresso and dark chocolate.

CHRISTIAN BALE ALE

Dry & Bitter, Gørløse, Zealand; 4.6%

More bitter than dry, this single-hop (Mosaic) session-strength IPA is easy-going with sharp bright flavours of grapefruit, peach, melon and tropical fruits, followed by a snappy bitter finish.

CLUB TROPICANA

Rocket, Haslev, Zealand; 5.2%

A fruity pale ale with tastes of grapefruit, mango and papaya accented by tart and peppery characteristics, creating in the process a quaffable and light orange-hued beauty.

COLUMBUS ALE

Det Lille, Ringsted, Zealand; 7.8%

Explore this hoppy ale and you will first be rewarded with a rich bitterness, followed and supported by malty fruitiness heavy on the mango notes.

DARK SIDE OF THE MOON

Kissmeyer, nomadic; 9.5%

From veteran brewer Anders Kissmeyer comes this Imperial porter loaded with flavours of dark chocolate, espresso, whisky and vanilla, accented by a refreshing cherry-ish tartness.

DOPPEL BOCK

Krenkerup, Sakskøbing, Zealand; 8.3%

A traditional Bavarian-style *doppelbock* with a lovely and warming mouthfeel, caramel flanked by chocolate and dried fruit and a subtly hoppiness on the finish.

EXTRA PILSNER

Jacobsen [Carlsberg], Copenhagen; 5.5%

From Carlsberg's craft beer sub-label, this organic pilsner with added sea buckthorn is well hopped in the Bavarian style with a full rather than crisp body given added tartness from the berries.

ESB

WinterCoat, Sabro, Jutland; 6.1%

A strong, dark amber-coloured English-style bitter in which caramelly and biscuity malt are the predominant flavours, accented by floral hop and red-berry notes and culminating in a notably bitter finish.

FOUR

Coisbo, nomadic; 10%

A strongly floral Imperial stout – rich in lavender – with a massively malty mix of roasted and chocolaty flavours with prune notes, yet with unusual quaffability and an appealing dryness.

FROKOST

Fur, Fur, Jutland; 2.6%

Despite its low strength, this simple and refreshing pale ale offers an ambitious bitterness surrounding elements of biscuity malt, citrus and elderflower. Refreshing and highly, perhaps surprisingly, satisfying.

HØKER BAJER

Hancock, Skive, Jutland; 5%

As fine an example of a simple, refreshing Czech-style pilsner as you will find in Denmark, full in body with a round rather than crisp maltiness and a floral character from the use of exclusively Saaz hops.

HUMLEFRYD

Skands, Brøndby, Zealand; 5.5%

A fine crossover of a Czech and Bavarian approach to pilsner, crisp, clean and lively with a taste of mildly sweet malt, grass and hay, with the hoppiness pairing perfectly with the malt sweetness.

LE SACRE

Ebeltoft, Ebeltoft, Jutland; 6.7%

A light orange-hued *saison* with considerable wild yeast characteristics, such as notes of barnyard, hay, leather and sour apples, plus a rustic tartness and hints of strawberries and banana.

LIMFJORDSPORTER

Thisted, Thisted, Jutland; 7.9%

A smooth, oily and rich stout brewed with liquorice and smoked malt, with

CAN'T-MISS BREWERIES

AMAGER

Copenhagen

Brewer of bold and mostly forcefully hoppy ales, although with rising interest and proficiency in Imperial stouts. In the former class is **The Lady of Cofitachequi** (7%), an IPA with grassy, resinous and grapefruity aromas and flavours, while **Double Black Mash** (12%) leads the latter camp with an elegantly warming, chocolate and coffee character. Others on the IPA side include **Todd The Axe Man** (6.5%), with understated maltiness and tropical-fruit hoppiness, and **Winter in Bangalore** (6%), a modest, crisp and very well-balanced IPA with caramel and grapefruit notes in perfect harmony.

BEER HERE

nomadic

Founder Christian Skovdal Andersen can seem at times like the most gifted and versatile brewer in Denmark. Testament to his skills are beers like the hearty and creamy milk stout **Ammestout** (6.5%); **Nordic Rye** (8%), a rustic, dark ale loaded with fresh maltiness; and **Kama Citra** (7%), a brown ale well seasoned with its signature hop. **Infant Øl** (2.8%) derives low-alcohol complexity from six different malts, while **Hopfix** (6.5%) relies on a mix of hops for its resinous flavours of grapefruit, mango and pineapple.

CAN'T-MISS BREWERIES

●●●●●●●●●●●●●●●●●

BØGEDAL

Vejle, Jutland

Situated on an old farm and employing ancient brewing techniques, this may be the most charming
brewery in Denmark, producing equally charming beers that are each unique and often difficult to define by style. **No. 505** (7.7%) is a rich dark ale with added liquorice root, full of fresh malts and only discreet bitterness; **No. 459** (8.1%) is a light, strong ale with considerable maltiness and greater hoppiness than that usually found in the brewery's beers; and **Hyld** (6.6%) is seasoned with elderflower. **Jul#1** (6.7%) is a dark-brown Christmas ale with a solid base of malt and flavours of orange, coffee and caramel.

HERSLEV

Herslev, Zealand

An organic and terroir-focused brewery from farmer–brewer Tore Jørgensen, one of the pioneers of the Danish beer revolution. Cider-ish **Mark Fadlagret** (11%) is an unhopped ale fermented with wild yeast cultivated from hay; Czech-style **Økologisk Pilsner** (5.5%) is strongly malty, but neither does it lack any refreshing crispness; **Økologisk Stjernebryg** (9%) is a powerful but smooth, milk-chocolaty Christmas beer spiced with star anise and coriander; and **Birk** (5.5%) is a Belgian-wheat-beer-ish brew made with every part of a freshly harvested birch tree, from bark to sap to leaves.

flavours of dark chocolate, roasted malt, liquorice, smoke and tobacco all accenting a mouth-coating character.

MDXX DET STOCKHOLMSKE BLODBAD

Kongebryg, Næstved, Zealand; 11%

An almost flat mahogany barley wine with elements of roasted malt, caramel, sherry, dried plums and cherries. Composed of a grain bill that includes malted rye and oats.

MØRK MOSEBRYG

Grauballe, Silkeborg, Jutland; 5.6%

A dark, reddish brown Scottish-style ale from Grauballe with subtle tones of smoke hidden among the dunes of exquisite roasted maltiness and flavours of chocolate and dark fruits, with hops only providing balance.

PÁSKA BRYGGJ

Föroya Bjór, Klaksvik, Faroe Islands; 5.8%

This amber-coloured and highly quaffable Easter beer is an easy-going *bock* with sweet maltiness in focus, rich with caramel maltiness and raisin notes.

PERIKON

Kølster, Humlebæk, Zealand; 5.7%

An amber ale brewed with malt from the brewery's own malt house, seasoned with St John's Wort foraged from the surrounding forest. A solid base of fresh, rustic maltiness with herbal and bitter elements and hints of liquorice and hay.

BREWERIES TO WATCH

ALEFARM

Køge, Zealand

The brewery's fast journey to cultish status is due to its takes on IPA and *saison*, hazy and juicy beers loaded with interesting accents and tropical-fruit flavours, exemplified by **Funk Orchard Farmhouse Ale** (7%) and **Kindred Spirits Lactose** IPA (6%).

BRUS

Copenhagen

A brewpub concept from To Øl (*see* page 142) with a great variety of beers heavy on hip and hoppy styles, such as **Walk'n the Park** (4.8%), a pleasant IPA packed with Citra and Mosaic hops, and **Das Fruit** (8.4%), a sneaky strong, cleverly hopped double IPA.

WARPIGS

Copenhagen

A collaboration between Mikkeller (*see* page 137) and 3 Floyds designed to "bring a US-style brewery to Denmark", featuring many one-offs and regulars like the tropical-fruity IPA **Lazurite** (7.4%) and berry-ish, hoppy ESP **Illuminaughty** (6%).

PHISTER DE NOËL

Flying Couch, Copenhagen; 6.7%

A Christmas Imperial stout brewed with a touch of vanilla and dark sugar. A deep black and creamy body offers flavours of dark chocolate, roasted malt, vanilla and lactose.

RAVNSBORG RØD

Nørrebro, Copenhagen; 5.5%

From a near-legendary brewpub that has perhaps seen better days, this organic red ale is roasty with notes of dried fruits, caramel and pine.

RAZOR BLADE

Ghost, nomadic; 10%

Flavours of pine, grapefruit and tropical fruits are ever present in this black IPA, though they are the supporting cast to those of roasted malt, liquorice and candied sugar with hints of coffee, all leading to a dry and bitter finish.

RED ALE CELEBRATION

Ugly Duck, Nørre Aaby, Funen; 8.6%

A reddish-brown Imperial with notes of roasted and bready malt, caramel, fruit syrup and woodiness. The sweetness of this barrel-aged and dry-hopped ale has a tart edge to it.

ROUGH SNUFF II

Midtfyns, Årslev, Funen; 9%

A mahogany-coloured, Belgian-inspired strong ale with complex flavours of caramel, liquorice and tobacco accented by notes of tar, raisins and seaweed.

ROULV

Frejdahl, Assens, Funen; 9%

A full-bodied, creamy and sweet porter, slightly smoky with blackcurrant and rum hints mixing alongside more prominent elements of chocolate and raisins, all leading to a lasting bitterness in the finish.

SORT DESSERT ØL

No5, Holbæk, Zealand; 14%

What happens when *schwarzbier* meets barley wine; deep brown and evocative of a fine port stuffed with flavours of prunes, plums and raisins, and accented by tones of coffee and chocolate.

SORT MÆLK

To Øl, nomadic; 10.6%

The added lactose is the key to this deep brown and very full-bodied Imperial stout aged in whisky barrels. The notes of cream from the lactose blend perfectly with intense flavours of roasted malt, tobacco, toffee and coffee.

SPELT BOCK

Indslev, Nørre Aaby, Funen; 7%

A dark brown *bock* with a twist, brewed not only from barley malt and spelt, but also rye and wheat. A fresh and grainy maltiness introduces the beer, and notes of coffee and chocolate carry through the body.

VADEHAV

Fanø, Nordby, Fanø, Jutland; 6.5%

A masterful take on the challenging task of brewing a delicate brown ale, smooth and close to full-bodied with flavours of fresh roasted malt, lightly sweet caramel and mildly bitter nuttiness.

NORWAY

Spurred forward by the success of Nøgne Ø in 2002 (*see* page 145), Norwegian brewers convinced their country's beer drinkers to pay well above the already high price of local, uninspired lagers for beers of character and depth, and in so doing took one of Europe's more hidebound beer markets and evolved it into one of the most exciting.

A DAMN FINE COFFEE IPA

Ego, Fredrikstad, Østfold; 7.4%

Hazy and deep copper in colour, this unique IPA has an aroma that balances tropical fruit and coffee, while the body positions notes of papaya and mango on top of flavours of dark roasted coffee, chocolate and caramel with a dry, hoppy finish.

ALSTADBERGER KLOSTERGÅRDEN,

Tautra, Frosta, Nord-Trøndelag; 6.5%

A unique Norwegian-style ale known as *stjørdalsøl*, which is brewed with smoked local barley malt. The smoky, foresty aroma also boasts tones of freshly tanned leather, while the body adds caramel, smoked grain, honey and vanilla to the mix.

APARTE

Hadeland Håndverksbryggeri, Gran, Oppland; 4.5%

An unusual take on a *hefeweizen* fermented with *kölsch* yeast to a spicy, green-grape-accented aroma and grassy, malty body, all leading to a balanced, medium-dry finish.

BELGISK GYLLEN

Færder, Tønsberg, Vestfold; 8.5%

A forcefully fruity Belgian-style strong blond ale with dried fruit, raspberries, strawberries, mango and sweet lemon on the nose, and a vibrant fruitiness with red apple, honey, melon and mango in the body, finishing rather astonishingly dry.

BERGEN PALE ALE

Balder, Leikanger, Sogn og Fjordane; 5.7%

The joke here is that with no plans to export to India, the brewery named this US IPA-style beer after the west coast town of Bergen, where they do sell a considerable amount of beer. Hoppy in aroma, well balanced and refreshing.

BIPA

Aja, Drammen, Buskerud; 4.7%

The "B" stands for "Belgian", which is the yeast used to ferment this low-strength session IPA to its spicy, fruity, tea-leaf-accented aroma and dry, nutty body carrying notes of leather and nutty prune.

BIRKEBEINER

Rena, Østerdalen, Hedmark; 4.7%

A classic Norwegian light lager in the pilsner style from a small brewery located in the deep woods. A fresh, dry and hoppy aroma introduces a beer that is much the same, with light maltiness and easy-going hops. Well balanced.

BLÅBÆRSTOUT

Austmann, Trondheim, Sør-Trøndelag; 6%

A stout brewed with Norwegian wild blueberries, black in colour with a predictably blueberry-ish aroma

accented by dark chocolate and coffee, and a body that follows suit, ending medium-dry.

BLÅND

Trondhjem, Trondheim, Sør-Trøndelag; 4.7%

A US-style blond ale, slightly hazy with aromas of fruit candy, spice and wheat. The body features a soft, wheaty graininess and elements of melon and white gooseberry, with hoppiness growing to the finish.

BOCK

Aass, Drammen, Buskerud; 6.5%

Long-surviving Scandinavian *bock* with a deep reddish-amber colour, notes of roasted walnut and chocolate in the nose and a complex but quaffable palate of caramel and mocha accompanied by tones of prune and fig. A Norwegian classic.

BØKERØKT

Larvik, Larvik, Vestfold; 7.2%

A smoked malt, dark ale brewed by a small brewery established in 2011. Aromas of open fire, roasted malt, wet earth and leather lead to flavours of coffee, chocolate, caramel and nuts.

BOKKØL

Borg, Sarpsborg, Østfold; 6.6%

An award-winning, copper-brown *bock* with a roasted aroma of chocolate and coffee, a taste of caramel, bitter chocolate and dark roasted coffee and a slightly sweet and faintly fruity finish.

BOKKØL

Frydenlund [Ringnes-Carlsberg], Gjelleråsen, Oslo; 6.5%

A classic Norwegian *bock* beer, deep reddish brown in colour with an aroma of chocolate, dried berries and coffee. The berry notes carry through to the body alongside roasted malt, finishing with dark chocolate and coffee.

BØVELEN

Kinn, Florø, Sogn og Fjordane; 9%

This deep gold and hazy Belgian-style *tripel* has a fruity aroma of white melon, honey, orange peel and almonds, with a body of orange-peel marmalade, honey and exotic spices leading to a complex and warming finish.

BRETT FARMHOUSE

Lindheim, Gvarv, Telemark; 7%

Part of this fruit-farm brewery's Farmer's Reserve series, this sees the regular, *saison*-style Farmhouse Ale conditioned with *Brettanomyces* and apple fruit to a complex fruitiness and an off-dry and hoppy finish.

CORVUS

Nøisom, Fredrikstad, Østfold; 10.2%

Aromas of port wine, blackberry, chocolate and espresso characterize this cross between a *saison* and an Imperial stout by Nøisom, with a rich and forceful body carrying flavours of fig, prune, berries, dark chocolate, coffee and caramel.

ICONIC BREWERY

NØGNE Ø [HANSA BORG]

Grimstad, Aust-Agder

The most award-winning craft brewery in Norway, founded by Kjetil Jikiun of Bådin (*see* page 147), who left the company not long after its purchase by Hansa Borg in 2013. It is still acknowledged as a Norwegian craft beer market leader, and highlights from the lengthy portfolio include **Imperial Stout** (9%), with notes of espresso, dark chocolate and roasted nuts; **#100** (10%), a barley wine of impressive complexity; the lightly smoky, apricot-ish **Tiger Tripel** (9%); and **#500** (10%), a double IPA crafted from five malts and five hops to commemorate the brewery's 500th brew.

CROW'S SCREAM ALE

Crowbar, Oslo; 4.7%

In the steam beer style, this hazy and orange brew has a gently fruity hoppiness on its aromatic nose and a palate of grapefruit, orange and caramelly malt, finishing dry and hoppy.

DRENGENS DEBUT

Moe, Trondheim, Sør-Trøndelag; 4.7%

A hazy golden and quite floral ale with citrus on the nose, and a refreshing, malt-led body with elements of sweet lemon, green apple and gooseberry, finishing off-dry.

FISH & SHIPS MARITIM PALE ALE

Grim & Gryt, Hareid, Møre og Romsdal; 4.7%

A light copper-coloured and very fruity pale ale from an all-organic brewery on the Norwegian coast, this offers notes of peach and grapefruit in the nose and a citrusy mix of peach, apricot and melon in the body.

HAAHEIM GAARD RØYKT IPA

Lysefjorden, Ytre Arna, Hordaland; 7%

This amber-hued, smoked malt IPA offers aromas of wet wool, wood smoke, roasted malt and caramel to introduce a smoky body carrying flavours of chocolate, caramel, date, fig and dried blueberries.

HARDT STYRBORD

Baatbryggeriet, Vestnes, Møre og Romsdal; 6.4%

A strong version of the brewery's 4.6% Styrbord pale ale, this is amped-up and citrusy, with plenty of hoppy fruit in the nose and spicy pine added to the mix in the malt-forward body.

HELVETESJØLET QUADRUPEL

Geiranger, Geiranger, Møre og Romsdal; 10%

Brewery-aged for over six months, this strong Belgian-inspired abbey-style ale exudes aromas of banana, raisin, nougat and nutty marzipan, with a complex palate of fruity chocolate and caramel, and a long and warming finish.

HUMLEHELVETE

Veholt, Skien, Telemark; 8.5%

A double IPA from an award-winning, family-owned farm brewery. Pine and tropical-fruit notes on an otherwise grapefruity nose, and a complex and warming body with roasty and caramel malt buttressed by fruity flavours of citrus, mango and pear.

HVETEØL

Reins Kloster, Rissa, Sør-Trøndelag; 4.6%

A *hefeweizen* brewed on an ancient farm that was for centuries also a monastery. Aromas of banana, wheat and lemon introduce this lean and quaffable beer, with tones of melon, banana and tropical fruit in the body.

IPA

Telemark, Skien, Telemark; 6.5%

Very much in the classic US style, this cloudy orange IPA has tropical-fruit aromas, including papaya, pink grapefruit and melon, and a richly malty and citrusy-fruity body that finishes very dry and hoppy.

JULIE INDIA SAISON

Amundsen, Oslo; 6%

A successful brewpub, now expanding to brew greater quantities of beers like this tropical-fruity *saison* with a full and floral, citrus-and-tropical-fruit and moderately dry finish.

KJELLERPILS

Sundbytunet, Jessheim, Akershus; 4.5%

A German-style *kellerbier* brewed in small batches by the award-winning brewer Frank Werme. Lightly cloudy with a balanced aroma of malt, florals and fresh hops, and a faintly fruity palate of grain, honey and apples at the finish.

KJETIL JIKIUN INDEPENDENT STOUT

Bådin, Bodø, Nordland; 8.5%

A black and oily stout with complex aromas of nuts, dark bitter chocolate, roasted coffee and dried berries, and a body of strong coffee, dark fruit, cherries and vanilla.

KNURR

Tya, Øvre Årdal, Sogn og Fjordane; 7%

A single hop – Centennial – US-style IPA with a grapefruity aroma holding notes of papaya and a balanced body with marmalade tones layered over dry maltiness.

KØLA-PÅLSEN

St Hallvards, Oslo; 6.2%

Porter with a complex aroma of herbs and chocolate, coffee and liquorice, and a luscious body of coffee and dried dark fruits, made by a crowd-funded brewery with its very own fields of barley and hops.

KVERNKNURR

Små Vesen, Valdres, Oppland; 6.5%

From a defunct brewery revived in 2015, this British-style ESB is dark copper in colour with an aroma of caramel, dry toffee and dark fruit, and a balanced body of chocolate and caramel, vanilla and honey that finishes medium-dry.

KVITWEISS

Inderøy, Inderøy, Nord-Trøndelag; 4.5%

This *weissbier* pours a hazy light gold with a rich collar of foam and tones of wheat and banana in the aroma. The refreshing body offers bright notes of red apples, honey and melon, leading to a medium-dry finish.

LØKKA SITRONGRESS SAISON

Grünerløkka, Oslo; 6%

A *saison* brewed with added lemongrass, this has a spicy, grassy nose accented by lemon and tropical spices, and a fresh and vibrant body with elements of lemon and grain, finishing hoppy and off-dry.

MELKESTOUT

Eiker, Mjøndalen, Baskerud; 5.5%

The name translates to "milk stout", which is precisely what this sweet, nutty and caramelly stout is, with roasted coffee and cream notes on the nose, and chocolate and those of vanilla adding to the flavour.

NAKENBAD

Atna, Atna, Hedmark; 4.7%

Unpasteurized and unfiltered organic pilsner brewed in a small village in central Norway. The aroma is floral and lightly grainy, while the body offers soft bready malt tones and a moderate hoppiness.

NEPTUN

Berentsens, Egersund, Rogaland; 4.7%

A Belgian-style wheat beer that is very light of hue with a fruity aroma of orange peel, grapefruit, coriander and pine needles, and a fresh and fruity body balanced between fruity and wheaty notes, ending with a slight hoppiness.

OREGONIAN

Voss Fellesbryggeri [Norbrew], Voss, Hordaland; 6%

A US-style pale ale, as evidenced by its name, with a deep copper colour, a hoppy, fruity, spicy and slightly bready aroma and a fine balance between its malty tropical fruitiness and reserved hop flavour.

PALE ALE

Nua, Mandal, Vest-Agder; 4.7%

A light and refreshing pale ale, with a fruity nose of fresh grass, floral citrus, papaya and mango, and a medium body with tropical-fruit notes leading to a dryly hoppy finish.

RATATOSK

Ægir, Flåm, Sogn og Fjordane; 9%

A double IPA produced by a brewery located on a fjord, this is emblematic of the brewery's many successes, with a richly fruity aroma and a complex, fruity and malty body, loaded with hoppiness on the finish.

ROASTY ROAST

Schouskjelleren, Oslo; 6%

A popular brewery located at a historic brewing site making impressive ales like this espresso- and vanilla-scented stout with a full, moderately sweet body carrying notes of coffee, chocolate and

gentle liquorice and finishing with a
burst of hoppiness.

SJEF

Skavli, Evenskjer, Troms; 4.7%

A US-style amber ale with a fruity
aroma of berries and a balanced body
weighing out roasted malt, honey, fig
and red berries. Brewed by the lady of
the house.

SLOGEN ALPE IPA

Trollbryggeriet, Liabygda, Møre og
Romsdal; 4.7%

A deep golden IPA with a light character
and sessionable strength, tropical fruit,
pine and grapefruit in the nose and a
fresh citrus–spicy body with a hop-
fuelled finish.

SPITSBERGEN STOUT

Svalbard, Longyearbyen, Svalbard; 7%

From the world's northernmost brewery
hails this strong stout with rich aromas
of nut, caramel, chocolate, toffee and
dark rum, and a malty, roasty body with
chocolate, liquorice and nutty flavours.
Well balanced with a creamy finish.

STEAMER

Oslo, Oslo; 4.7%

The bestseller at the first craft
brewery established in Scandinavia, in
1989. Aromas of dried forest berries,
plum and caramel characterize this
take on the steam beer style, with a
lightly roasty maltiness, more fruity
berry notes and moderate hoppiness
in the body.

CAN'T-MISS BREWERIES

● ● ● ● ● ● ● ● ● ● ● ● ●

HAAND

Drammen, Buskerud

One of the first successes among
craft breweries in Norway, established
in an old knitting factory inherited by
the founder Jens Maudal. **Norwegian
Wood** (6.5%), probably the brewery's
best-known beer, is a smoked malt ale
with a malty body of smoke, charred
wood, whisky and dry caramel, but also
not to be missed are **Dark Force** (9%),
an Imperial wheat stout; **Tindved** (7%),
a tangy ale rich with Norwegian berries;
and **Ardenne Blond** (7.5%), a Belgian-
style strong blond ale with tropical-fruit
elements and a rich hoppiness.

LERVIG

Stavanger, Rogaland

An accomplished brewery on the
southwest coast well known for its
Rye IPA (8.5%), a hazy, amber ale with
complex notes of spicy rye grain, dried
fruit and berries. Other stellar picks
from the brewery's lengthy portfolio
include **Konrad's Stout** (10.4%), a
rich, full and complex Imperial stout;
Galaxy IPA (6.5%), single-hopped with
Galaxy for a full, tropical fruit character;
and **Lucky Jack** (4.7%), a citrusy,
sessionable US-style pale ale.

STORHAVET

Lauvanger, Tennevoll, Troms; 4%

A brown ale brewed with seaweed, this unusual Lauvanger beer has a lightly smoky nose with elements of wood, caramel and roast, while the body brings interesting tones of smoked almonds and roasted caramel.

STOUT

Smøla, Smøla, Møre og Romsdal; 4.7%

A young brewery on a western island is responsible for this coffee-ish, dark chocolaty stout with hints of liquorice in the nose and vanilla and caramel in the body, finishing dry, roasty and bitter.

TRAA

Voss, Voss, Hordaland; 4.7%

An unfiltered blond ale with a slightly fruity and yeasty nose, lightly malty and gently fruity body and enough hoppiness to make it eminently quaffable.

TYST

Fjellbryggeriet, Tuddal, Telemark; 4.75%

A light and refreshing *saison* of the type one might want to drink when working the fields, with fresh grass and floral citrus on the nose, and a crisply malty body that grows spicy toward its dry finish.

ULRIKEN DOUBLE IPA

7Fjell, Bønes, Hordaland; 8.5%

Although relatively light in strength for the style, this double IPA displays all the

hoppy notes of its type, with grapefruit and pine in the aroma and a fruity and dry body with elements of orange peel, pine resin, papaya and mango.

VIKING WARRIOR

Lindesnes, Lindesnes, Vest-Agder; 7.2%

Brewed at the southern tip of Norway, this is a rich and heavy IPA designed for Norwegian cuisine, with exotic fruit on the nose, a malty and fruity body featuring dried berries, fig and plum and a strongly hoppy finish.

WINTER WARMER BATCH # 1

Backyard Hero, nomadic; 7.1%

Riffing on the famous BrewDog slogan, this *doppelbock* brewed at Grünerløkka and aged three months in aquavit barrels is billed as "Beer for Underdogs". Complex with flavours of coffee, caramel, dried plum and chocolate.

SWEDEN

The sometimes shocking cost of beer in Sweden has not dampened the enthusiasm of its brewers, who have created one of the most dynamic markets in Europe despite the price hurdles. Certainly of some benefit is the state liquor store system, which is quite supportive of craft breweries, although the rest is all grit, determination and apparently boundless imagination.

AMARILLO

Oppigårds, Hedemora, Dalarna; 5.9%

This citrusy, quaffable IPA, from a brewery that has grown organically into a major operation, is one of the mainstays of the Swedish beer scene and a go-to IPA for many.

BARONEN

Hantverksbryggeriet, Västerås, Västmanland; 9–12.7%

A deeply malty barley wine with some variation between the annual releases. Intense raisiny malt character combines with mild peppery heat in a beer that ages with grace.

BIG BLIND

All In, nomadic; 7.9%

This beer is a real hop feast, delivered by an up-and-coming contract brewer with high ambitions. Passion-fruit, lychee and mango notes grab all the attention in this double IPA with unusually high quaffability.

BLACK JACK

Monk's Café, Stockholm; 7.5%

Chocolate and liquorice meet blackcurrant in a dense version of an Imperial porter made by a prolific brewpub that over the years has attracted at one time or another some of the country's top brewing talent.

ICONIC BREWERY

NÄRKE KULTURBRYGGERI
– med anor från allra första början –

Kaggen!
STORMAKTS PORTER 2008

Kraftig och värmande Imperial Stout bryggd med ljunghonung från Närke och lagrad på ekfat i 2,5 månader. Serveras med fördel i små kupor vid lägst 14°C. Den bryggdes i december 2008 och går bra att lagra i många år.

OG 1.112   Öl är Konst!   ABV 9,5%

NÄRKE

Örebro

With a curious sense of humour and an experimental mindset, but still deeply in touch with brewing traditions, Närke announced its arrival on the global beer scene with **Kaggen! Stormaktsporter** (10%), an outstanding heather honey Imperial stout. While that particular beer has since been retired, variations such as **Kaggen Stormaktsporter Börb'nåhallon** (9%) continue to be brewed and are complemented by **Tanngnjost & Tanngrisnir XXX** (9.5%), a juniper wood-smoked strong ale brewed in *Gotlandsdricke* tradition; **Jontes Atgeir** (4.7%), a well-hopped pale ale named after the brewer's son; and **Mörker** (4.9%), a mellow yet rich porter.

BLACK RYE IPA

Sälens Fjällbryggeri, Sälen, Dalarna; 6.5%

Liquorice and citrus notes dominate this partially rye-based black IPA, designed as a peppery *après ski* warmer at this resort brewpub. The chocolaty, rounded malty body enhances the experience.

BLACK SOIL IPA

Sigtuna, Arlandastad, Stockholm; 7.5%

Blackcurrant, tar and liquorice combine with grapefruit zest and treacle in this full-flavoured and hoppy black ale, brewed in, of all places, a shopping outlet in the vicinity of Arlanda Airport.

BOURBON MASH BEER

Rådanäs, Mölnlycke, Västra Götaland; 6.7%

An unconventional beer from an otherwise conventional brewer – strong ale brewed from malted barley, rye and corn, using bourbon-soaked oak chips during fermentation to deliver evident oaky tones while remaining relatively light.

BYSEN NO:1

Barlingbo, Visby, Gotland; 5.5%

A turbid amber beer, loosely based on the brewing traditions of the region, made by one of many new breweries on this Baltic island. Phenolic banana and other yeast-induced flavours meet light juniper smoke.

FROM SKÅNE WITH LOVE

CASSIS

An elegant and fruity sour ale, fermented with loads of black currants. *Brettanomyces* yeast and lactic acid bacteria add a great complexity.

BREWED & BOTTLED BY THE THREE EK BROTHERS

BREKERIET BEER AB

LANDSKRONA - SWEDEN

CASSIS

Brekeriet, Landskrona, Skåne; 5.2%

This mainly *Brettanomyces*-fermented ale, refermented with blackcurrant, took the market by storm upon release. While this was the first from a brewer solely brewing "wild" beers, it is widely regarded as their best.

CHRISTMAS ALE

Åre, Järpen, Jämtland; 7.3%

A spiced, medium-strength ale evidently modelled after that of California's Anchor Brewing (*see* page 201), crafted by a tiny brewer near Sweden's premier skiing resort, and delivering a punch of nutmeg and cardamom atop a toasty body.

FOR REAL ALE

Klinte, Klintehamn, Gotland; 5.8%

Tangerine, key lime, gooseberry and mango meet the nose at first encounter with this pearl of a US-style pale ale. A seductively creamy maltiness is followed by a distinctly piney bitterness.

GOLDEN ALE

West Coast, Gothenburg, Västra Götaland; 4.5%

A crisp and light golden ale with rich tropical-fruit hop character and a highly refreshing quality from one of several promising upstart breweries in Gothenburg.

HALF IPA

Örebro, Örebro; 5%

A juicy, but fairly light ale, packed with papaya, tangerine and dill flavours from a brave new brewery located in Örebro with high ambitions and a fiercely progressive attitude.

HALF THE STORY

Södra Maltfabriken, Handen, Stockholm; 7%

A suburban brewery provides this malty strong ale with evident inspiration from Britain. Designed to complement Jura whisky, it is doing that astonishingly well in an unexpected way. Rather than delivering smoke and awe, it relies on rich maltiness and mild hay-like hops.

HERRGÅRDSPORTER

Skebo Bruksbryggeri, Skebobruk, Uppsala; 5%

An English-style porter from Sweden's finest producer of cask ales. Mildly earthy with some liquorice flavours, and as soft and pleasant as you would get from traditional English brewers.

HOLD THE BUNS

Költur, Hölö, Stockholm; 5.9%

A coffee stout rich with the taste of espresso, yet treacherously mild with a seamless, soothing flavour profile, made by a tiny brewery on the far outskirts of Stockholm.

H W SÖDERMANS PILSNER

Ångkvarn, Uppsala; 4.6%

The one fixed entry on an otherwise ever-rotating taplist at this new brewpub is a solid, smooth, malty Czech-style pilsner with mild grassy notes.

IDJIT

Dugges, Landvetter, Västra Götaland; 9.5%

A concentrated, potent, relatively dry Imperial stout with plenty of coffee, liquorice and vanilla in the taste from a long-standing craft brewery, edgeless and harmonious in spite of its richness.

KB STOCKHOLM STOUT

Kungsbryggeriet, Älta, Stockholm; 4.5%

A velvety, chocolaty dry stout from a start-up brewery. Despite concentrated coffee and chocolate flavours, it retains the desired quaffability for a beer of its style.

LEUFSTA BLONDE

Leufstabruk, Lövstabruk, Uppsala; 6%

Immigrant Wallonian brewing traditions persist in the mining areas in northern Uppland, where family-brewing roots can date back centuries. This Belgian-style blond ale is a harmonious, down-to-earth beer with mild yeasty bubblegum notes.

LJUS BELGO

Ryentorps, Falun, Dalarna; 9.6%

A seductive, treacherously strong golden ale where Belgian yeast character and peppery heat are emphasized. Its balance and depth make it stand out among Belgium-inspired ales in Sweden.

LUNATOR

Grebbestad, Grebbestad, Västra Götaland; 7.9%

An annually released seasonal, this nut-brown *doppelbock,* which is rich with sticky malt accented by notes of fig, toffee and grass, is practically a west coast institution.

MÄLARÖ KYRKA

Adelsö, Adelsö, Stockholm; 10%

A sherry-barrel-aged Imperial porter from a small brewery in the inland archipelago. Featuring liquorice and oak flavours, it has the expected depth of a well-made high-strength beer and a warming, peppery finish.

MÖRK LAGER JULÖL

Nääs, Ydre, Östergötland; 5.3%

Dark Christmas lagers are traditional in Sweden and this updated interpretation features citrusy hops rather than the more usual spices, all on a delightful toasty malt base.

CAN'T-MISS BREWERIES

MALMÖ

Malmö, Skåne

A brewpub and production brewery that a few years into existence suddenly started putting out world-class beers. **Canned Wheat** (7%) is a citrusy hop bomb partially based on wheat malt. **Limpic Stout** (12.2%) and **Acoustic Porter** (14.2%) cater, with their sweet and heavy richness, for those in need of warmth in the wet Scandinavian winters. **Grand Crew** (6.2%) is a lambic-style ale, aged in Cognac barrels, complete with cobwebs and citric acidity.

NYNÄSHAMNS

Nynäshamn, Stockholm

One of the oldest craft breweries in the country, with one foot solidly in the British tradition and the other in the US genre. The marmalade-ish house character is evident in **Bedarö Bitter**

(4.5%), the brewery's most popular beer, and the British influence runs deep in **Bötet Barley Wine** (9.1%) and **Smörpundet Porter** (5.9%). **Pickla Pils** (4.8%), a summer favourite, breaks with the brewery's standard approaches and embraces instead central European traditions.

QVÄNUM MAT & MALT

Kvänum, Västra Götaland

Rural, somewhat rustic ales produced at a farm on the fertile plains between Sweden's largest lakes, including hearty **Ambassadörsporter** (7.8%), an earthy Imperial porter; the peppery, phenolic **Helgas Hembrygd** (7%), an ale brewed from local barley, rye, oat and spelt, using only local hops; **Jonsson** (5.8%), a spicy ale, brewed with rye from the neighbours' fields; and the Czech-influenced **Q Lager** (5.1%) with bready malt and a touch of butteriness.

NEBUCHADNEZZAR IIPA

Omnipollo, Stockholm; 8.5%

An immensely popular, intensively citrusy, full-bodied IIPA. Combining the design and marketing talents of this contracting brewer with the clinical execution of Belgium's Proef brewery.

NYA TIDENS IPA

Pite, Piteå, Norrbotten; 6.9%

A small brewery from the northern Bothnian coast produces this straightforward, bronze-coloured IPA with ample hoppy notes of grapefruit and hay atop a solidly malty body.

OATMEAL PORTER

Jämtlands, Pilgrimstad, Jämtland; 4.8%

From a small village deep within the taiga forests, this wonderfully crafted, light but roasty porter brought the modern Swedish beer scene to life in the mid-1990s.

OKTOBERFESTLIG ÄNGÖL MÄRZEN

Ängö, Kalmar; 5.8%

An amber-coloured Oktoberfest beer with lovely creamy, deep malt character, balanced sweetness and subdued grassy–spicy bitterness. Obviously designed for gulping rather than sipping.

OUD BRUIN

Stockholm (Sthlm) Stockholm; 6%

A copper-coloured, woody and vinous *oud bruin* with notes of oak and lemon and light grape-stone bitterness from an inner-city brewer that in 2016 defied local legislation to open a taproom.

PALE ALE

Electric Nurse, nomadic; 4.6%

A nicely citric US-style pale ale with lychee and grapefruit flavours from a successful contract brewing operation run by a young couple, he an electronic designer and she a nurse, made at the Dugges brewery, which is owned by the nurse's father.

PALE ALE

Skäggalösa, Växjö, Kronoberg; 5.3%

A dry and zesty pale ale with citrus, blackcurrant and a long, piney bitter finish, produced in a tiny village in the Swedish forests of the deep south.

PERDITION

Tempel, Uppsala; 8.3%

A sour raspberry stout with balsamic vinegar elements made by a brewer focusing solely on so-called "sour" beers. Fresh cherry tartness balances liquorice and tobacco flavours.

PILSNER

Lycke, Mölnlycke, Västra Götaland; 5%

A crisp and distinct north German-style pilsner from a youthful brewery in Gothenburg's suburbs. Grass and citrus notes combine with a dry and grainy breadiness for a refreshing experience.

THE RED SLOPE

Remmarlöv, Eslöv, Skåne; 8.5%

Copper coloured with a bold and forthright maltiness and a wealth of Seville-orange, tea and caramel flavours, this is possibly the best Swedish example of modern US-style strong ales.

RÖKÖL

Helsinge, Söderhamn, Gävleborg; 5%

A *rauchbier* from a brewery focusing solely on German beer styles, an unusual entity in Sweden. With a very traditional approach and relatively subtle smoke, it is aiming for approachability.

RÖTT MEN INTE SÖTT – BARREL AGED

Sahtipaja, Sätila, Västra Götaland; 4.4%

A juicy modern-style *Berliner weisse* with lots of raspberries, subsequently aged on bourbon barrels with vanilla pods and cinnamon. Despite an onslaught of concentrated flavours, it remains curiously harmonious.

BREWERIES TO WATCH

STIGBERGETS

Gothenburg, Västra Götaland

It took only a year for this brewery to jump from solid, well-made beers to outstanding hop-heavy examples such as the IPA **GBG Beer Week 2016** (6.5%) and malt-focused gems like **Wee Heavy** (10%).

WENNGARN

Sigtuna, Stockholm

A new microbrewery situated at the ancient Wenngarn Castle, starting out in valiant fashion. Among the early releases are **De la Gardie Porter** (9.5%), a rich Imperial porter rested in bourbon barrels, and **Lager Nr. 1** (5.2%), a hoppy *zwickelbier*.

SVAGDRICKA

Hjo, Hjo, Västra Götaland; 2%

One of a handful of remaining traditional examples of a "table beer" style once produced by hundreds of brewers and consumed in quantity, this showcases restrained sweetness and accessibility.

SVARTKROPP

Modernist, Stockholm; 8.4%

Mildly peaty with a full body replete with chocolate, liquorice and leather notes, this is a relaxed, yet full-flavoured Imperial stout with personality.

T-56 STOUT

Fjäderholmarnas, Lidingö, Stockholm; 8%

Potent and chocolaty, this warming stout from a brewpub located on an islet in the harbour inlet to Stockholm leaves distinct impressions of liquorice and citrus.

TREUDD SAISON INSIDIEUX

Nyckelbydal, Ekerö, Stockholm; 7.2%

A tart, blond ale brewed true to the Wallonian *saison* traditions by a small family brewery. Elegant and mildly spritzy with harmonious, focused flavours of curaçao with honey and a mild tartness.

TRIPEL

Eskilstuna Ölkultur, Södermanland; 9%

A full-bodied and fruity *tripel*-style ale with bubblegummy and mildly peppery heat, evocative of a fine brandy. It is best enjoyed in situ at the scenic riverfront brewpub.

WEE HEAVY

Octabrew, Fagersta, Västmanland; 8.7%

A mature and mellow strong ale with a mildly warming finish, this Scottish-inspired beer boasts rich maltiness with notes of bread, toffee, prune and ripe fruit.

WHAT THE DUCK!

Klackabacken, Kristianstad, Skåne; 7.8%

Although it is packed with flavour, including elements of blueberry, liquorice, dark chocolate and coffee, this Imperial porter never grows overwhelming, remaining instead concentrated and delightful.

FINLAND

Facing the highest alcohol taxes in the European Union, a government store system that has exclusivity to the sale of all beers greater than 4.7% ABV and an attitude that can be hostile toward small breweries, together with a flood of cheap beer arriving daily aboard the Estonian ferries, it takes a lot to make it as a Finnish craft brewer. Still, many have prevailed, and despite it all, Finland's craft beer making scene is not only surviving but bordering on thriving.

BLACK PILS

Mallaskosken, Seinäjoki, Southern Ostrobothnia; 5.5%

A hybrid between *schwarzbier* and pilsner, with the label emphasis on the latter, there is a rich roastiness to this beer, even hints of coffee, but in the end it is the hoppiness that has the last say.

BLACK TIDE

Hopping Brewsters, Akaa, Pirkanmaa; 6.4%

While billed as a black IPA, this ale has a toasty, almost burned roastiness with notes of dark fruit and liquorice more reminiscent of a stout, all balancing and occasionally dominating its not-insignificant hoppiness.

BREWER'S SPECIAL SAISON

Saimaan, Mikkeli, Southern Savonia; 6%

Quite floral and perfumey with hints of citrus and fresh-cut grass on the nose, this light and refreshing ale offers the drinker a wheaty, fruity and faintly peppery palate.

BUSTER-JANGLE

Radbrew, Kaarina, Southwest Finland; 7%

With a wealth of citrus notes from the Cascade and Mandarina Bavaria hops used, this US-style IPA offers a firm, caramelly maltiness and a quaffability disproportionate to its strength.

STYLE SPOTLIGHT

SAHTI – POSSIBLY THE ULTIMATE FOLK BEER

Sahti entered public awareness outside Finland after beer scribe Michael Jackson began exploring and writing about it in the 1970s and 1980s. Sometimes described as the closest thing to what the Vikings drank and possibly as old as Nordic civilization itself, it was once purely a farmhouse brew, mashed in a hollowed-out tree trunk and heated with the addition of red-hot stones.

The defining feature of the beer, which is made from barley malt and up to 50% or more rye, is arguably less its grain make-up than the juniper boughs through which it is filtered, the berries and the branches acting as both flavouring and antibacterial agent. Or perhaps the more important characteristic is the baker's yeast typically used for fermentation. Or maybe it is the freshness that is all but essential to its enjoyment.

The flavour of most sahtis will tend toward the highly fruity, with banana notes frequently dominant and a spiciness also key to its character. The majority will also be higher strength, as with **Lammin Sahti**, a rich though mellow mélange of fruity, honey-ish and juniper tones. Closer to what traditional "feast" versions of the drink would have been is the **Finlandia Sahti**, full of toffee and banana flavours with a more biting juniper spiciness, while harder to find but a classic is **Hollolan Hirvi Kivisahti**, a full and velvety *sahti* still heated with hot stones according to traditional techniques.

CAN'T-MISS BREWERY

PLEVNA

Tampere, Pirkanmaa

Though it started by simply breathing some life into simple lager styles, this brewery–restaurant has moved with the times and demonstrated that it can master a variety of styles. The succulent **Amarillo Weizen** (5%) is a full-bodied and hoppy *weizen*, blending the signature hop's fruitiness with that from the yeast; **Petolintu** (5.4%) is a bready lager high in both hop aromatics and bitterness; **Weizenbock** (7.5%) is rich with banana esters; and **Siperia** (8%) is a massive Imperial stout with unusually high hop aroma and bitter hopping.

HELSINKI PORTTERI

Suomenlinnan, Helsinki, Uusimaa; 5.6%

A respectful nod to the classic English porter, this chocolaty interpretation may seem on the light side, particularly for a Scandinavian beer, but reaches its zenith when occasionally found in cask-conditioned form.

HUVILA ESB

Malmgård, Malmgård, Uusimaa; 5.2%

Richly malty with a gentle East Kent Golding hop bitterness, this remains true to its English extra-special bitter designation with a fruity malt character tempered by its hops.

ISOPORTTERI

Pyynikki, Tampere, Pirkanmaa; 7.3%

A rich, chocolaty porter with a gentle touch of both smokiness and woodiness, and a dryness and bitterness that exceeds those of many – perhaps most – other Finnish strong porters.

JULMAJUHO

Teerenpeli, Lahti, Päijänne Tavastia; 7.7%

With sweetish and slightly woody aspects that are almost reminiscent of barrel-ageing, this smoked porter is a marvel of malt construction, with a mellowness that belies its strength and a peaty and liquorice-ish finish.

KIEVARI IMPERAALI

Laitilan, Laitila, Southwest Finland; 9.2%

An Imperial stout with a roasty, plummy and raisiny aroma accompanied by a

body that is sweet, burned and even a touch phenolic, evoking thoughts of baked raisin cookies.

KOFF PORTER

Sinebrychoff, Kerava, Uusimaa; 7.2%

Stands out as unusual among Baltic porters today as a top-fermented beer, in contrast to the lagers now typical, with a rich and oily mouthfeel, chocolate–caramel notes in a full body and a roasty, bitter finish.

MALTAAN HAUKKA

Olutpaja, Laitikkala, Pirkanmaa; 4.7%

Brewed to the *altbier* style, this has a sweet and bready maltiness holding a touch of nuttiness and a soft, drying rather than bittering hoppiness.

MOOOD

Maistila, Oulu, Northern Ostrobothnia; 5.8%

A mellow and balanced stout that comes with a sweetness evocative of double cream and a cakey and quaffable body holding notes of burned sugar and hints of raisins.

MUFLONI SINGLE HOP SIMCOE

Beer Hunter's, Pori, Satakunta; 3.5%

One of a wide range of single-hop and lower-alcohol beers from the brewery, this fruity and resiny session IPA delivers plenty of character and avoids the wateriness of some of its style.

PASKA KAUPUNNI

Sonnisaari, Oulu, Northern Ostrobothnia; 7.1%

Made with four malts and six varieties of hop, this IPA is packed with tropical-fruit notes in the aroma and a rich and full maltiness in the body, with a lingering, resinous hoppy finish.

PILS

Helsinki, Helsinki, Uusimaa; 4.5%

Crafted by a German head brewer, this is a perhaps surprisingly malty pilsner with bready tones and a well-balanced herbal bitterness.

PILS

Rousal, Rosala, Southwest Finland; 4.6%

With citrusy, peppery hoppiness, this pilsner deviates slightly from convention, but satisfies nonetheless with a crisp and refreshing body culminating in a long and lingering bitter finish.

PLÄKKI

Hiisi, Jyväskylä, Central Finland; 6.3%

With a "hotness" that makes it seem stronger than it actually is, this shippable black IPA has a highly chocolaty roastiness contrasted by a notably citrusy hoppiness.

SAVU KATAJA

Vakka-Suomen, Uusikaupunki, Southwest Finland; 9%

With both a fair proportion of smoked malt and added juniper, this could easily be an overwhelming ale. It is, however, designed to be more approachable and satisfies with its luscious, rich palate, which ends in a sweet, smoky finish.

SAVU PORTER

Maku, Tuusula, Uusimaa; 5.9%

Although made with smoked malt, the smoky aspect of this balanced beer is kept mellow and accessible by a rich and chocolaty maltiness culminating in a drier and more roasted finish.

ULTIMATOR

Stadin, Helsinki, Uusimaa; 8%

From one of Finland's oldest modern craft breweries, this rich *doppelbock* is fruity with citrus and pine notes when young, but develops a raisiny hint as it ages and has a beautiful winey and woody flavour either way.

VEHNÄ

Koulu, Turku, Southwest Finland; 5.4%

From a brewery–restaurant built in a former school near the city centre, this well-executed *hefeweizen* has a decidedly wheaty, malty character, with banana and citrus notes providing the refreshment.

ICELAND

Although very late to end the country's extended flirtation with Prohibition, with full-strength beer made legal only as recently as 1989, and even later to join the craft beer movement, Iceland has been moving forward quickly to establish its own space within the world of beer. Some of its brewery creations have been little more than cries for attention – smoked whale testicle ale, anyone? – but many more have been genuinely interesting, uniquely Icelandic takes on the world of brewing.

ICELANDIC NORTHERN LIGHTS

Steðja, Borgarnes, Western Region; 5.3%

From the brewery responsible for the notorious whale testicle beer comes this significantly more conventional brew – a crisp, deep amber lager flavoured with liquorice to a sweet, smooth and well-balanced character.

ICELANDIC TOASTED PORTER

Einstök, nomadic; 6%

Having its beers brewed at Viking Ölgerd in Akureyri allows this export-driven company to focus on the clever marketing of some occasionally impressive beers, including this coffee-accented porter with vaguely smoky chocolate elements.

LAVA

Ölvisholt, Selfoss, Southern Region; 9.4%

Named after an active volcano visible from the brewery, this smoked malt Imperial stout has a sweet, roasted malt smokiness, on the line between subtle and assertive, with dark, dried-fruit notes and hints of liquorice.

PALE ALE

Gæðingur, Skagafırði, Northern Region; 4.5%

Brewing on Iceland's northwest coast, a fair distance from the population centre of Reykjavík, this young operation has managed to craft some of the country's deftest hoppy beers, including this clever pale ale with an approachable, floral character.

CAN'T-MISS BREWERY

● ●

BORG

Reykjavík

Although not the first Icelandic brewery to make an impression outside of its home country's borders – that title goes to Ölvisholt (*see* above) – this offshoot of the Ölgerðin beer and soft drinks producer and distributor has certainly made the biggest noise. Brands identified by number include **Nr. 3 Úlfur India Pale Ale** (5.9%), with its spicy–grassy–citrusy balance; the raisiny, walnutty **Nr. 19 Garún Icelandic Stout** (11.5%); the chocolaty, faintly herbal **Nr. 13 Myrkvi Porter** (6%); and the herbal, heathery and slightly mossy **Nr. 32 Leifur Nordic Saison** (6.8%), among many, many others.

CENTRAL & EASTERN EUROPE

THE CZECH REPUBLIC

The current explosion of independent small breweries in the Czech Republic is comprised mostly of pub breweries, more often than not focused on traditional lager styles that, even in small brewhouses, often undergo the laborious process known as decoction mashing, considered by many an essential component of Czech lagers. Meanwhile, ale traditions are regrowing, with early stages of fusion styles emerging that appear to give pale ales, porters and wheat beers a distinctively Czech edge.

12° SVĚTLÝ LEŽÁK

Rezek, Zásada, Liberec; 5.5%

A pils with presence – a little stronger, a little louder, with a heavier charge of hops than usual, yet very well balanced and almost surprisingly grown-up for a beer that comes from a young brewery big on attitude.

450

Svijany, Svijany, Liberec; 4.6%

Something Czech drinkers value the most in a pale lager is its *říz*, roughly translating as "zest". The best way to understand what that means is with a pint of this rich gold and floral, Saaz-hopped lager, brewed to celebrate the brewery's 450th anniversary.

ALBRECHT INDIA PALE ALE 19%

Frýdlant, Frýdlant, Liberec; 7.9%

As classy as the restored brewery that makes it, this IPA boasts a wonderful blend of complexity, balance and approachability, with intense notes of orange peel and tangy tropical fruit that will captivate even wine drinkers who have never before encountered an IPA.

ASFALT

Zhůřák, Zhůř, Plzeň; 7.2%

An Imperial stout as dark as its name implies stands out not only thanks to its impressive quality but because it is made by a Californian brewer in a small village near the cradle of pale lager, Pilsen.

B:DARK

Budějovický Budvar, České Budějovice, South Bohemia; 4.7%

While its pale sibling gets all the attention, in part due to its US Budweiser doppelgänger, this *tmavý ležák* (dark lager) has a roasted, drier character and towers above the competition from the larger Czech breweries.

BESKYDIAN BANDIT

Beskydský Pivovárek, Ostravice, Moravia Silesia; 5.1%

This brewery from the far east of the Czech Republic is better known for its range of pale ales, but they also know how to lager, as this rich, unctuous, nutty *polotmavé* shows with great panache.

BLACK I.P.A.

Permon, Sokolov, Karlovy Vary; 5.7%

Anyone insisting that black IPAs are just hoppier stouts may find support in the roasted flavours of this one. Others will simply find a solid, well-balanced beer that gets everything right, from one of the best Czech ale brewers.

BŘEZŇÁK 12°

Velké Březno [Heineken], Velké Březno, Ústí nad Labem; 5.1%

The Czech subsidiary of Heineken makes this superb *světlý ležák* with a crisp mouthfeel and notes reminiscent of sweet herbs and fresh grain in a brewery they have kept as a sort of living museum.

ICONIC BREWERY

MATUŠKA

Broumy, Central Bohemia

When Martín Matuška opened his brewery in 2007, it became one of the first widely distributed new Czech breweries. When he was joined by son Adam, it also became one of the first famous for the quality of its ales, including **Raptor IPA** (6.3%), almost a national benchmark for the style; **Apollo Galaxy** (5.5%), a US-style pale ale with flavours that are both balanced and intense; **California** (5.3%), an elderflower-accented ale that speaks to its namesake state; and **Černá Raketa** (6.9%), a powerful black IPA that equally evokes Oregon.

ICONIC
BREWERY

ÚNĚTICKÝ

Únětice, Central Bohemia

Restored in 2011 after over 60 years of idleness, the brewery was an immediate success thanks to their only two year-round beers, both pale lagers: **10°** (3.8%), providing proof that, in good hands, ordinary-seeming beers can pack flavour and character; and **12°** (5%), with all a proper Bohemian pils should have and then some. Seasonals include the almost criminally quaffable **Masopustní Bock** (6%), brewed for the outdoor winter revelries of the Czech Mardi Gras; and **Posvícenský** (4.6%), a rye amber lager with a complex blend of malts taking centre stage, brewed for the village's Parish Fair.

BRNĚNSKÁ 11

Hauskrecht, Brno, South Moravia; 4.5%

From the former brewmaster at a major brewery, now running his own business, comes this *světlý ležák*. Nothing innovative – just sweet grains with fragrant herbs and flowers making it a classic Bohemian pils done as it should be.

ČERNÁ SVINĚ

Šnajdr, Kostelec nad Černými lesy, Central Bohemia; 5.2%

If anyone were to be given this blind and told that it was an English-style porter, nobody could fault them for believing it, even though it is, in fact, a dark lager with notes of prune, hints of liquorice, roast and chocolate and a full quaffability.

ČERNÝ LEŽÁK

Bernard [co-owned by Duvel Moortgat], Humpolec, Vysočina; 5.1%

Renowned in several countries, this lager has become a true classic and remains one of the best available in the country, coming across like a lightweight Baltic porter able to keep a firm grip on your palate.

CHOTOVINSKÝ STOUT

Chotoviny, Chotoviny, South Bohemia; 5.3%

A beer to bring to mind a block of bitter chocolate dissolved in a cup of strong and very good espresso. Complex and rewarding, and the sort of stout that begs for your palate's attention.

DALEŠICKÁ 11°

Dalešice, Dalešice, Vysočina; 4.3%

Classic and traditional are overused
words, but it is hard to find better ones
for this bready pale lager boasting notes
of dandelion honey and embodying all
the attributes of a classic and traditional
Czech beer.

DUŠIČKOVÝ STOUT

Falkenštejn, Krasná Lípa, Ústí nad
Labem; 5.7%

Brewed each year for early November,
when Czechs honour their dead, it
brings everything you expect from the
style, with an intriguing yet warming
note of freshly ground black pepper.

ESO

Konrad, Vratislavice nad Nisou, Liberec;
4.6%

In the darker side of the *polotmavý*
spectrum, this conversational amber
lager from Northern Bohemia demands
to be drunk in half-litre portions so
that you can fully appreciate its subtle
harmony of caramel, hazelnuts and
herbal bitterness.

FABIÁN 12°

Fabián, Hostmice, Central Bohemia;
4.6%

Made by the former head brewer of
Dalešice (*see* above) in a resurrected
brewery located not far from Prague,
this is a textbook example of how round
and floral a proper *světlý ležák* can be,
with hints of honey and far from boring
and bland.

FLEKOVSKÝ LEŽÁK

U Fleků, Prague; 4.6%

Ignoring any possible modern trend,
Prague's oldest pub brewery produces
only one beer, the same since 1843 or
so they claim – a superb dark lager full
of notes of chocolate, sweet coffee,
dried fruit and history.

GYPSY PORTER

Kocour, Varsndorf, Ústí nad Labem;
7.1%

Born from a collaboration with an
English brewer brokered by a local beer
writer, the success of the first batch
convinced the brewery to add it to its
regular portfolio. Muscular, complex
and weighty.

H8

Hendrych, Vrchlabí, Hradec Králové; 3.3%

The brewery produces a solid range
of beers, but it is in this case in
particular that the brewer shows his
craftsmanship by brewing a lightweight
pale lager with enough flavour to keep
you entertained for either one glass or
the whole day.

HIBISCUS

Krkonošský Medvěd, Vrchlabí, Hradec
Králové; 6.8%

A *weizenbock* infused with hibiscus
flowers and lemongrass, the flowers
bringing principally the beer's pink
colour, while notes of the herb appear
almost fleetingly toward the finish,
contrasting with the flavour and
inspiring curiosity.

HRADEBNÍ TMAVÉ

Měšťanský Pivovar v Poličce, Polička, Pardubice; 3.9%

A *tmavé výčepní* that calls to mind a dark mild, with notes of dark fruit and sweet coffee and hints of roast. An exception within a style mostly associated with the sweet, uninspired products of macro breweries.

HUBERTUS PREMIUM

Kácov, Kácov, Central Bohemia; 4.7%

Inexpensive doesn't have to mean low quality where Czech is concerned, as proven by this *světlý ležák* produced in a small regional brewery near Prague. It is a terrific quaffer, with grassy, honey-ish and bready malt notes.

JANTÁR 13°

Vinohradský, Prague; 5.5%

This *polotmavý* (amber lager) is an all-evening quaffer that makes you wonder whether it is possible to make an infusion of silk and dose it with a dash of summer fruit and the nectar of autumn flowers.

JISKRA

Radniční, Jihlava, Vysočina; 3.8%

When it first came out, this citrusy session ale tasted like a beginner's home-brew project. Its massive improvement is a testament to the dedication and perseverance of its brewers, who took the criticism as a motivator and not a deterrent.

KANEC

Břeclav, Břeclav, South Bohemia; 5%

Tasting of everything you could desire in a *světlý ležák*, this offers a solid, almost croissant-like malt base and confident yet subdued notes of noble hops. Perfect.

KLOSTERMANN

Měšťanský, Strakonice, South Bohemia; 5.1%

First brewed in 2008 to honour its namesake Austrian-born writer, this is a full-bodied *polotmavé* packing caramel-coated nuts and dried apricots with a pinch of roast and herbs in a very attractive finish.

KOUNIC

Uherský Brod, Uherský Brod, Zlín; 4.6%

Anton Dreher (*see* page 68) would probably love this superb Vienna lager with a round and smooth body supporting subtle notes of caramel and nuts that slowly open the path to an aromatic and floral finish.

KRÁLOVSKÁ ZLATÁ LABUŤ

Dvůr Zvíkov, Zvíkov, South Bohemia; 11.8%

After spending up to 15 months in the cellar, this bottom-fermented interpretation of the barley wine style with an appealing mahogany colour feels almost like drinking a mildly carbonated amontillado sherry or tawny port.

CAN'T-MISS BREWERIES

ANTOŠ

Slaný, Central Bohemia

A brewery making lagers and ales with equal skill at two locations. **Slánský Rarach** (4%) is a near-perfect *desítka* to tempt even the most conservative drinker; **Polotmavá 13%** (5.5%) boasts a blend of floral, autumn fruit and nut flavours; **Tlustý Netopýr** (7%) is a rye IPA that brings appealing spiciness to the mix; and **Choo-choo** (7.8%) is a powerful and complex black IPA that completes an interesting and rewarding beer voyage.

BŘEVNOVSKÝ KLÁŠTERNÍ

Vojtěcha, Prague

Located within the walls of the oldest monastery in Bohemia, the beers are sold under the Benedict name, including **Klasická Dvanáctka** (5%), a *světlý ležák* seasoned with Saaz hops from a 75-year-old hopyard, and **Imperial Lager** (8.5%), with a quaffability that belies its strength. **Klášterní IPA** (6.5%) has more of an English character with juicy tropical-fruit notes, while **Russian Imperial Stout** (8.5%) drinks like a study on the style, also coming in a whisky-barrel-aged version.

KLÁŠTERNÍ

Strahov, Prague

One of the Czech Republic's best, brewing under the Svatý Norbert name. Year-round beers include: **Jantár** (5.3%), a *polotmavé* with a stunning balance of malt and hops; **Speciální Tmavé** (5.5%), almost chewy and full of roastiness, but with a surprisingly hoppy finish; and the truly world-class **IPA** (6.3%) on top – intense and aromatic, but perfectly balanced. Of their many other brews, two autumn beers stand out, **Antidepressant Ale** (6.3%) and **Antidepressant Lager** (6.3%), brewed from the same dark malt bill, though with different hopping.

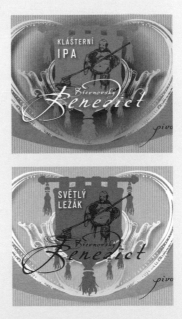

KRUTÁK 12°

Továrna, Slaný, Central Bohemia; 5%

When beer snobs complain that Czech pale lagers "lack personality", they are not thinking of this beer with freshly kilned grain notes supporting a bouquet of summer flowers.

MAGOR

Zichovecký, Zichovec, Central Bohemia; 6.2%

Fortunately, it doesn't honour its name – Czech for "lunatic" – but carefully and sanely chooses the best bits of Vienna lager, *märzen* and *bock* to create an impressive strong *polotmavé* that qualifies as dangerously quaffable.

PARDUBICKÝ PORTER

Pernštejn, Pardubice; 8%

It might be the novelty of "foreign" styles or because it is a classic everyone takes for granted, but this Baltic porter doesn't get the attention it deserves. Smooth, rich and reminiscent of tawny port with a drop of umami.

PILSNER URQUELL

Plzeňský Prazdroj, Plzeň; 4.4%

They say it is a shadow of its former self, perhaps with some justification. But it's still the most iconic Czech beer and, doubters notwithstanding, remains the benchmark of *světlý ležák* (pale lager), one that few smaller breweries are able to reach.

PODLESKÝ LEŽÁK

Podlesí, Příbram, Central Bohemia; 5.5%

Full flavoured, smooth and floral – adjectives that, while accurate, don't do justice to a beer sufficiently impressive that it will make you want to travel to a suburb of an ugly former mining town.

POLOTMAVÉ VÝČEPNÍ

Bakalář, Rakovník, Central Bohemia; 4.5%

A beer named after and of a style native to the Czech lands, yet so rare as to be almost unknown. Subtle notes of nuts coated in caramel, dark bread crust and herbs; simple and complex at the same time.

POLOTMAVÝ 11°

Všerad, Všeradice, Central Bohemia; 4.6%

You don't need big, bold flavours to make a beer with interest and complexity, and this example provides ample proof. Full appreciation requires contemplation and more than a sip or two, but rewards with peppery, herbal and malty elements.

POLOTMAVÝ LEŽÁK

Bašta, Prague; 4.8%

Once this brewpub found the god of consistency, their beers fulfilled all the promises of those first batches, and this subtle, caramelly amber lager with notes of stone fruit and nuts and a flowery finish became something to pursue.

PORTER

U Bulovky, Prague; 6.1%

An English-style porter that in one pint
will take you back to the late Victorian
age, while a second will have you return
to the present enjoying its malty mix of
roast, black sugar, prunes and dried figs.

PORTER

Uhřiněves, Prague; 6.8%

Baltic porter is an underrated style all
over the world, and the Czech Republic
is no exception. Which is a shame, as
we need more dark lagers like this
one, which brings to mind Christmas
fruitcake soaked in amontillado sherry.

POSTŘIŽINSKÉ FRANCINŮV LEŽÁK

Nymburk, Nymburk, Central Bohemia;
5%

The Nymburk brewery was the
birthplace of writer Bohumil Hrabal,
whose face adorns the label of this
excellent, everyday drinker, with a fuller
body than usual for the style, but no
less quaffability.

PREMIUM TMAVÝ LEŽÁK

Bohemia Regent, Třeboň, South
Bohemia; 4.4%

Criminally underrated and almost
forgotten in favour of the wave of new
breweries and styles, this classic boasts
chocolaty notes that masterfully walk
the fine line between sweet and roasty
without missing a step.

CAN'T-MISS BREWERIES

● ● ● ● ● ● ● ● ● ● ● ● ●

KOUNICKÝ

Kounice, Central Bohemia

Owned by the renowned malting
company Klusáček, which naturally
produces the excellent Bohemian
floor malts that are the foundation
of the brewery's beers. **Světlý Ležák
12%** (4.9%) proudly displays the
quality of these house-made malts,
complemented by the finest Saaz,
while the ginger-infused **Ginger Ale**
(5%) uses Premiant hops to make a
surprisingly quaffable beer. **Rauch**
(5.6%) is smoked beer for introducing
people to the style, while **Melon 15°**
(6.5%) is one of a changing line of
ales, each brewed from pilsner malt
with a single hop variety and named
after the hop.

KOUT NA ŠUMAVĚ

Kout na Šumavě, Plzeň

Brewery with an almost cult-like status
among fans of proper lagers, which is
all that they brew. **Koutská Desítka**
(4.2%) is a pale lager that laughs in the
face of the category's stereotype of
bland and boring beers, with **Dvanáctka**
(5%) being a contender for the title of
ultimate *světlý ležák*. The dark **Koutský
Tmavé** (6%) pumps up the volume with
strength and complexity, while **Tmavý
Speciál** (8.2%) could be considered the
Tmavý on steroids.

BREWERIES TO WATCH

CLOCK

Potštejn, Hradec Králové

Principally an ale brewery, although also making lagers, with beers such as the textbook US-style pale ale **Clock** (5%); **Twist** (6.2%), a reddish IPA; and **Rišaví Zmikund** (7.8%), a massive and muscular red ale that feels like falling asleep in a basket full of summer.

RAVEN

Plzeň

Australian-led ale specialist making excellent beers like the nutty, soothing **Brewhemian Cream Porter** (6.3%); a balanced, light-on-the-palate **White IPA** (6.3%); **Laid to Waste** (8.2%), a strong ale named after a heavy metal band; and **Gunslinger** (6.4%), an IPA that shoots.

PRINC MAX X

Vysoký Chlumec, Vysoký Chlumec, Central Bohemia; 4%

In the upper gravity range of the *desítka* pale lager category, this has a fuller body than most, dominated by freshly dried cereal notes. The hops are solely to provide some balance to the relatively generous maltiness.

PŠENIČNÝ SPECIÁL 16°

U Vacků, Chlumec nad Cidlinou, Hradec Králové; 6.4%

A *weizenbock* by any other name, with all the warm, autumnal characteristics of the style and a surprising flash of wild strawberry by the finish that will make you crave another round.

RAMPUŠÁK

Dobruška, Dobruška, Hradec Králové; 4.9%

Made with the brewery's own floor maltings, it offers the sensory gamut of a proper *světlý ležák* – freshly baked white bread, flowers, herbs, grain, honey and caramel –with a subtlety that will reward every sip.

RYCHNOVSKÁ KNĚŽNA

Rychnov, Rychnov nad Kněžnou, Hradec Králové; 5.2%

At first encounter, it seems no different than any other decent *světlý ležák*, but a sharper bitterness than most sets it apart and will have the drinker hurrying for another round.

SEDM KULÍ

Ferdinand, Benešov, Central Bohemia; 5.5%

Named after the seven bullets that whacked Archduke Franz Ferdinand, founder of the brewery, this *polotmavý* infused with herbs doesn't pack a murderous punch, but a range of subtle yet complex flavours that seem to change with every sip.

SINGLE HOP

Velický Bombarďák, Velká nad Veličkou, South Moravia; 5%

Single-hop beers are becoming popular among Czech brewers, often with mixed results, but not in this case. Each beer in the series brings out the best of the hop used without neglecting the other ingredients.

SMOKED AMBER ALE

Mordýř, Dolní Ředice, Pardubice; 5.5%

Smoked malts often get lost in hop-forward beers, but not here, with bacon appearing at the end of the first sip and gaining intensity with each subsequent mouthful yet never overwhelming the fragrant Cascade hops.

STALKER IPA

Falkon, nomadic; 6.9%

Jakub Veselý, the young brewer behind this beer, is proud of his "flying brewery" and has impressed from the start – which happened to have been this IPA – with bold hopping of varying varieties depending on what Veselý can get his hands on.

STAROKLADNO 10,8°

U Kozlíků, Kladno, Central Bohemia; 4%

At the strong end of its generally low-alcohol style, this *desítka* will have you believing that you are drinking something considerably stronger. Full and richly flavourful for a lager of its diminutive strength, session beer hardly gets any better than this.

ŠTĚPÁN SVĚTLÝ

Dům, Prague; 5%

From one of the first craft breweries in the Czech Republic comes this still solid *světlý ležák*, full of herbal notes on a solidly malty base, which remains one of the finest examples of the Czech-born style.

SVĚTLÝ LEŽÁK

Poutník, Pelhřimov, Vysočina; 5%

A slice of freshly baked white bread – without the crust – spread with a thin layer of mild honey with bitter spring herbs. Beautiful in its simplicity.

SVĚTLÝ LEŽÁK

Purkmistr, Plzeň; 4.8%

When you are making a pale lager in Pilsner Urquell's town, it had better be damn good, as is this one, with grain, honey and floral notes dialled up a notch, almost as if the brewer were trying to show the creator of the style how it should be done.

SWEET JESUS

Sibeeria, nomadic; 8%

When an Imperial stout is designed and commissioned by a bar called BeerGeek, you know subtlety won't be one of its features. Still, there is surprising balance and complexity provided mostly by the blend of malts.

TAMBOR 11°

Tambor, Dvůr Králové nad Labem, Hradec Králové; 4.5%

A classic, working-class Bohemian pils, unpretentious, grassy, a bit drier than the average and a beer to build an evening around.

TEARS OF SAINT LAURENT

Mamut/Wild Creatures, Mikulov, South Moravia; 6%

An unremarkable South Moravian brewery run by winemakers who decided to make the first Czech "lambic", maturing this one for two years with Saint Laurent grapes in casks used for that same wine and yielding remarkable results.

TMAVÝ SPECIÁL

Herold, Březnice, Central Bohemia; 5.3%

The best way to describe this Bohemian dark lager is a blend of the best of stout, *dunkel* and *schwarzbier*, with typical Czech character. A beer that doesn't demand attention, but will reward anyone who will pay heed.

TORPID MIND

Bad Flash, nomadic; 10.5%

An Imperial stout that is brewed with a grain bill that includes smoked wheat malts and proves that contract brewing can produce unique beers, especially when commissioned by two pub owners who understand beer as well as many brewers.

TRIBULUS

U Dobřenských, Prague; 6%

Named after the herb it is brewed with – *Tribulus terrestris*, also known as puncturevine – this has the quality of a pale ale brewed with exotic hops. The flagship of a brewery specializing in herbal ales.

VÍDEŇSKÝ SPECIÁL

Harrach, Velké Meziříčí, Vysočina; 6.2%

A couple of sips of this reddish-amber-coloured lager makes one wish there were more brewed exclusively with Vienna malts. Silky, with notes of dark honey and lightly toasted white bread, and a pinch of floral hoppiness.

VIMPERSKÝ SVĚTLÝ

Ležák Šumavský, Vimperk, South Bohemia; 4.9%

Brewed by the same person who teaches secondary school children in Prague how to brew, this is, naturally, technically perfect. A beautiful, flowery, smooth, rewarding Czech pils from start to finish.

WEIZENBIER

Primátor, Náchod, Hradec Králové; 4.8%

One of the oldest wheat beers still on the market, and the first to come out in bottles, with classic notes of banana and clove and a smooth mouthfeel that can compete as an equal with the best Bavaria has to offer.

YERBA MATE'S 13°

U Bizona, Čižice, Plzeň; 5.25%

This amber lager is an excellent example of how to use an unconventional ingredient – yerba mate or *Ilex paraguariensis*, a member of the holly family – while avoiding the gimmick. Anyone familiar with Argentina's national beverage will recognize it at once; the rest will be intrigued by its earthy tones.

ZAJÍC 12°

Kynšperský, Kynšperk nad Ohří, Karlovy Vary; 5.2%

Resurrected breweries are a Czech phenomenon and tend to produce very good, mostly classic beers, and this *světlý ležák* is no exception, featuring notes of crushed dried flowers, herbs and slightly sweet bread.

ESTONIA

Rife with influence from Scandinavia – the three largest breweries in Estonia are all owned by Scandinavian brewing concerns – Estonia was perhaps well set to become one of the first Baltic states to fully embrace craft brewing, beginning with Põhjala (*see* opposite) and evolving quickly from that pioneering operation.

DR. JONES

Anderson's, nomadic; 6.5%

Very much a classic example of modern IPA, this offers jammy and juicy fruitiness upfront and a lovely zesty aspect to the finish. Citrusy and full of character, yet still refreshing and quaffable.

EV98 PORTER

Must Lips, Tallinn, Harju; 7.7%

This was originally brewed in 2016 for the 98th anniversary of the Estonian Republic and the number will be adjusted accordingly. What will not change is the rich and chocolaty roastiness and smooth palate that disguises its strength.

GAMBRINUSE ÕLLEPOOD RADIAATOR

Vormsi, Norrby, Lääne; 7.5%

This rich *doppelbock* was brewed initially for the Gambrinuse beer shop in Tartu, but is now widely available. It showcases bold, sweet, bready malts, dryly bitter hopping and a raisiny element that stands up well to cellaring.

HOP TVOYU MAT

Käbliku, Palutaja, Põlva; 7.9%

Introducing Belgian yeast to a double IPA recipe, this beer offers a potent mix of fruity, rich hoppiness in the aroma and body with a sweet, caramelly malt backbone, rounded off by a drying bitter finish.

MÄRZEN SPEZIAL

Beer House, Tallinn, Harju; 4.4%

This is a crisp and refreshing unfiltered lager that belies its relatively low strength with a solid bready maltiness and generous hopping. Characterful but, like all of this brewpub's offerings, remaining true to tradition.

MÜNCHEN VASKNE

Sillamäe, Sillamäe, Ida-Viru; 6.3%

A full-bodied amber lager worthy of the city mentioned in its name, Munich, this is gently hopped with light herbal notes, but its standout characteristic is a rich grainy taste that brings the phrase "liquid bread" to mind.

ÖÖ

Põhjala, Tallinn, Harju; 10.5%

This potent Imperial stout, billed as a Baltic porter but ale-fermented with roasty, chocolatey maltiness and a drying finish, is the grandfather of the Estonian craft beer scene, providing inspiration for a family of variants, including heady barrel-aged versions.

PIHTLA ÕLU

Taako, Pihtla, Saare; 7.6%

Similar to a Finnish *sahti*, this is filtered through juniper branches, which gives it a herbal bite and strong yeastiness. However, without any rye content, it is more bready and wheaty. A true Estonian farmhouse brew.

CAN'T-MISS BREWERY

● ● ● ● ● ● ● ● ● ● ● ● ● ●

PÜHASTE

Tartu

Nomadic until 2016, one of the earliest craft brewers in Estonia now has a brewery of its own and is building a strong reputation. Notable beers include the fruity **IPA Mosaiik** (6.9%), dry-hopped with the Aussie hop newcomer Vic Secret; **Patt** (6.6%), a rich and chocolaty porter; and the suitably named **Dekadents** (11.2%), a strong and sweet Imperial stout aged on raisins and rum-soaked vanilla pods. A new arrival is **Sosin** (6%), a black IPA with richness from rye and other darkly roasted malts alongside a spruce-tip and citrusy hoppiness.

OAK AGED PORTER

SUUR PAKS MASTIF

Lehe, Keila, Harju; 9.6%

This barley wine in the English tradition is rich, sweet, raisiny and nutty, matured for a full year prior to release and with the potential for much more ageing.

RUKKI KUNINGAS

Õllenaut, Saue, Harju; 7.7%

From the brewery recognized for its mastery with malts, this rich rye beer is cakey with hints of dried fruit and mellowed by long maturation. An excellent dessert beer.

WINTER GORILLA

Sori, Tallinn, Harju; 7%

A soft, velvety porter with a hint of liquorice to its roasted maltiness, this is dosed with enough coffee to notice, but not so much that it becomes the overwhelmingly dominant trait.

SAUNA SESSION

Tanker, Vaida, Harju; 4.7%

Brewed with birch leaves, this is intended to evoke thoughts of the sauna with its unique aroma and atmosphere, offering a pleasant herbal character at a quaffable strength ideal for sauna sessions.

HUNGARY

Following a mid-1990s boom in brewing, Hungary saw the majority of its new and hopeful breweries close by the turn of the century. Today, however, the comeback is well underway, buoyed by beer fests like Budapest's Főzdefeszt and the establishment of a small brewers association, Kisüzemi Sörfőzdék Egyesülete.

BLACK ROSE

Szent András, Békésszentandrás, Southern Great Plain; 9%

The oldest bottled craft beer in Hungary is this *doppelbock* from Szent András in the southeast, slightly fruity in its sweetish aroma and medium-bodied with a gentle, sweet maltiness and warming finish.

BRETTANNIA BRUT SOUR ALE

Legenda, Budapest; 5.3%

A highly fruity ale broadly in the Flemish red style, with cherry and other berry notes in the aroma and a hint of balsamic vinegar in its complex, sweet-and-sour body.

FORTISSIMA IMPERIAL STOUT

Széles & Széles, Balassagyarmat, Northern Hungary; 9.5%

So called after the nickname that the city earned in the First World War, "the bravest", this has a pleasing aroma of roasted malt and mocha backed by fruity hoppiness and a full, slightly oily body with a lingering finish.

FRANKY FOUR FINGERS

MONYO, Budapest; 13%

A British-style barley wine brewed from renowned Maris Otter malt aged in the bottle for a year prior to release. Toffee-ish in the aroma with notes of

CAN'T-MISS BREWERY

BORS

Győrzámoly

One of the old-style "microbreweries" from the 1990s, surviving well into the new century with core beers inspired by the legend of Robin Hood, such as **Tuck Barát** (7.7%), a heavily malty *dubbel* with notes of dried fruit; **Maid Marian** (6%), a honey-ish *hefeweizen*; and **Sherwood** (6.5%), a slightly sweet, earthy stout. Most promising are the beers of the emerging Seven Sins series, such as **Wrath** (5%), a well-hopped black IPA with a creamy, rounded mouthfeel.

dried fruit, and medium-rich on the palate with impressive complexity.

FREAKY WHEATY GRIBANC

armando_otchoa, nomadic; 7%

A spin-off from this contracting brewer's flagship Grabanc IPA, this is brewed without wheat but fermented with a *hefeweizen* yeast, then infused with raspberries for a delicately tart, creamy and citrusy body.

GREYJOY DOUBLE IPA

Balkezes, nomadic; 9%

Infused with bergamot oil and Earl Grey tea, the focus of this quaffable, tea-like brew is balance and harmony between tea, hops, malt and citrus elements, which it accomplishes admirably.

INSTEAD OF INNOCENCE IPL

zip's, Miskolc, Northern Hungary; 6.5%

A full-bodied "Imperial pale lager" with tremendous hop complexity, mixing herbal-resiny, citrussy and fruity flavours, supported by a firm maltiness and leading to a sweetish, lingering long aftertaste.

ISOTONIA

Hedon, Balatonvilágos, Southern Transdanubia; 5.3%

A refreshing, pale-gold summer seasonal *gose* with a wheaty aroma sporting light coriander notes, a spritzy, slightly grassy and faintly salty body and a touch of thirst-quenching sourness on the finish.

JAM 72

Mad Scientist, Budapest; 7.2%

Although billed as American in style, this IPA opens with a fruity aroma that is more tropical than citrusy, a characteristic that continues in the medium-full, slightly sticky body and lingering, moderately bitter finish.

MAIBOCK

Rizmajer, Budapest; 6.5%

A seasonal homage to Germany, this has a sweet and biscuity aroma backed by herbal hop notes and a well-balanced character with just enough hop to support the sweet, bready maltiness.

ONE NIGHT SEDUCTION

Synthesis Brewlab; Budapest, 8.2%

A creamy, chocolaty, biscuity Imperial stout made with malted rye, there is a delicate and fruity hoppiness and notable rye-derived spiciness to this beer; truly seductive.

ROMANOV RUSSIAN IMPERIAL STOUT

Fóti, Fót, Budapest; 12%

Not quite black in colour with a sweet and spicy aroma accented by liquorice and a whiff of alcohol. The body is multi-layered and complex, with molasses and sweet coffee notes and a warming finish.

TÁVOLI GALAXIS

Rothbeer, Nagykovácsi, Budapest; 6.1%

As the name suggests, this IPA is hopped with Galaxy only, giving it a tropical-fruit and citrus aroma and a flavourful, hoppy-fruity body supported by an elegant maltiness.

BREWERY TO WATCH

HOPTOP

Budapest

The first Hungarian brewery to earn a medal at the European Beer Star competition, with beers like **Green Zone** US-style IPA (6.4%), spicy with a earthy maltiness, and the award-winning, chocolaty **Midnight Express Foreign Extra Stout** (6%) boding well for its future.

LITHUANIA

While breweries have for several years now been seen starting up in Lithuania, particularly in the capital, Vilnius, the country is perhaps more rewarding to the adventurous beer trekker who is willing to venture into the countryside in search of the fascinating, indeed challenging authentic beer style of the land.

GREEN MONSTER IPA

Apynys, Kaunas; 6.3%

This likeable, fruity take on a US-style IPA is the most accomplished beer yet from a small brewery of growing confidence in the country's second city.

IMPERIAL STOUT

Sakiškių, Vilnius; 9.2%

Rising star already making spot-on beers in straightforward styles at their self-built brewhouse near the capital, including this rich, balanced and misleadingly quaffable strong stout.

PORTERIO

Aukštaitijos Taruškų, Trakiškis, Panevėžio; 6%

The best new beer from the recent amalgamation of Aukštaitija breweries is this occasional limited-edition fusion of herbal-edged folk ale and light, well-attenuated Baltic porter.

STYLE SPOTLIGHT

KAIMIŠKAS

The *kaimiškas* beers of northeastern Lithuania were hidden for decades from Soviet officialdom, their production method becoming along the way unique, including: a grain bill that can encompass most cereals; hops boiled separately in sealed containers, sometimes in underground cellars, making a concentrated tea that is added after mashing; and a rapid fermentation by naturally selected yeasts that have survived reuse for a century or so.

The result is not so much a beer as a cultural entity, ill-fitted to a world that celebrates the clean character of its great ales. This beer is earthy, edgy, technically flawed and created for low-paid locals. Their lone "export" market is seen as the cluster of bars called Šnekutis in Vilnius. Variants include brews that veer toward mead and ales called *keptinis*, made from caked spent grain.

On a faltering journey from traditional to modern, better examples of the former are the enigmatic **Jovaru** by the brewery of the same name and its honeyed variant **Medumi**, while prized among the newer breed are Joalda's semi-rustic **Joniškėlio Respublika 1919** and the plainer **Seklyčios** from Piniavos. A recent amalgamation of five Aukštaitija breweries has seen **Aukštaitijos Bravorų** appear in stoppered flagons and a revival of the sweetish, darkish **Kupiškėnų Keptinis**.

CAN'T-MISS BREWERY

DUNDULIS

Panevėžys

The driving force and inspiration behind the country's revived brewing culture, creating beers in global craft styles, traditional local ones and a few fusions from two breweries in the same town. A tasting journey begins with ruddy-brown, burned-toast **Kurko Keptinis** (5.2%), thence to the tidy, refreshing Anglo-American **Humulupu IPA** (5.5%), the bravely authentic, sweetish **Syrne** (6%), made with pea flour, and ending with a tar-black, peat-smoked and unrelenting stout, **Kovarnių** (6%).

POLAND

New Polish brewing has advanced beyond the ubiquitous IPA variants to build on its Baltic porter tradition, old ways of brewing with rye, the practice of mashing with smoked grain and a revival of local session styles like *grodziskie* (*see* page 189) and perhaps *schöps*. An unusually high proportion of flashier new players are nomadic, but some are putting down roots.

AFICIONADO

Kingpin, nomadic; 7%

At the avant-garde end of pale ale, this is a beer that survives a chaotic recipe. Aromatic from Ethiopian coffee and smoky from peated malts and pine-smoked Lapsang Souchong tea, it has a remarkably appealing finish.

ALBERT

Wąsosz, Konopiska, Silesia; 4.9%

One of the own-brand beers from a southern brewery that also makes ales for over a dozen nomadic craft brewers. This clove- and banana-tinged *hefeweizen* would pass as classic Bavarian were it not for its splash of Mosaic hop.

BIO HAZARD

Hopkins, nomadic; 7.5%

A "whisky" porter from Gdynia on the Baltic coast that is the best of a range of black beers from a beer designer that has proved it has mastered the art. Its intense peaty aroma heralds a well-delivered smoky character.

DYBUK

Golem, nomadic; 6.5%

This reliably excellent rye porter has a touch of cola behind its sweet chocolaty aroma and wider-ranging, coffee-tinged and more caramelly taste, from a sometimes hit-and-miss range commercialized by a craft beer pub in Poznań.

FUNKY WILD FRUIT WIŚNIA BA

Jan Olbracht Rzemieślniczy, Piotrków Tyybunalski, Łódź; 5.6%

This is the cherry beer from the Piotrek z Bagien series. Fruit-steeped beer is barrel-aged with cultured *Brettanomyces*, creating horse-blanket aromas and a sour taste, but a nice cherry character. Refreshingly new and wild!

HOPFACE KILLAH

Piwne Podziemie, Chełm, Kuyavia Pomerania; 6.4%

One of the lasting brands from a prodigiously inventive husband-and-wife brewery near the Ukrainian border, influenced by 10 years in Atlanta, as tasted in this intensely but cleverly hopped, bitter but drinkable IPA.

NAFCIARZ DUKIELSKI

Brokreacja, nomadic; 6.3%

A uniquely designed beer named after the oil miners of Dukla. Whisky malt and rye are brewed into a double brown recipe and porterized with Goldings to create a full-bodied ale with a peaty, almost diesel aroma and oily texture.

PORTER BALTYCKI WEDZONY 24°

Gościszewo, Sztum, Pomerania; 9.6%

Another huge Baltic porter, in this case from the 55 series from a northern brewer of numerous top-quality beers. Subtly smoked to create a cacophony of flavours vying for attention, but none dominant.

ICONIC BREWERY

KORMORAN

Olsztyn, Warmia-Masuria

Among the first of the new wave breweries established in 1993, Kormoran has kept steadily to a line of making off-mainstream beers, its grand cru exemplars appearing as Podróże Kormorana brands. Experiments with different cereals, hops and fruits has led to a range of well-balanced beers respected by consumers, connoisseurs and competitors alike. Among the best are IPA **Plon Niebieski** (6.2%) made with fresh Sybil and Marynka hops, which are also found in "noble" blond lager **Warmińskie Rewolucje** (5.2%). At the heavier end are multi-award-winning straight Baltic porter **Warmiński** (9%) and **Imperium Prunum** (11%), an aged variant lavishly flavoured with heavily smoked dried plums.

CAN'T-MISS BREWERIES

ARTEZAN

Błonie, Masovia

The first of Poland's nomadic craft brewers to have their own brewery, opened in 2012 west of Warsaw. Its dizzying scatter of interesting one-off beers has topped 100, complementing the regular pilsner are the clean, exotically hopped **Pacific Pale Ale** (5%), hoppy, spicy-wheat **Białe IPA** (5.6%), barrel-aged rye porter **Kazimierz** (6%) and Christmas's chocolate-orange stout **Too Young to be Herod** (8%).

PINTA

nomadic

The release of robustly hopped US-style IPA **Atak Chmielu** (6.1%) in March 2011 marked the start of the craft beer revolution in Poland.

Remaining a trendsetter, highlights of its wide offer today include gentle birch-sap-infused wheat beer **Son of a Birch** (3%), high-hopped and lactified "double India sour" **Kwas Epsilon** (6%) and authentically constructed *sahti* tribute act **Koniec Świata** (7.9%).

PRACOWNIA

Modlniczka, Lesser Poland

Set up in 2013 on the outskirts of Kraków and developing a reputation for collaboration brews, it nonetheless keeps faith with its own beers, like cleverly nuanced, grassy wheat beer **Hey Now** (3.8%), classically Polish smoked stout **Cent-US** (4.7%), dark herbal *saison* **Magic Dragon** (5.9%) and pitch-black, coffee–chocolate and tobacco-toned Imperial stout **Mr. Hard's Rocks** (9.5%).

BREWERIES TO WATCH

MARYENSZTADT

Zwoleń, Masovia

Rapidly expanding small brewery near Warsaw producing the fruity, Mosaic-hopped pilsner **Wunder Bar 13** (5.4%); **Polish Hop(e)** (5.5%), an amber ale brewed from locally sourced ingredients; and the coffee-fuelled Imperial stout **RaiSa Espresso** (9.4%).

URSA MAIOR

Uherce Mineralne, Subcarpathia

An ambitious small brewery with a developing range of two dozen beers, including the citrusy wheat beer **Rosa z Kremenarosa** (4.8%), spicy, toasty "Indian summer ale" **Carynki z Caryńskiej** (5.2%) and malt-driven IPA **Pantokrator** (6.5%).

ROWING JACK

AleBrowar, nomadic; 6.2%

One of the first US IPAs on the Polish market back in 2012. This is beer well done, with new wave hops, 80 IBU of bitterness and nice citrus and resinous aromas, yet managing to retain drinkability.

THE SPIRIT OF SONOMA

Widawa, Chrząstawa Mała, Lower Silesia; 6.2%

New Polish beer has advanced far enough to host this US-style IPA dry-hopped and aged in Sauvignon Blanc barrels, one of the more successful creations from an inconsistent but inventive and talented brewer.

SZCZUN

Szałpiw, nomadic; 8.1%

Unashamedly flashy and eye-catching operation creating beers in a wide variety of styles, from whisky-soaked quadrupels to light session beers via this ester-popping, slightly phenolic Polish take on a US-hopped Belgian-style tripel.

ŻYWIEC PORTER

Zamkowy Cieszyn [Heineken], Cieszyn, Silesia; 9.5%

This is a huge beer from a huge brewery group, made at one of its smaller breweries. Typical of the Polish take on Baltic porter – deep ruddy brown, heavy and grain dominated with some hop balance.

STYLE SPOTLIGHT

GRODZISKIE – RISING STAR FROM A BYGONE CULTURE

Grodziskie is like a little-known 19th-century watercolourist whose work has been rediscovered and is now found in modish galleries and auction houses. Identical to German grätzer, it probably originated in the Polish town of Grodzisk Wielkopolski near Poznań.

For 500 years, across much of central Europe beer was defined as brown or white, the latter referring to wheat beers. This bright, yellowish and highly carbonated variant is light in body and low in alcohol, but stands out for its oak-smoked grain mash.

Supporters of grodziskie hail it as a distinctive old-fashioned summer quencher, while detractors see it as a beer for another era. Known since the 14th century, it was out of production between 1993 and 2010, but today **Grodzisku Wielkopolskim Piwo z Grodziska** is brewed in the town and **Nepomucen Grodzisz** up the way in Jutrosin, with **Profesja Mnich** and **Olimp Sophia** also impressing.

RUSSIA

If there is a "Wild East" in global craft beer, it is in Russia. With some nomadic brewers operating out of several different breweries and even outside of the country, others appearing overnight and disappearing almost as quickly, and still others brewing quantities so small as to be almost insignificant, even the most informed of the local beer cognoscenti have no idea of how many breweries are in operation. What they do agree upon is that, despite overall beer production numbers falling steadily since 2008, they will witness continued craft beer growth for the foreseeable future.

BALTIC PORTER

Knightberg, Saint Petersburg; 6.8%

Almost black in colour with a light tan head, this offers an aroma of spicy, roasted malt that translates into the body, with flavours of cinnamon, chocolate, light citrus and ripe fruit along with earthy notes.

BASTILSKIJ PORTER

ID Jons, nomadic; 7%

"Bastille Porter" is in fact a Baltic porter first brewed on the French Bastille Day holiday, with roasted malt and a hint of chocolate in the nose, and a sweet, slightly burned-tasting body that lends itself to quaffability.

COWBOY MALBORO

Plan B, Yaroslavl; 6.5%

A deep gold US-style IPA with bright, fresh, bready aromas of orange and earth, from a combination of Mosaic and Citra hops, and a formidably hoppy, citrusy and floral body with a lingering and bitter finish.

CRAZY MOOSE

Konix, Zarechny, Penza Oblast; 5.5%

A very citrusy, medium-bodied US-style pale ale with tropical-fruit tones in the aroma and a spicy, grassy flavour accented by notes of grapefruit, bitter orange and pine.

ЭНС 28%   АЛК 13,2%

ЛЕНИНГРАДЕЦ

ОВСЯНО-ЯЧМЕННОЕ ВИНО

БАКУНИН

ПИНТА МЁБИУСА

INVISIBLE PINK UNICORN

Mager, nomadic; 10.5%

An old ale made from both honey and barley malt in the style of a braggot, this is amber-red with a toasted malt aroma and medium-bodied with sweet flavours of caramel, berries, herbs, honey and smoke.

KRÜGER PREMIUM PILS

Томское (Tomskoe), Tomsk; 5%

From a Prussian brewery founded in 1876 by Carl Krüger, this is, in Russian terms, an unusually hoppy pilsner, with a bold flavour profile comparable to Germany's best.

LENINGRADER (ЛЕНИНГРАДЕЦ)

Bakunin, Saint Petersburg; 13.2%

A deep red barley wine with an aroma of dried fruit, caramel and fruit jam introducing a sweet, medium-full body

CAN'T-MISS BREWERY

● ● ● ● ● ● ● ● ● ● ● ●

МОСКОВСКАЯ ПИВОВАРЕННАЯ КОМПАНИЯ)

Mytishchi, Moscow Oblast

Large but reliable brewery creating traditional beers like **Zhiguli Barnoe (Жигули Барное**; 4.9%), an award-winning Bohemian-style pilsner, so successful that illegal knock-offs are sometimes found, and the solid, clean pale ale **Shaggy Bumblebee (Мохнатый Шмель**; 5%). Craft division Wolf's Brewery (Волковская пивоварня) gets more creative with the slightly nutty, moderately sweet porter Port Arthur (**Порт Артур**; 6.5%), the Mosaic-hopped Belgian-style wheat beer **Blanche de Mazay (Бланш де Mazaй**; 5.9%) and **American Pale Ale** (5.5%), fresh and fruity with mango and tropical-fruit notes.

BREWERIES TO WATCH

JAWS

Zarechny, Sverdlovsk Oblast

One of the earliest craft breweries of Russia with exciting beers including **Nuclear Laundry** (Атомная прачечная; 7.2%), a golden amber IPA with notes of tropical and citrus fruits, and **APA** (5.2%), a floral, hoppy pale ale with balanced bitterness.

STAMM

Krasnaya Pakhra, Moscow

Creative brewery making diverse beers like the outstanding Imperial stout **Urals** (10%), chocolaty with hints of vanilla, liquorice and blackcurrant; **Red River** (5.5%), a fruity pale ale; and the US-style IPA **Hop Gun Eldorado & Citra** (7%), seasoned with the hops of its name.

with notes of red berries, warming alcohol and a touch of citrus.

LOBOTOMY 777 (ЛОБОТОМИЯ 777)

AF Brew, Saint Petersburg; 12.7%

This coffee-infused Imperial stout pours a dark brown and offers aromas of coffee, chocolate and toffee and a sweet, creamy mouthfeel with flavours of coffee, roasted malt and oak.

MIDNIGHT MOSCOW IPA

Zagovor, Moscow; 5.6%

Golden and quite hazy in appearance, this brightly hoppy IPA is hugely fragrant with its Amarillo, Simcoe and Centennial hops, but more malty in the body with a light sweetness accented by citrus and spruce notes.

PORTER

Afanasy, Tver; 8%

A solid, rich, deep brown Baltic porter with a bready aroma holding soft liquorice notes and a medium-weight, sweet body with an elegant bitterness and a hint of sourness in the aftertaste.

PRYANIK STOUT 5.0 EDITION

Salden's, Tula; 6.5%

A dark brown stout with a spicy, caramelly aroma accented by coriander, ginger, cinnamon and nutmeg and a flavour that follows suit with ginger cookie, milk chocolate and hints of clove, finishing dry and spicy.

VICTORY ART BREW

Red Machine IPA

OG 1.068   IBU 65   Alc 6.9

RED MACHINE IPA

Victory Art Brew, Ivanteevka, Moscow Oblast; 7%

This US-style IPA from a most prolific brewery is double dry-hopped but remains nevertheless balanced with a herbal, citrusy hoppiness on a broad, caramelly maltiness and a moderately bitter finish.

RYZHAYA SONYA (RED SONYA or РЫЖАЯ СОНЯ)

Odna Tonna, Zhukovskiy, Moscow Oblast; 6.2%

An IPA that is flavoured with ginger, this amber-coloured ale has a floral, herbal aroma of tropical fruit and a lightly spicy and citrusy body with moderate bitterness.

RIZHSKOE BEER (РИЖСКОЕ ПИВО)

Vyatich, Kirov; 4.9%

This pilsner from a brewery founded in 1903 by the German brewer Carl Otto Schneider was formerly a favourite beer of the Soviet elite. Delicate and floral on the nose, but more assertively hoppy in the body.

ZOLOTOJ YARLYK (GOLD LABEL)

Velka Morava, Moscow; 5.4%

A revival of an old Russian variety of *märzen* made by the Trekhgorny brewery, honoured at the time by Tsar Nicholas II. Biscuity and slightly fruity on the nose, with caramel and citrus on the palate leading to a hoppy finish.

REST OF CENTRAL & EASTERN EUROPE

While proceeding at a much slower pace than that of many of their surrounding countries, these nations are nevertheless making forward strides into modern craft brewing, usually centred in the cities and sometimes led by expat brewers from the Western world, both tendencies that are increasingly common in emerging beer lands.

CROATIA

ALJAŠKI MRGUD

Vunetovo, Hvar, 5.9%

Named after the brewer's dog, an Alaskan malamute, this black IPA boasts notes of roasted malt and slightly herbal citrus on the nose and a somewhat mellow, dark malt-led body with herbal and fruity hop flavours.

FAKIN IPA

Medvedgrad, Zagreb, 7%

Well-established brewery producing a solid line-up of dependable beers, including this flagship IPA with an aroma of overripe fruit, a malty body with a slightly medicinal quality and a grassy, citrusy finish.

PALE ALE

Zmajska, Zagreb, 5.3%

A quartet of hops gives this amber-hued US-style pale ale a fruity nose with plenty of grapefruit and lemon notes, while a light caramelly maltiness in the body provides great balance to a moderately bitter, fruity hoppiness.

LATVIA

GAIŠAIS

Užavas, Užava; 4.6%

A refreshing and bready lager with crisp grassy hopping and delicate floral-honey sweetness. Packaged unfiltered and always at its best when served as fresh as possible.

LENTENU KĀVĒJS

Labietis, Rīga; 7.2%

A beer with the name "Tapeworm Slayer" had best be good to avoid ridicule, and this black IPA accomplishes the task with chocolaty roastiness and tingling citrusy hops combining to produce a deceptive quaffability.

TREJLEDUS

Valmiermuižas, Valmiermuiža; 8%

Occasionally tipping the scales at up to 9%, this eisbock is a caramelly and fruity classic, with sweet raisiny notes that are reminiscent of barley wine and a woody bitterness that keeps the sweetness in check.

CAN'T-MISS BREWERY

MALDUGUNS

Rauna

A versatile brewery working well in many styles, including **Stokholmas Sindroms** (6.3%), a soft, rich porter with a mocha twist and a tempting hint of chilli; **Lauvas Pacietība** (8.9%), a piney, citrusy double IPA with great balance; and an ongoing series of single-hopped IPAs, **Zaļā Bise** (6.3%), where emphasis is always on hop character and approachability. A seasonal pumpkin beer, **Pa Ķirbi** (7.7%) adds pumpkin flesh and spice notes to a luscious porter base.

SERBIA

BREWERY TO WATCH

KABINET

Nemenikuče, Sopot

The consensus leader in Serbian craft brewing, this still-young operation is making waves with beers like the hemp-fuelled **Rufaro** (5.2%); a series of single-hop pale ales and IPAs including **Mozaik** (5.2%); and the flagship **Kolaboracija 02** caramel stout (10%), aged six months in apple-brandy barrels.

SLOVAK REPUBLIC

ANCIKRIST IPA

Hellstork, Senica; 6–6.5%

Even with a supposed bitterness of 66.6 IBU, this is a nicely balanced IPA with tropical-fruit notes defining the aroma and an earthy maltiness in the body to support its bitterness. Dangerously drinkable, perhaps, but hardly evil.

PETER SVETLÝ ALE IPA

Wywar, Holíč; 5.7%

Australian Galaxy hops yield a full and tropical-fruity hop aroma that travels through to the body in a moderate and balanced way, blending nicely with crisp and elegant hoppiness.

STRANGE LAND IPA

dUb, Bratislava; 6%

The founder of this accomplished brewery pub had at publication left the operation, so it is only hoped that this spicy–citrusy ale built on a firm, biscuity malt base does not change except for the better.

CAN'T-MISS BREWERY

LANIUS BREWERY

Trenčín

Built in a 17th-century butcher's shop, this tiny operation brewing in 200-litre (44-gallon) batches is turning out some of the Republic's most interesting beers. Nutty, dark **Mild Ale 9°** (4%) demonstrates the brewer's dedication to traditional styles, while the raisiny, dried-fruit character of the *eisbock* known simply as **Eis 36°** (17%) shows an adventurous side. **Belgian Abbey Tripel 21°** (10%) boasts a spicy–sweet body with a dryly hoppy finish, and **Red Rye IPA** (6.9%) offers plenty of spicy rye character and a moderately bitter finish. Many other beers are made on a rotational basis.

SLOVENIA

BATCH #50 IMPERIAL STOUT

Reservoir Dogs, Nova Gorica; 9%

With the brewery transitioning from a hotel-based brewery to a stand-alone one, it is hoped that this liquorice-accented stout with notes of tar and bitter chocolate will only get better.

QUANTUM DIPA

Pelicon, Ajdovščina; 8%

An impressively nuanced double IPA from a young and rapidly improving brewery, this has an aroma of ripe fruit and a flavour that layers yellow fruit with citrus and caramelly malt, all leading to a hop-edged finish.

CAN'T-MISS BREWERY

HUMANFISH

Vrhnika

Slovenia's leading craft brewery since 2008, run by an Australian expat, this operation southwest of Ljubljana has branched out from basic ales like their crisp, aromatic **Pale Ale** (4.5%) and chocolaty, creamy, medium-bodied **Stout** (4.5%) to more adventurous beers such as the formidable **Russian Imperial Stout** (8.2%), with rich aromas of molasses and dark chocolate and a jammy, oily palate, and **Combat Wombat** (4.8%) session IPA, with an earthy, citrusy aroma and a malt-driven creamy body.

NORTH
AMERICA

USA

At the start of 2017 the USA was home to more than 5,000 breweries, most of which were the small, artisanal operations known as craft breweries. When and where this number will reach saturation is the subject of much debate, but with a market share of over 12% and a dollar volume stake in excess of 20%, there is little question that US beer drinkers are shifting their beer preferences in droves, fuelling not just the expansion of the craft brewing industry but also the growth of beer specialist bars, brewery taprooms and domestic beer-focused tourism.

2X4

Melvin, Alpine, Wyoming; 9.9%

A ginormous wallop of hops grabs hold of you and never lets go. Luckily, it is perfectly balanced and paradoxically delicate despite the Imperial IPA's heft, layered with juicy citrus, resiny pine, orange zest, grapefruit and mango.

5 BARREL PALE ALE

Odell, Fort Collins, Colorado; 5.2%

Perhaps best described as a pale ale with a foot in each world, this sophisticated quaffer has a citrusy, US hop character layered over a more British-style, earthy–biscuity malt base.

ADAM

Hair of the Dog, Portland, Oregon; 10%

The brewery's first release and still its unlikely flagship, this traditional ale takes the drinker from a gingerbread start through a subtly spicy, roasted apple and raisin mid-palate to a long, warming and lingering finish.

ALPHA KING PALE ALE

Three Floyds, Munster, Indiana; 6.66%

Once considered the king of ultra-hoppy beers, the recent IPA bitterness arms race has lessened the impact of this ale's notable US hop character, but has done nothing to detract from its balance and beauty.

ANGEL'S SHARE

The Lost Abbey, San Marcos, California; 12.5%

From southern California's barrel-aged beer specialist comes this massive ale named after the alcohol lost from the cask in a distiller's warehouse. Complex, densely malty with vanilla threads and a warming, dried-fruit finish.

ARCTIC DEVIL BARLEY WINE

Midnight Sun, Anchorage, Alaska; 13.2%

Monstrously malt-forward and vanilla-accented from its time in oak barrels, this northern legend combines earthiness with fruity malt for a kaleidoscope of flavours that mix and mingle for what seems an eternity.

AROMA COMA

Drake's, San Leandro, California; 6.75%

One whiff should put the most ardent hophead into a summer slumber, with complex aromas of citrus, pine, grapefruit, herbs and flowers. This summer seasonal IPA hits you with fresh hop flavours, big fruit notes and great balance.

ARROGANT BASTARD ALE

Stone, Escondito, California and other locations; 7.2%

One of the first craft beers to combine copious quantities of malt with high hoppiness and significant strength, this ale did, and still does, it brilliantly, with shocking balance and high quaffability for such a potent brew.

AUTUMN MAPLE

The Brucry, Placentia, California; 10%

An autumn seasonal of a different ilk, brewed with large quantities of yam, various spices and maple syrup for a sweet, clove-ish and spicy, earthy beer with nutty hop notes and a long, soothing finish.

BARNEY FLATS OATMEAL STOUT

Anderson Valley, Boonville, California; 5.8%

A revivalist stout from the earlier days of California craft brewing. Deep black and silky smooth, with a gently porridge-y sweetness and mild roasted-malt character carrying notes of soft berry fruits and coffee.

BARREL AGED SHIPWRECK PORTER

Arcadia, Kalamazoo and Battle Creek, Michigan; 12%

Aged 10 months in bourbon barrels, this is a heady brew redolent with aromas of roasted malt and vanilla, chocolate and plum, along with chocolate, rum-soaked raisin and vanilla in the body.

BEAR WALLOW BERLINER WEISSE

Arizona Wilderness, Gilbert, Arizona; 3.2%

This beer highlights both local ingredients, some foraged, and the wild yeast character of kettle souring. Delightfully complex combination of fruity elements; decidedly tart, though softened by white Sonora wheat.

BED OF NAILS BROWN ALE

Hi-Wire, Asheville, North Carolina; 6.1%

A toasted malt aroma introduces this wonderfully balanced, mid-weight brown ale from Hi-Wire. Brown sugar and date notes leading to a slightly winey, dry finish.

BEING THERE

Right Proper, Washington, DC; 5%

Although this newish brewery has a well-deserved reputation for mixed fermentations and the use of botanicals, it is hard to resist the unpretentious beauty of this *kellerbier*; floral, bready, spicy and dry.

BENDER

Surly, Minneapolis and Brooklyn Center, Minnesota; 5.1%

English ale yeast and oatmeal soften this somewhat silky brown ale with notable complexity, the roasty coffee-and-cream nose giving way to a chocolate, caramel and tart-fruit body.

BERNICE

Sante Adairius, Capitola, California; 6.5%

A golden straw colour with a pillowy white head, this US take on a Belgian farmhouse ale is brightly effervescent, with a wonderfully sophisticated mélange of tart lemon and zesty spices, soft flavours and a dry finish.

ICONIC BREWERY

ANCHOR [SAPPORO]

San Francisco, California

By most accounts, US craft brewing got its start when Fritz Maytag bought the floundering Anchor brewery in the late 1960s and, with zero background in brewing, set about reversing its course in dramatic fashion. First came the revival of **Steam Beer** (4.9%), which mixes ale and lager characteristics in a most refreshing fashion, followed by **Liberty Ale** (5.9%), arguably the first modern American IPA, and equally pioneering **Old Foghorn Barleywine Style Ale** (8–10%). Still eagerly anticipated is the annual **Christmas Ale** (6.5%), a spiced beer brewed to a different recipe for each of its more than 40 years.

ICONIC BREWERIES

BELL'S

Kalamazoo and Comstock, Michigan

First known for its oversized portfolio of porters and stouts, numbering about a dozen, Bell's has gone on to claim adherents on several fronts, including those who await the summer arrival of the spicy–hoppy wheat beer **Oberon** (5.8%), and others who swear by the complexly fruity bitterness of their IPA **Two Hearted Ale** (7%). For the rest, there are such delights as the leafy hop-driven and underrated **Amber Ale** (5.8%), the plum and cinnamony **Third Coast Old Ale** (10.2%) and, not to forget the dark stuff, the densely fruity, oily and complex **Expedition Stout** (10.5%).

BOSTON BEER

Boston, Massachusetts and elsewhere

The largest craft brewery in the USA, responsible for often good, sometimes great and occasionally just okay beers grouped under the Samuel Adams brand name. Pay little heed to the gimmicky Nitro Project ales and focus instead on the dry and toasty original **Boston Lager** (5%); "Barrel Room" beers like the winey *tripel* **New World** (10%); the robustly flavourful seasonal **Octoberfest** (5.3%); and, of course, the outstandingly complex and almost ludicrously strong **Utopias** (28%), blended to a differing intensity every year or two.

BITTERSWEET LENNY'S R.I.P.A.

Shmaltz, Clifton Park, New York; 10%

Named after the late comedian Lenny Bruce, this potent rye IPA packs considerable spicy punch into a beer that is as complex as it is warming, and which is worth storing in the cellar for a year or two.

BLACK BAVARIAN LAGER

Sprecher, Glendale, Wisconsin; 5.86%

The picture of balance in a black lager, this is both one of the first US-brewed *schwarzbiers* and among the oldest continually brewed brands in this Germanic specialist brewery's portfolio.

BLACK TULIP TRIPEL

New Holland, Holland, Michigan; 8.8%

While New Holland is better known for its Mad Hatter line of IPAs, this gently spicy–herbal Belgian-inspired strong ale is at least as deserving of note, particularly given its smooth progression to a dry, lightly bitter finish.

BOAT BEER

Carton, Atlantic Highlands, New Jersey; 4.2%

This American Pale Ale looks and smells like exotic fruit juice; juicy hops, including flavours of grapefruit, pineapple and mango, are balanced by resin and pine. Soft malt middle notes slide easily into a dry finish.

BOURBON COUNTY BRAND STOUT

Goose Island [AB InBev], Chicago, Illinois and other locations; 13.8%

One of the earliest bourbon barrel beers in modern America, this remains a complex, chocolate–vanilla–spice beauty despite some infection issues in 2016.

BUTT HEAD BOCK

Tommyknocker, Idaho Springs, Colorado; 8.2%

This reddish-brown ale has the strength of a *doppelbock*, but the gentle malt profile of a lighter *bock*, with spicy caramel in the nose, a floral–spicy toffee body and a warming, off-dry finish.

CAMPFIRE STOUT

High Water, Stockton, California; 6.5%

Imagine you are in the woods, beside a roaring campfire over which you have just roasted marshmallows to put with chocolate pieces in between two graham crackers. Now imagine that s'more were a beer.

CAPELLA PORTER

Ecliptic, Portland, Oregon; 5.2%

A stellar porter from the former long-time Full Sail brewer John Harris, this is more London than West Coast USA, with chocolate and liquorice in the nose, nutty cocoa along with a drying bitterness in the body and a faintly spicy finish.

CAVATICA

Fort George, Astoria, Oregon; 8.5%

A standout Imperial stout from the brewery that celebrates Stout Month every February. Smooth and silky, with notes of dark chocolate, coffee and char, this black beauty is named after the spider in E B White's children's classic, *Charlotte's Web*.

CERASUS

Logsdon, Hood River, Oregon; 8.5%

This barrel-aged Flemish-style red ale sees two pounds (a kilogram) of sweet and tart local cherries added per US gallon (3.8 litres) of beer, contributing a lovely burgundy colour and anticipated cherry tones to complement oak and balsamic flavours.

CHERRYTREE AMARO

Forbidden Root, Chicago, Illinois; 9%

Brewed as an homage to the Italian herbal liqueur amaros, a wide range of botanicals including cherry stems, bitter orange peel, lemon peel, cinnamon, coriander, basil and almond flavour this still highly beer-like beer, as with the other beers in the portfolio.

CHING CHING

Bend, Bend, Oregon; 4.5%

Pomegranate and hibiscus lend a stunning pink hue and contribute a gentle, tasteful tartness to this beautiful, gently wheaty take on a *Berliner weisse*.

CHINGA TU PELO

5 Rabbit Cerveceria, Bedford Park, Illinois; 4.8%

This former Trump Hotel exclusive had a rebirth and name change following Donald Trump's negative comments about Mexicans, emerging a splendid and solid golden ale quaffer with a slightly rude Spanish name.

CITRA DOUBLE IPA

Kern River, Kernville, California; 8%

A big beer with a bright amber colour. It pours a generous white head and boasts a pungent Citra nose, with signature floral and citrus aromas and tropical-fruit flavours nicely balanced with a honeyed malt backbone.

CITRAHOLIC

Beachwood, Long Beach, California; 7.1%

A standout IPA from a brewery that has burst onto the scene with a remarkable range of quality offerings, this one blending four varieties, emphasizing Citra, into a beautifully nuanced and balanced hop monster.

CITY WIDE

4 Hands, St. Louis, Missouri; 5.5%

A pale ale brewed to benefit the city of St. Louis and sold only in St. Louis in a can decorated by the city's flag. Showcases US hops balanced properly by moderately sweet malt.

COUNTER CLOCKWEISSE

Destihl, Bloomington, Illinois; 3%

Demand for German-style sour beers like this one has fuelled brewery expansion. Refreshingly wheaty, smelling of yogurt and lemon and pleasantly tart on the palate.

CRASH LANDED

Begyle, Chicago, Illinois; 7%

Billed an "American pale wheat ale", this medium gold beer has an approachability that contrasts favourably with its strength, its tropical fruitiness being tamed to an appealing dryness by herbal hoppiness.

CUVEE DE CASTLETON

Captain Lawrence, Elmsford, New York; 7%

Barrel-ageing, muscat grapes and *Brettanomyces* transform the brewery's popular Liquid Gold into an enormously complex experience, with juicy tropical fruit at the front of all the flavours expected in a "wild" beer.

DAILY WAGES

Saint James, Reno, Nevada; 6.7%

Goldenrod in colour and pouring a thick, pillowy head with great lacing, this big, Americanized *saison* is funky and herbal, with tart citrus notes and spiced with green peppercorns.

DAISY CUTTER PALE ALE

Half Acre, Chicago, Illinois; 5.2%

Flagship brand from this now landmark Midwestern success story, with a floral and fragrant, citrus-filled aroma and likewise grapefruity and lemony body with solid balancing malt.

DAYLIGHT AMBER

Track 7, Sacramento, California; 6.25%

Clear copper colour, with toffee and toast aromas. Malt-forward with toffee, caramel and soft biscuity character, but balanced with aggressively big, spicy and grapefruit hops.

DEAD CANARY LAGER DORTMUNDER-STYLE EXPORT

Ol' Republic, Nevada City, California; 4.8%

Light gold colour with a biscuit malt nose and delicate aromas of light sweet corn, honey and whole-grain bread. Crisp, refreshing flavours that are mildly sweet with a clean, noble hop finish.

ICONIC BREWERY

NEW BELGIUM

Fort Collins, Colorado and Asheville, North Carolina

Now a misnomer, since this brewery's impressive portfolio features many beers well outside of the Belgian style set, including hop-forward but soft-finishing **Voodoo Ranger IPA** (7%) and gluten-reduced **Glütiny Pale Ale** (6%). For their best, however, one should still explore the limits of the Belgian-inspired oeuvre, like the pleasingly estery **Trippel** (8.5%), the caramelly **Abbey** (7%), cast in the style of a well-executed *dubbel*, and the tartly fruity, complex **La Folie** (7%), aged one to three years in the large oak barrels known as foeders.

ICONIC BREWERY

SIERRA NEVADA

Chico, California and Mills River,
North Carolina

A powerhouse brewery that dates
as one of the earliest of the craft
beer renaissance and remains one of
the best. Beers include the definitive
US-style pale ale **Sierra Nevada Pale
Ale** (5.6%); a more recent IPA arrival
Torpedo Extra IPA (7.2%), which
portrays hop complexity brilliantly;
the seminal hop-forward barley wine
Bigfoot (9.6%); **Nooner Pilsner**
(5.2%), a crisp lager that can stand with
Germany's best; and a host of special
releases, collaboration brews and
seasonal brands.

DEATH AND TAXES

Moonlight, Santa Rosa, California; 5%

Some say this is a *schwarzbier*, while
others think it's a black lager. But given
that few things in life are certain, we
can attest that this light-bodied, highly
drinkable beer with a taste of iced
coffee is always delicious.

DOG ATE MY HOMEWORK

West, San Pedro, California; 7%

Deep purple colour with a full pink
head. Yeasty *saison*-like nose with
strong blackberry fruit aromas.
Well-integrated tart fruit flavours,
lightly spiced, with blackberry jam
and vinous notes, finishing dry.

DORTMUNDER GOLD LAGER

Great Lakes, Cleveland, Ohio; 5.8%

The late beer-writing maven Michael
Jackson described the Dortmund style
of lager as bigger and sweeter than a
pilsner, but drier than a *helles*, which
pretty much describes this refreshing
lager to a tee.

EASY UP PALE ALE

Coronado, Coronado, California; 5.2%

One of the San Diego area's best-
balanced beers, this medium gold ale
offers a dry, leafy aroma with hints of
citrus and a round, more citrusy and
highly quaffable, dry body accented
by slight peppery tones.

ELEVATED IPA

La Cumbre, Albuquerque, New Mexico; 7.2%

Although the La Cumbre brewery makes a more pungent IPA called Project Dank, the flagship is brimming with US hop character – complexly fruity with tongue-coating resins, and robust bitterness that balances all that hop flavour.

EXPONENTIAL HOPPINESS

Alpine, Alpine, California; 11%

Even in a brewery known for its hop monsters, this beer stands out exponentially, with fresh hop aromas and tastes; herbal, pine, blood orange, apricot and grapefruit, yet surprisingly smooth and well balanced throughout.

EXTRA PALE ALE

Summit, St. Paul, Minnesota; 5.2%

Thirty years old and considered an English-style pale ale these days, EPA is distinctive without being overpowering, citrusy at the outset with toasted malt and fruity character mid-palate and a firmly bitter, lemon-scented finish.

FIELD 41 PALE ALE

Bale Breaker, Yakima, Washington; 4.5%

Hailing from the hops motherland of the USA, this light and refreshing pale ale stands out among the brewery's other delicious hoppy offerings for its smooth, balanced bitterness of grapefruit, tangerine, honeydew and pine.

FIREBRICK

August Schell, New Ulm, Minnesota; 5%

A classic Vienna lager from the USA's second-oldest family-owned brewery, showcasing toasted malt from start to finish. Rich, almost regal, but clean and crisp, balanced by firm hop bitterness.

FIRST FROST WINTER PERSIMMON ALE

Fullsteam, Durham, North Carolina; 10%

The brewery rewards patrons who forage for persimmons with this caramelly, cinnamony winter warmer that grows better with a year or more of ageing.

FIST CITY

Revolution, Chicago, Illinois; 5.5%

Bright gold with a very floral aroma, this quencher offers crisp fruitiness mixed with brown spice and a drying, medium-bitter finish. Like a fine ESB, except seasoned with US rather than British hops.

FLORA RUSTICA

Upright, Portland, Oregon; 5.2%

From this Pacific Northwest Belgian and French style specialist comes their particular take on a *saison*, a hazy blond ale brewed with yarrow and calendula for a floral–peppery aroma and complex, spicy–herbal flavour.

CAN'T-MISS BREWERIES

ALLAGASH

Portland, Maine

Unabashedly Belgian-centric in its approach to brewing, this East Coast stalwart has been turning out sometimes unexpectedly excellent beers since 1995. Mainstay is the superbly balanced Belgian-style wheat beer **White** (5.1%), the success of which enables the production of more "out there" beers, such as the surprisingly subtle, oak-aged *tripel* **Curieux** (11%), also stunning in non-barrelled form as the regular **Tripel** (9%), and the spicy, pear-accented **Saison** (6.1%). An ongoing spontaneous-fermentation project has yielded such impressive results as the plummy–oaky–herbal **Coolship Resurgam** (6.3%).

BOULEVARD [DUVEL MOORTGAT]

Kansas City, Missouri

This early achiever in the heart of the Midwest has progressed from an early wheat beer, now the refreshing **Unfiltered Wheat Beer** (4.4%), to the tangerine-accented **Single-Wide IPA** (5.7%). Along the way, a line of more esoteric beers called the Smokestack Series was developed, producing such beers as the fruity, tart and much sought-after **Love Child No. 7** (8–9.5%) and the spicy and misleadingly quaffable **Tank 7 Farmhouse Ale** (8.5%).

BROOKLYN

Brooklyn, New York

Born from contract brewing, this East Coast mainstay has gone on to become a pivotal force in craft brewing, partly thanks to its charismatic head brewer, Garrett Oliver. Mainstay **Lager** (5.2%) is an underrated Vienna lager with a dry finish, but greater excitement is generated by regulars like the slightly nutty **Brown Ale** (5.6%); seasonals such as the deeply rich, chocolaty **Black Chocolate Stout** (10%), the flavour of which is all from malt; and big-bottle releases like the botanically influenced **Improved Old Fashioned** (12.8%).

FORTUNATE ISLANDS

Modern Times, San Diego, California; 5%

Think hybrid wheat IPA, aggressively hopped with Citra and Amarillo. The result is a massive tropical-fruit nose and hop flavours of mango, guava and passion-fruit smoothed out wonderfully by the wheat malt.

FREAK OF NATURE

Wicked Weed [AB InDev], Asheville, North Carolina; 8.6%

Loyalists were up in arms when this stellar operation was sold to AB InBev in early 2017, and it is hoped that changes do not befall beers such as this intense, herbal–citrus double IPA with plenty of oily hoppiness and sufficient malt to hold it all together.

FÜNKE HOP FARM

Sudwerk, Davis, California; 6.5%

For a brewery that is best known for its lagers, this funky wild one is brewed with three yeasts and aged on different wine barrels, giving it amazing complexity with soft fruit and a tart farmyard earthiness.

GRAND CRU

Alesmith, San Diego, California; 10%

If you choose not to age this immensely cellar-friendly ale, your experience will be one of spicy raisin, cocoa and brown spice on the nose and a body filled with massive dried-fruit notes and bittersweet chocolate.

GREEN PEPPERCORN TRIPEL

The Brewer's Art, Baltimore, Maryland; 10%

Effervescent, nuanced, subtle banana and floral pear skins are played against peppery phenols and peppercorns, and brightened by lively acidity.

HEAD HUNTER

Fat Head's, Middleburg Heights, Ohio and other locations; 7.5%

An IPA that other brewers judge their own against, beginning with the citrus/tropical hop punch at the outset. Hop bitterness and flavour are perfectly intertwined.

HEADY TOPPER

The Alchemist, Stowe, Vermont; 8%

One of the original New England cult beers, folks still line up to buy this double IPA with a perfume of florals in its aroma and citrusy, spicy, lightly tannic hoppiness held just in check by robust orange–caramel malt.

HEFEWEIZEN

Live Oak, Austin, Texas; 5.3%

The beers here lost none of their Old World character when the brewery began packaging in cans in 2016. This one is wheat-rich with a harmonious blend of banana, clove and vanilla.

HEFEWEIZEN

San Tan, Chandler, Arizona; 5%

Built for the southwest heat with a bright carbonation and a light wheat body showcasing classic Bavarian character alongside notes of pear and lemon-lime, which add complexity to expected banana aroma and flavour, matched by peppery cloves.

HELL OR HIGH WATERMELON WHEAT

21st Amendment, San Francisco/San Leandro, California; 4.9%

Only available during the warmer half of the year, fresh watermelon juice is added to wheat beer for a second fermentation, creating a uniquely refreshing fruit beer that is delicate and not overpowering.

HELLES

Kansas City, Kansas City, Missouri; 5%

Great beers in the *helles* style have aromas of perfumey grain and gentle, malty sweetness on the palate, like this fine lager. Arguably a touch fuller than the style would dictate, but no less refreshing for it.

HUNAHPU'S IMPERIAL STOUT

Cigar City [Oskar Blues], Tampa, Florida; 11%

The brewery has built a festival around the release of this beer, a truly Imperial stout infused with and flaunting the flavours of cacao nibs, vanilla pods, Ancho and Pasilla chillies and cinnamon.

IMPERIAL COCONUT HIWA PORTER

Maui, Kihei, Maui, Hawaii; 9.4%

A rich mocha head rises out of this ash-black beer, with a nose redolent of coffee roast and, naturally, fresh coconut. With a very smooth and creamy mouthfeel, the beer maintains its balance in spite of being loaded with coconut flavour.

INCEPTUS

Three Taverns, Decatur, Georgia; 6%

A "Georgia Wild Ale", fermented with yeast captured during a rare snow storm and then aged for several months in wine barrels, creating complex fruity and grapey flavours before a brightly tart finish.

JET STAR IMPERIAL IPA

No-Li, Spokane, Washington; 8.1%

Pine forest meets toasted lemon peel in the aroma of this big beer that deftly combines biscuit and British-style maltiness with US hop-forwardness, producing a malty–citrusy–peachy ale with an off-dry finish.

KATY

2nd Shift, St. Louis, Missouri; 5.4%

Fermented and aged in barrels inoculated long ago with a strain of *Brettanomyces*, Katy is beholding to no style. Brightness from zesty lemon at the outset leads to lightly bready, stone-fruit elements adding complexity mid-palate and a tart finish.

KILT LIFTER

Four Peaks [AB InBev], Tempe, Arizona; 6%

The brewery's flagship, showcasing its UK influence in a Scottish ale that is rich and malty throughout, with a taste of caramel and toffee and a hint of smoke on top.

LA GUARDIA RUBIA

Cruz Blanca, Chicago, Illinois; 6.8%

An early success from this *cervecería* owned by celebrated chef Rick Bayless, this is a spicy, medium gold-hued treat based on the *bière de garde* style, with food-friendly citrus accents and a mildly bitter finish.

LE PETIT PRINCE

Jester King, Austin, Texas; 2.9%

Those who complain about the difficulties of getting full flavour from a low-alcohol beer have never met the Little Prince. With a citrusy floral aroma, this sublime thirst-quencher is peppery and mildly bitter, and finishes bone dry.

CAN'T-MISS BREWERIES

●●●●●●●●●●●●●●●●

DESCHUTES

Bend and Portland, Oregon

One of the handful of early Pacific Northwest breweries to emerge as a national leader, Deschutes seems to excel at almost everything they turn their hands to. Flagship **Black Butte Porter** (5.2%) sets the standard for American porters, while **Mirror Pond Pale Ale** (5%) is a laudably floral take on the style pioneered in California. Cocoa-accented, spicy **Jubelale** (6.7%) is a much-anticipated winter seasonal, while special Reserve Series releases like the intense anniversary ale **Black Butte XXVIII** (XXIX in 2017; 11.5%) and liquorice-accented Imperial stout **The Abyss** (11.1%) are not to be missed.

FIRESTONE WALKER [DUVEL MOORTGAT]

Paso Robles, California

Founded as the meeting place of British and US brewing, the flagship Double Barrel Ale, now **DBA** (5%), marks the territory marvellously, with a rich yet refreshing mix of fruit and caramel malt drying finely on the finish. **Union Jack IPA** (7%) continues the brewery's cross-continental ways with juicy fruit upfront and citrusy hop bitterness in the back, while the quenching, spicy **Pivo Hoppy Pils** (5.3%) demonstrates the brewery's skills in lager fermentation. Yearly **Anniversary Ale** (12.5–13.5%) releases are always complex blends and are seldom less than exceptional.

LIL' HEAVEN

Two Roads, Stratford, Connecticut; 4.8%

Brewed with four designer hops, producing the exotic tropical aroma and rich juicy taste expected of a modern IPA on a satisfyingly firm malt base, despite its lower alcohol and "session IPA" label.

LITTLE JUICE IPA SMOOTHIE EDITION

Three Magnets, Olympia, Washington; 6.6%

Joining the cloudy IPA craze, this hazy offering delivers on the promises of its aromas of tropical-fruit cocktail and oranges, later bringing a citrus-peel note and residual juicy, fruit flavours intermingled in a slightly creamy body.

LOOSE CANNON HOP3

Heavy Seas, Baltimore, Maryland; 7.25%

From the brewery formerly known as Clipper City comes this hops cocktail of an IPA, brimming with tangerine, grapefruit and pine aromas and flavours, lightly toasted bread slathered in alcoholic orange marmalade.

LUPULIN LUST

Rip Current, San Marcos, California; 9%

Referred to as a San Diego-style IPA, this light golden-hued ale has all the anticipated grapefruit and tangerine aromas with floral notes. It is also easy-drinking, being beautifully balanced with a dry, bitter finish.

CAN'T-MISS BREWERIES

FOUNDERS

Grand Rapids, Michigan

Fame may have come to the company on the back of their rich and complex Kentucky Breakfast Stout, renamed **KBS** (11.8%) following a Kentucky-based lawsuit, but this is a brewery solid throughout their portfolio. From the single-hop, grapefruit–apple–redcurrant **Centennial IPA** (7.2%) to the dark rye breadiness of **Red's Rye I.P.A.** (6.6%); and the wonderfully aromatic, raisin-and-fig **Old Curmudgeon Ale** (9.8%) to the well-named, quenching **All Day IPA** (4.7%), it's hard to go wrong with a Founders brew.

NEW GLARUS

New Glarus, Wisconsin

The bestselling brand is the slightly chewy, quaffable **Spotted Cow** (4.9%), yet fame resides in its many only-in-Wisconsin brands including balanced fruit beers like the whole-cherry-flavoured **Wisconsin Belgian Red** (4%) and the apple–cherry–cranberry **Serendipity** (5.1%). Seasonals bring further highly deserved accolades, as with the strong, clove-and-pepper **Dancing Man Wheat** (7.2%) and nutty brown ale **Fat Squirrel** (5.5%). Some of the finest spontaneous fermentation in the USA results in occasional releases such as the **R&D Vintage 2015** (5%).

MAD ELF

Tröegs, Hershey, Pennsylvania; 11%

Cherries and local honey take a strong Belgian ale literally to 11 (% ABV), imbuing it with a menagerie of fruity and spicy aromas and tastes that glow a bright dark red.

MÄRZEN

Gordon Biersch, San Jose, California; 5.7%

Bright amber orange in colour with aromas of toasted pretzels, dried fruit and sweet malt. Refreshingly authentic version of a German Oktoberfest beer with clean, rich malt flavours and a caramel sweetness balanced by classic noble hop character.

MÉLANGE À TROIS

Nebraska, Papillion, Nebraska; 11.3%

Six months in Chardonnay barrels add all the flavours you would expect to an already rich and fruity blond Belgian ale, as wood tannins merging with peppery phenols and residual wine provide a crisp acidity.

RUSSIAN RIVER

Santa Rosa, California

Run by the husband and wife team of Vinnie and Natalie Cilurzo, the brewery excels in both hoppy and so-called sour beers, producing the definitive double IPA **Pliny the Elder** (8%), on the former side, and mixed-fermentation, barrel-aged beers such as the wine-ish, sour cherry **Supplication** (7%) and surprisingly nuanced blond ale **Temptation** (7.5%) on the latter. Dryly fruity **Damnation** (7.75%) is an homage to the Belgian ale Duvel, while **Blind Pig IPA** (6.25%) is a solid and sturdy India Pale Ale.

CAN'T-MISS BREWERY

● ● ● ● ● ● ● ● ● ● ● ● ● ● ● ●

VICTORY

Downingtown, Pennsylvania
and other locations

Brewing multiple styles since before it
was cool, Victory has long exhibited skill
in both ale and lager fermentation, their
deliciously crisp **Prima Pils** (5.3%) and
deftly hopped, piney **HopDevil India
Pale Ale** (6.7%) being among their
early successes. A similarly early foray
into Belgian influence yielded the fruity,
almost nectar-ish **Golden Monkey**
(9.5%), while more aptitude on the
Germanic side is shown in the newer
Helles Lager (4.8%).

MIAMI MADNESS
J Wakefield, Miami, Florida; 3.5%

The state's brewers have staked out
Florida *weisse*, a *Berliner* beer infused
with fruit, as their own style. This
version, one of several that the brewery
makes, balances mango, guava and
passion-fruit sweetness and lemonade-
like tartness.

MODUS HOPERANDI
Ska, Durango, Colorado; 6.8%

From a musically minded brewery in the
south of the state, this IPA offers the
familiar mix of citrus and pine aromas
and flavours typical of its style in the
USA, but with a softening finish that
accentuates its refreshing character.

MONK'S INDISCRETION
Sound, Poulsbo, Washington; 10%

Consistently award-winning Belgian-style
strong ale that nods to its West Coast
upbringing, with tropical-fruit flavours
canoodling alongside more conventional
banana, herbal, spicy and lemon notes,
leading to a pleasantly dry finish.

MOSAIC SESSION IPA
Karl Strauss, San Diego, California; 5.5%

This relatively restrained IPA, at least
for the West Coast, is still loaded with
grapefruit and tropical-fruit aromas.
Satisfying mouthfeel with mango,
tangerine and guava, plus a noticeable
malt presence underneath it all.

MOTHER OF ALL STORMS

Pelican, Pacific City, Oregon; 14%

A world-class barley wine from a consistently award-winning brewery, aged in bourbon barrels for deep flavours of toasted malt, bourbon and oak, with a sublime finish of vanilla, toffee, caramel and a touch of alcoholic warmth.

MT. NELSON

Cellarmaker, San Francisco, California; 5.4%

This American pale ale stands atop the mountain of impressively hoppy offerings at which Cellarmaker excels, and its single hop, Nelson Sauvin, manages to introduce a complex array of flavours, from grapes and lemon to guava and mango.

MULLET CUTTER

Revolver [Molson Coors], Granbury, Texas; 9%

An unusual take on an American double IPA with spicy rather than citrusy hops dominating the nose and an earthy, spicy–herbal and slightly resinous body, culminating in a citrusy hop finish.

NOYAUX

Cascade Barrel House, Portland, Oregon; 9.29%

A blend of blond ales aged in white wine barrels on raspberries and apricot stones produces a sublime, almondy–berry-ish beer with a tart and drying palate of great fruity complexity and a rosé Champagne-esque finish.

OAK AGED YETI IMPERIAL STOUT

Great Divide, Denver, Colorado; 9.5%

One of several versions of the brewery's trademark Imperial stout, this one rounds off the borderline sharp roastiness of the regular Yeti with whiskey-barrel-derived vanilla notes and a softened hop bitterness.

OKTOBERFEST

Real Ale, Blanco, Texas; 5.7%

One of the best Oktoberfest märzens brewed in the USA, this has a bready, toasted-grain aroma and a caramelly, off-dry maltiness in the body that effectively bridges the gap between traditional and modern styles.

OLD RASPUTIN RUSSIAN IMPERIAL STOUT

North Coast, Fort Bragg, California; 9%

A "gentle giant" of an Imperial stout, with luscious chocolate- and coffee-accented maltiness and just enough hop to keep the sweetness in check. Deservedly an iconic American stout.

PALO SANTO MARRON

Dogfish Head, Milton, Delaware; 12%

Ageing in vats made from Paraguayan woods gives this brown ale a nose of cinnamon, vanilla and other aromatic spices, while a load of malt bestows flavours of chocolate fudge and rum-soaked raisins.

PEEPER ALE

Maine, Freeport, Maine; 5.5%

Certainly a beer that is not shy about its US hopping, this golden Maine pale ale has nonetheless a deep and rich maltiness that instead evokes the British approach to brewing hop-forward beers.

PETIT DESAY

de Garde, Tillamook, Oregon; 5%

This wild-fermentation brewery uses the coastal region's microflora to ferment its beers traditionally in a *koelschip* before transferring to barrels. A refreshingly tart farmhouse ale with notes of apricot and pineapple, a touch of oak and a lemony finish.

PIKE IPA

Pike, Seattle, Washington; 6.3%

In 1990, there were few IPAs brewed in the USA, but there was this beer, built on a solid base of dry, caramelly malt and floral, citrusy hoppiness with an almost note-perfect balance between the two.

PILS

Heater Allen, McMinnville, Oregon; 4.9%

Brewed in wine country, this earthy, spicy take on a Bohemian-style lager is slightly more golden in colour and rounder in body than many versions, while finishing dry. No wonder it's a favourite among local winery workers.

PILS

Lagunitas [Heineken], Petaluma, California; 6%

The brewery's typical irreverence is set aside for this foray into Czech-style *světlý ležák*, which offers a classically floral aroma, firm maltiness and crisp refreshment, albeit with more bitterness and strength than is typical.

PILS

Trumer, Berkeley, California; 4.9%

Pale golden, bright and clear, with a dense white head. Signature Saaz hop nose and classic German-style pilsner flavours make this one of the best authentic pilsners brewed in the USA using a centuries-old Austrian recipe.

PILSNER

Marble, Albuquerque, New Mexico; 4.7%

Unfiltered, and a frequent award winner in international competitions as a *zwickelbier*. Floral and spicy hops create a delicate perfumey aroma and persist into the taste, blending seamlessly with bready malt, finishing dry and bitter.

PIPEWRENCH

Gigantic, Portland, Oregon; 7.8%

Ageing Gigantic's already tasty IPA in Ransom Old Tom gin barrels creates an entirely different entity that is surprisingly refreshing, with bright citrus and fruity notes alongside juniper, spice and oak.

POINT REYES PORTER

Marin, Larkspur, California; 6%

Inky black with a tight tan head, a nose thick with chocolate and coffee aromas and a creamy mouthfeel. The flavour profile is dry with rich espresso and chewy chocolate character, finishing cleanly with a velvet smoothness.

PORTER

The Duck-Rabbit, Farmville, North Carolina; 5.7%

Robust dark malt flavours from a dark beer specialist, with creamy middle notes (perhaps from the addition of oats) creating an intriguing juxtaposition with dry chocolate and roasted coffee bitterness.

PORTER

Stoneface, Newington, New Hampshire; 5.5%

With an aroma of chicory-accented mocha plus a whiff of liquorice, this solid and sessionable black beer from Stoneface boasts elements of raisin and date mixed with a hint of espresso toward its off-dry finish.

PRAIRIE STANDARD

Prairie Artisan, Krebs and Oklahoma City, Oklahoma; 5.6%

Not as strong as most of its stable mates, this *saison*-style ale shares much of its relatives' complex funkiness, stone and citrus fruits and spicy finish, in this case with a bit of lime zest thrown in.

PSEUDOSUE

Toppling Goliath, Decorah, Iowa; 5.8%

An American pale ale that serves as an advertisement for the Citra hop, the only variety used to make it, checking all the boxes for bold citrus-, tropical- and stone-fruit aromas and flavours.

PUMPKIN LAGER

Lakefront, Milwaukee, Wisconsin; 5.8%

Pumpkin sceptics may be forgiven for approaching this beer with trepidation, but Lakefront makes it all work with soft spice in the aroma and a clove-accented body boasting soft, creamy, vaguely peppery richness.

RACER 5 IPA

Bear Republic, Healdsburg, California;
7.5%

Atypically brewed from malted barley
and wheat, which adds a fragrant and
floral, even slightly spicy aspect to the
US hops that otherwise shine their
citrusy light throughout this quaffable
ale from Bear Republic.

RASPBERRY EISBOCK

Kuhnhenn, Warren, Michigan; 15.5%

With outrageous complexity and
massive fruit flavours, this very big
lager is no shrinking violet, mixing
raspberry notes with chocolate cream
and orange brandy. Delicious on release,
but also highly cellar-worthy.

THE REVEREND

Avery, Boulder, Colorado; 10%

The nose of this massive deep purplish
burgundy *quadrupel* is dark fruit – raisins,
dates, prunes, currants – while the body
is rich and intense, with molasses, plum,
burned raisins and chocolate, as warming
as a thick blanket on a cold night.

ROBUST PORTER

Reuben's, Seattle, Washington; 5.9%

A spot-on porter from a brewery
known for its flawless interpretations
of styles. Rich caramel, roasted coffee,
cocoa and a hint of liquorice, with a dry,
cracker-y finish.

ROBUST PORTER

Smuttynose, Hampton, New Hampshire;
6.2%

While decidedly chocolaty in its aroma,
this full and coffee-ish ale is drier than
one might expect and, in fact, quite
dry in its mocha-ish finish. A tasty
mixture of US and British approaches
to the porter style.

ROGGENWEISSWINE

Coachella Valley, Thousand Palms,
California; 10%

Made from wheat and rye malts
comprising an astonishing 96% of its
grain bill, the nose is full of spiced plum,
vanilla and charred oak, while the palate
brings boozy lemon peel, dried fruits
and peppery spice.

THE RUSTY NAIL

Fremont, Seattle, Washington; 13.2%

A beer so deeply complex that it begs
hours of contemplation, with a base
of Imperial smoked oatmeal stout aged
on cinnamon bark before spending 15
months in 12-year-old bourbon barrels.
Delicious at release, it promises to
improve with age.

RYE PALE ALE

Terrapin [Molson Coors], Athens, Georgia; 5.3%

The brewery came to life around this beer, one of the USA's original rye ales. Spicy rye enhances an impression of dark bread, earthy and citrusy bitterness leading to a dry finish.

SAHALIE ALE

Apothecary, Bend, Oregon; 9–10%

Flagship wild ale from this rustic, mixed-fermentation brewery where mashing, open fermentation, conditioning and dry-hopping all take place in oak, resulting in notes of pineapple, apricots and citrus that dance sublimely with pithy, earthy and herbal undertones.

SAISON

Casey, Glenwood Springs, Colorado; 5.5%

The base beer for other wildly popular brands such as the Fruit Stand series stands up just fine on its own, with aromas and flavours of funky fruitiness, wet hay and bright citrus backed by fresh, tart and lively acidity.

SAISON ATHENE

Saint Somewhere, Tarpon Springs, Florida; 7.5%

The first beer that this smallish brewery bottled is brimming with house character – a bit wild, spicy lemon zest on the nose, stone fruits lingering beneath, mingling with grainy malt. Ultimately tart and dry.

BREWERIES TO WATCH

BAERLIC

Portland, Oregon

With a name meaning "of barley" in old English, this young outfit shows great promise with unusual brews like the creamy **Eastside Oatmeal Pilsner** (6%), classics including the porridge-y **Noble Oatmeal Stout** (6.3%) and a straight-up, spicy, dry-finishing **Invincible India Pale** (6.7%).

BAGBY

Oceanside, California

Multiple award-winning brewer Jeff Bagby turned a former car dealership into a brewpub, where he brews a dizzying line-up, from Belgian-style mini blond **Yvankë** (4%) to tropical-fruit-forward **Dork Squad IPA** (6.8%) and the dark chocolaty **Reconnoiter Porter** (7.4%).

BIG DITCH

Buffalo, New York

Brewery–restaurant that is part of downtown Buffalo's ongoing renaissance, with beers ranging from **Low Bridge** (4.8%) "hoppy golden ale" to the intense **Deep Cut Double IPA** (8.5%).

BREWERIES TO WATCH

BLACK PROJECT

Denver, Colorado

Wildly experimental brewery devoted to spontaneous fermentation in varied forms, producing beers like the lemony, solera-style **Dreamland** (5.7%) and the dry and dry-hopped **Jumpseat** (6.2%)

CENTRAL STANDARD

Wichita, Kansas

There are big ambitions from this young outfit formed by five friends, who are brewing such diverse beers as the creamy **Extra Medium Pale Ale** (5.3%), the tangy and quenching **Wally Funk** (7%) and the floral, gingery **Red Cicada** (4.5%) *gose*.

CLOUDBURST

Seattle, Washington

Former Elysian brewer Steve Luke has released completely new and different IPAs every two weeks since opening his new brewery in January 2016, along with other gems like "bastardized German Pilsner" **Happy Little Clouds** (5.1%) and "toasted brown ale" **Two Scoops** (5.8%).

SAISON DE LIS

Perennial, St. Louis, Missouri; 5%

The addition of camomile flowers adds a tea-like twist to a fruit-and-spice character central to many of the often adventurous beers made here at Perennial. Lively, floral, earthy, complex but never overbearing.

SAISON DU FERMIER

Side Project, Maplewood, Missouri; 7%

No longer just a side project, the intense stouts and lively *saisons* from this brewery generate equal excitement. Fermented and aged with local cultures in Chardonnay barrels and wrapped in a fog of fruity funk finished by bright acidity.

SAISONHANDS

Tired Hands, Ardmore, Pennsylvania; 4.8%

First known as FarmHands, this is a tribute to farmers and a nod to four grains – barley, rye, wheat and oats – in the grist. Brightened by lemon zest and stone-fruit aromas, with yeasty funk adding satisfying complexity.

SARA'S RUBY MILD

Magnolia, San Francisco, California; 3.8%

The inspiration for Magnolia's mild came during an English vacation; malt-forward throughout, it has a silky mouthfeel. Especially fine on cask, with lightly roasted malt, dark fruit and delicate flavours.

SAWTOOTH ALE

Left Hand, Longmont, Colorado; 5.3%

The brewery's original flagship beer, a not-so-simple amber ale combining toasty biscuit malt with sweet chocolate and caramel notes, finished with citrus-tinged bitterness and mineral-like dryness.

SCALE TIPPER IPA

Bosque, Albuquerque, New Mexico; 6.5%

Part of a family of IPAs that quickly established hop-forward intentions here. A fresh, tropical bouquet along with hints of pine and camphor leads to a firm, bready maltiness balanced by lingering bitterness.

SCULPIN IPA

Ballast Point [Constellation], San Diego, California; 7%

A near-perfect West Coast IPA, especially when fresh, with a mountain of hops that somehow still manages to maintain great balance. With strong grapefruit aromas and flavour, it is lightly spiced and highly drinkable.

SCURRY

Off Color, Chicago, Illinois; 5.3%

Deceptive in its chocolate, liquorice and molasses aroma, which is akin to that of a bigger ale, this honey beer has a creamy brown ale character, chocolaty with notes of hazelnut and an off-dry, food-friendly finish.

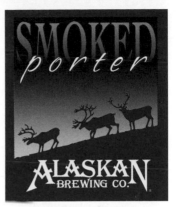

SLESS' OATMEAL STOUT

Iron Springs, Fairfax, California; 8%

Strong, smooth stout with aromas of dark chocolate and roasted coffee. Velvety mouthfeel, delightfully softened by the oats, with flavours of bitter dark chocolate, espresso and a hint of liquorice.

SMOKE & DAGGER

Jack's Abby, Framingham, Massachusetts; 5.6%

An outstanding *rauchbier* from New England's lager specialists, mahogany hued with a lean, softly smoky nose that is reminiscent of smouldering balsawood and a complex, lightly smoky body with hints of black liquorice and burned walnut.

SMOKED PORTER

Alaskan, Juneau, Alaska; 6.5%

From a first batch made with malt smoked at a local salmon smokehouse

BREWERIES TO WATCH

CREATURE COMFORTS

Athens, Georgia

An almost instantly popular brewery that struggled early to keep up with demand for **Tropicália** (6.6%), a tropical (of course) and juicy IPA, but **Athena** (4.5%) *Berliner weisse* and several fruited versions thereof are equally impressive.

DOVETAIL

Chicago, Illinois

An oddball but so far outstanding brewery producing a wonderfully Munich-esque **Lager** (4.8%) and outstanding **Rauchbier** (5.3%) downstairs, while upstairs it conditions barrels of spontaneously fermented beers for much later release.

GRIST HOUSE

Pittsburgh, Pennsylvania

Destination brewery in the city's Millvale neighbourhood, making solid, straightforward ales like **Gristly Bear** (5.8%) American brown and **Camp Slap Red** (5.8%) American IPA.

to a craft beer legend, this slightly oily, smoky and utterly enticing and wonderfully balanced ale has changed little through the years, thankfully.

SMOKESTACK HERITAGE PORTER

East End, Pittsburgh, Pennsylvania; 5.7%

A smoked porter that is sublime in its smokiness, mixing with dark chocolate and raisin in the nose and dried fruitiness – prune, dates and raisins – in the body, with a refreshingly dry finish.

STICKY HANDS

Block 15, Corvallis, Oregon; 8.1%

Also known as The Hop Experience Ale, this double IPA, from which numerous variants are made, continues to draw fans, thanks to its aromatic blast of tropical fruit and citrus and an assertive yet balanced bitter finish.

SUE

Yazoo, Nashville, Tennessee; 9.2%

The first legal high-strength beer sold in Tennessee scrimps on nothing, with cherrywood-smoked malt dominating a big porter long on chocolate flavour and roasted bitterness, with dark figgy fruit providing complexity.

SUPER SAISON

pFriem, Hood River, Oregon; 9.5%

A beautiful meringue-like head floats atop juicy notes of pineapple, papaya, peppercorns and kiwi fruit that are well balanced with a touch of wood, citrus, barnyard funk and a slightly mineral finish.

STYLE SPOTLIGHT

AMERICAN PALE ALE & IPA

No beer has dominated the conversation since the start of the new millennium as much as has US-style IPA. And so it is easy to forget that as little as two decades ago it barely existed.

The US interpretation of India pale ale, or IPA, was born not out of the British original but as a spawn of the less-hoppy, weaker American pale ale, pioneered by Sierra Nevada Brewing and characterized by the citrusy twang of US-grown Cascade hops. As US-style pale ales, sometimes known as APAs, rose in popularity through the 1990s, they gave rise to the bigger, bolder, even more citrusy IPAs that would dominate the US craft beer market for the 2000s and 2010s.

Today, US-style IPAs are multitudinous and cross a vast range of flavour profiles and sub-styles, while after serving years as a distant second fiddle to their bolder stylistic offspring, American pale ales appear to be in fashion again. Classics among the former camp, not counting those already mentioned elsewhere in these listings, include Cigar City's flagship **Jai Alai** from Florida, with melon and peach notes joining the citrusy party, the fiercely aromatic **Susan** by Hill Farmstead of Vermont and the resinous **Pernicious** from Wicked Weed, in Asheville, North Carolina.

In the pale ale camp, established mainstays such as Missouri's subtle, nuanced **Schlafly Pale Ale** and the fragrant, quaffable Philadelphia standard **Yards Philly Pale Ale** are joined by more recent arrivals like the Boston area's tropical **Night Shift Whirlpool** and the floral-citrus **Bone-A-Fide** from Oregon's Boneyard Beer.

SURETTE

Crooked Stave, Denver, Colorado; 6.2%

From a brewer who wrote his master's thesis on *Brettanomyces* comes this dusty, herbal, modestly tart and earthy *saison* with controlled fruity acidity and impressive depth. Changes slightly from batch to batch.

SWEET POTATO CASSEROLE

Funky Buddha, Oakland Park, Florida; 7.9%

One of the funkiest beers from a brewery known for unique flavours, in this case "fresh out of the oven" spiced sweet potatoes and marshmallows swimming in a strong ale.

TEN FIDY

Oskar Blues, Longmont, Colorado and Brevard, North Carolina; 10.5%

One of the first strong beers to appear in a can, this pitch-black Imperial stout bears its potency proudly, with molasses and raisin on its boozy nose and a warming roastiness throughout.

TINY BOMB

Wiseacre, Memphis, Tennessee; 4.5%

An immigrant beer, drawing on Czech and German tradition, but adding local wildflower honey to create an American pilsner. Floral and spicy hops complement cracker-like honey malt and provide crisp bitterness.

TRINITY TRIPEL

Community, Dallas, Texas; 9%

Belgian in inspiration but indisputably New World in character, this strong and moderately hoppy ale boasts a unique and appealing mix of fragrant orange and tropical-fruit notes, with yeasty spice bringing it all together.

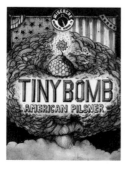

TRIOMPHE BELGIAN-STYLE INDIA PALE ALE

Vivant, Grand Rapids, Michigan; 6.5%

More sublime than most so-called Belgian IPAs, this beer has notes of sweet and floral apple throughout, with a restrained spiciness and bittering hop rising to the drying finish.

TRIPLE WHITE SAGE

Craftsman, Pasadena, California; 9%

Long before craft brewers were throwing everything but the kitchen sink into their beers, Mark Jilg was foraging wild white sage to bring a tremendously appealing peppery–herbal character to his dryish take on a *tripel*.

TROPIC KING

Funkwerks, Fort Collins, Colorado; 8%

A well-named *saison* with a rich and tropical-fruity aroma – notes of floral mango, papaya, pineapple and kiwi fruit, and a likewise richly fruity body that grows both spicier and drier as the flavour progresses to its peppery finish.

TRUTH

Rhinegeist, Cincinnati, Ohio; 7.2%

From the historic Over-the-Rhine brewing district, a very New World IPA, weaving fruit flavours such as grapefruit, pineapple and melon throughout, finishing dry and resiny.

URBAN FARMHOUSE

Commons, Portland, Oregon; 5.3%

Proving that less can be more, this mildly *Brettanomyces*-affected golden ale has a delicately floral aroma with musty notes and a gently fruity body with hints of funk upfront and a lengthy dry finish. Quenching and appetizing.

VELVET ROOSTER

Tallgrass, Manhattan, Kansas; 8.5%

A seasonal take on the *tripel* style, this light golden ale is dryly fruity of aroma, round and fruity with peppery spice in the body and with a super-dry finish, bringing it very close to the textbook ideal for the style.

VIENNA LAGER

Devils Backbone [AB InBev], Lexington and Roseland, Virginia; 5.2%

Delivers on the promise of the label, with rich, toasty Vienna maltiness paired with subtly spicy hops. A clean and crisp product of patient lagering.

WEE MAC SCOTTISH-STYLE ALE

Sun King, Indianapolis, Indiana; 5.3%

A beer some might argue exceeds what the Scots themselves are brewing in the style, this canned ale has an attractive sweetness that never grows cloying or sticky, but always invites another sip.

WEEDWACKER

Saint Arnold, Houston, Texas; 4.9%

A unique mash-up from the oldest craft brewery in Texas, its Fancy Lawnmower

BREWERIES TO WATCH

MANTRA

Franklin, Tennessee

Exciting operation founded by television chef Maneet Chauhan, crafting beers such as **Saffron IPA** (6.2%) and **Sun Salutation** *witbier* (4.8%) designed to complement Indian cuisine.

THE RARE BARREL

Berkeley, California

Calling themselves a "sour beer company", they take wort from nearby breweries and create liquid masterpieces in their home barrels, such as the dark **Ensorcelled** (6.2%), aged with raspberries, or **Soliloquy** (5.4%), a golden sour aged with rose hip and orange peel.

THE VEIL

Richmond, Virginia

An instant cult favourite helmed by much-lauded brewer Matt Tarpey. Early and exciting beers include **Crucial Taunt** (8%), a sneaky-strong double IPA, and the hugely aromatic, double dry-hopped **Broz Broz Day Day** (4.8%).

(*kölsch*) grist fermented with a *hefeweizen* yeast, the result hinting at banana bread but finishing crisp and peppery.

WEST COAST IPA

Green Flash, San Diego, California; 8.1%

Despite the audacity to call their IPA "West Coast", it does deliver on that promise, hitting all the right notes; with a big herbal and citrus hop nose, along with juicy hop flavour lasting for days.

THE WHALE

Community Beer Works, Buffalo, New York; 5.9%

A US take on the northern English brown ale (*see* page 13), this beer has a slightly austere maltiness, but in a way that really works for its flavour mix of burned nut, toasted malt and raw cocoa.

WITTE WHEAT ALE

Ommegang [Duvel Moortgat], Cooperstown, New York; 5.2%

It took Ommegang many years to brew up a *witbier*, but they nailed it when they did with this dryly spicy, wheaty brew offering whispers of fresh lemon juice and peel and a fully dry, peppery finish.

XQST KÖLSCH

Ruhstaller, Sacramento, California; 5%

Nice Californian interpretation of a German classic, with bright straw-gold colour and lasting lacing on a frothy white head. Biscuity malt and light floral hop flavours combine with a zesty and effervescent mouthfeel to make this satisfyingly refreshing.

XS OLD CRUSTACEAN BARLEY WINE

Rogue, Newport, Oregon; 10.6%

One of the early classic American barley wines, this presents a complex aroma of mixed berry fruit and spicy cigar tobacco, and a body that is aggressively hoppy and bitter. Will mellow with ageing.

ZONKER STOUT

Snake River, Jackson, Wyoming; 6%

A US standard-bearer for foreign-style stout, robust without being overbearing, hop bitterness balancing rich mocha-tinged malt. Pleasingly dry finish.

ZWICKEL

Urban Chestnut, St. Louis, Missouri; 5.2%

Unfiltered and hazy as per the style, this wonderfully yeasty lager is everything a *zwickel* should be, with a fresh and floral aroma, bready maltiness and a dryly bitter, refreshing finish.

CANADA

Canada came to what was then "microbrewing" not much later than the USA – the first modern brewpub in North America was actually Canadian – but lagged behind for some time due to the conservative nature of its brewers and, frankly, its citizenry. In recent years, however, the stereotype of the "cautious Canadian brewer" has been flipped on its head and the country has begun producing exciting, creative beers in almost every province.

AMNESIAC DOUBLE IPA

Phillips, Victoria, British Columbia; 8.5%

A spicy mix of citrus fruit, apricot and gentle nuttiness, this powerhouse-that-sips-softly is both one of the first and one of the best Canadian west coast double IPAs.

BACK HAND OF GOD STOUT

Crannóg, Sorrento, British Columbia; 5.2%

A wonderfully named and pleasingly roasty stout with hints of tobacco leaf from the BC interior's leading organic farm brewery, now also a resource for home hop-growers.

BEST BITTER SPECIAL

Granite, Toronto, Ontario and Halifax, Nova Scotia; 4.5%

The survivor Maritime brewery is now overshadowed by its Toronto offspring, from whence originated this deliciously appetizing, leafy and dry-hopped cask-conditioned best bitter, the equal of England's finest.

BLACK LAGER

Silversmith, Virgil, Ontario; 5%

This young wine-country brewery made a great first impression with this earthy, slightly liquorice-accented *schwarzbier* with hints of black pepper and burned citrus oil. Pleasingly roasty, dry-finishing and immensely satisfying.

BOB LEBOEUF

Brasseurs du Petit Sault, Edmundston, New Brunswick; 5.2%

There is considerable spiciness to this unspiced blond ale, with a brown-spice hoppiness in the nose and body that mixes favourably with just off-dry toffee-ish malt. Big flavours in a relatively small beer.

BOCK ME GENTLY

Big Rig, Kanata, Ontario; 7%

The name is a riff on a song by 1970s Canadian warbler Andy Kim, but this Big Rig beer is all business, with a dry toffee aroma and an off-dry body that is as soft and smooth as it is flavourful and warming.

BOSON DE HIGGS

Hopfenstark, L'Assomption, Québec; 3.8%

A stylistic mash-up of *rauchbier*, *Berliner weisse* and *saison* that this eccentrically minded brewery somehow manages to make work, with predictably smoky, tart flavours complemented by a yeasty spiciness.

LA BRITISH

À la Fût, Saint-Tite, Québec; 4.7%

Although nut free, there is a profound nuttiness to this bright brown ale crafted very much in the English tradition, with a hazelnutty aroma and off-dry body with faint chocolate notes upfront and a dry, nutty, roasty finish.

BRONAN IPA

High Road, nomadic, Ontario; 7.1%

A hazy-to-cloudy IPA in the so-called "Vermont style", meaning deeply fruity and, usually, turbidly cloudy, this draught-only beer is a refreshingly restrained take with citrus and mango notes, made for now at the Niagara College brewing school facilities.

LA BUTEUSE

Trou du Diable, Shawinigan, Québec; 10%

Sold in both regular and barrel-aged versions, this is a loose interpretation of a *tripel*, with a spritzy character and ample fruitiness subdued in the second half by peppery spiciness and a growing hoppiness. Wonderfully warming.

DECEPTION BAY IPA

Tatamagouche, Tatamagouche, Nova Scotia; 6.2%

From a promising young brewery, this is a hugely fragrant IPA offering mixed-citrus and tropical-fruit aromas and a similarly fruity, bitter body that is the picture of aromatic complexity in an IPA.

DOUBLE TEMPEST

Amsterdam, Toronto, Ontario;
11.9–14%

Variable from year to year, this weighty
version of Amsterdam Brewing's
Imperial stout is aged in bourbon barrels
to a fruity and mocha mix that is as
soothing as it is intoxicating.

FARM TABLE MÄRZEN

Beau's All-Natural, Vankleek Hill,
Ontario; 5.5%

A full and rich take on the style with
a toasted caramel and lightly nutty
character and a warming note of alcohol
on its mild to moderately bitter finish.
An autumn seasonal very well suited
to its season.

FARMHAND SAISON

Driftwood, Victoria, British Columbia; 5%

A spiced *saison* for those who dislike
spiced saisons, its black pepper does
present itself in both aroma and body,
but always in gentle harmony with the
orangey notes of the body and dryness
of the finish.

GLUTENBERG BLONDE ALE

Brasseurs Sans Gluten, Montréal,
Québec; 4.5%

From a brewery dedicated to gluten-
free beers comes this testament to
creativity with different grains, thin and
citrusy but with enough spiciness that
you almost forget the fact.

ICONIC BREWERY

UNIBROUE [SAPPORO]

Chambly, Québec

More than any other, the brewery that
brought Belgian brewing sensibilities to
Québec and, eventually, Canada, and
mercifully little has changed since its
purchase by Japan's Sapporo. Known
for a quenching and coriander-ish
Blanche de Chambly (5%); the spicy,
food-friendly strong amber ale **Maudite**
(8%); and a fine and fruity *tripel* that
was among the first brewed in North
America, **La Fin du Monde** (9%). Not to
be missed is the intense, almost brandy-
like *quadrupel* **Terrible** (10.5%).

CAN'T-MISS BREWERIES

CENTRAL CITY

Surrey, British Columbia

Perhaps better known as "Red Racer" after the name that adorns many of the brewery's brands, including the grassy, citrusy **Red Racer Pale Ale** (5%), one of the best in its style in Canada. Big brother **Red Racer IPA** (6.5%) is more aggressive, but no less appealing, while **Red Racer ISA** (4%) has a balance and structure much bigger than its moderate strength. Southern BC's rainy winters are made more tolerable by the arrival of the complexly spicy, orange-tangerine maltiness of the rich barley wine **Thor's Hammer** (11.5%).

DIEU DU CIEL!

Montréal and St-Jérôme, Québec

An impressive Montréal brewpub that expanded to a production facility north of the city, this is one of Canada's earliest and best beer innovators. Widely varied successes include the summery, hibiscus-flavoured wheat beer **Rosée d'Hibiscus** (5.9%), the densely fruity kumquat IPA **Disco Soleil** (6.5%) and the intense, coffee-accented strong stout **Péché Mortel** (9.5%). Seasonal releases include the stunningly balanced, black pepper-spiced rye beer **Route des Épices** (5.4%) and the dryly fruity, impressively reserved barley wine **Solstice d'Hiver** (10.5%).

HOYNE

Victoria, British Columbia

Helmed by veteran brewer Sean Hoyne and located in a rather industrial part of the generally pretty provincial capital, this is a brewery skilled in many styles. Highlights at the bottom of the fermenter include the lightly sweet, eminently quaffable **Pilsner** (5.5%) and the firmly malty **Helios Dortmunder Golden Lager** (6%), while ale fermentation yields the authentically British-style **Appleton Extra Special Bitter** (5.2%) and lean and sophisticated porter **Dark Matter** (5.3%), the last given a cold, lager-like conditioning for smoothness.

SIDE LAUNCH

Collingwood, Ontario

The offspring of Toronto's once-landmark Denison's Brewing, the plain names of this brewery's beer belie their frequent brilliance. **Wheat** (5.3%) is a lovely and fairly fruity example of the Bavarian *hefeweizen* style, while **Dark Lager** (5.3%) is a similarly authentic, toasty-nutty take on a Munich *dunkel* and **Mountain Lager** (4.7%) a superbly quenching *helles*-style beer with soft malty sweetness balanced by herbal hoppiness. Visit the brewery taproom for occasional treats like the deliciously spicy **Colossus Dunkelweizen Dopplebock** (8%).

GOLDEN ALE

The Exchange; Niagara-on-the-Lake, Ontario; 7.6%

A lovely example of the studious use of oak-barrelling to achieve a lighter beer style, mixing musty tones of *Brettanomyces* yeast in with pineapple, melon and pear fruitiness, finishing dry and gently warming.

GRAND BALTIC PORTER

Garrison, Halifax, Nova Scotia; 9%

A big-flavoured, deep purple beer from a stalwart of the "second wave" east coast craft brewing scene, suitably unfruity, rich and coffee-ish finishing in a pleasantly sweet, burned-sugar character. Thoroughly enjoyable.

HELLER HIGHWATER

Kichesippi, Ottawa, Ontario; 4.8%

From a brewery whose fortunes improved after the hiring of peripatetic brewer Don Harms, a nearly spot-on *helles* lager with a perfumey aroma and gentle malty sweetness.

KELLER PILSNER

Persephone, Gibsons, British Columbia; 5%

Only slightly hazy, but with a fresh, bright, wild-flower aroma and a grassy-bitter mid-palate with steadily advancing dryness. Lovely structure in a beer occasionally released in special single-hop versions.

KING HEFFY IMPERIAL HEFEWEIZEN

Howe Sound, Squamish, British Columbia; 7.7%

Even those with naught but distain for "Imperial" versions of traditionally lower-alcohol beer styles must appreciate the spice-accented roasted banana and tangerine of this sweet but never cloying beauty.

KITCHEN PARTY PALE ALE

Big Spruce, Nyanza, Nova Scotia; 5.0%

A copper-coloured ale with a perfumey aroma discernible from a foot away, rich with apricot, peach and tangerine. Add to that a mix of fruity toffee and faint, resinous herbals in the body and you have yourself a winner.

LEO'S EARLY BREAKFAST IPA

Dunham, Dunham, Québec; 6.2%

A successful collaboration with Danish brewer Anders Kissmeyer that has become a Dunham mainstay, this tropical-fruity, citrusy and spicy IPA is made with the addition of Earl Grey tea and guava purée.

LONDON STYLE PORTER

Propeller, Halifax, Nova Scotia; 5%

This is as English a porter as you are likely to find outside of the UK, with a slightly burned chocolate aroma and a dark chocolaty, toffee-ish body leading to an off-dry finish.

MAD TOM IPA

Muskoka, Bracebridge, Ontario; 6.4%

An IPA that speaks first to nose, then to palate, this brewery flagship offers a full, leafy, slightly forest-y aroma and a flavourful hoppiness that is a fragrant perfume, then a mouth-shattering bitterness, finally finishing dry and moderately bitter.

MITCHELL'S EXTRA SPECIAL BITTER

Spinnakers, Victoria, British Columbia; 5.2%

Long-standing mainstay at Canada's oldest craft brewery, very much in the character of an English ESB with a floral hoppiness and full and fruity malt profile. Usually even better in cask-conditioned form.

NECTAROUS

Four Winds, Delta, British Columbia; 5.5%

Billed a "dry-hopped sour", this enigmatic ale offers fresh tropical-fruit notes on the nose and a tangy mid-palate of complex tropical and citrus fruits. A beer to linger over, perhaps for several bottles.

NUT BROWN ALE

Black Oak, Toronto, Ontario; 5%

Aptly named and a survivor in a market not particularly enthusiastic about brown ales, this has a robustly nutty aroma, principally hazelnut, a just off-dry, slightly winey and still nutty flavour and a satisfyingly bitter finish.

OLD DEUTERONOMY BARLEY WINE

Alley Kat, Edmonton, Alberta; 10.3%

Released annually in frustratingly small amounts, this cellar-worthy ale has a slightly variable strength and complexity, but always features ample malty fruitiness and a lengthy, warming finish.

PILSNER

Steam Whistle, Toronto, Ontario; 5%

The lone product of this downtown brewery is a good one, more toward the *helles* than the pilsner style. Fragrant and floral in its aroma, with a gently sweet and grainy body that is well tempered by a drying hoppiness.

PORTER BALTIQUE

Les Trois Mousquetaires, Brossard, Québec; 10%

Almost jet black, this sweet espresso-scented beauty has a chocolate-raisin front leading to a complex mix of cinnamon-led spiciness and more dark

chocolate. Occasionally released in spirits-barrel-aged versions.

RED HAMMER

Paddock Wood, Saskatoon, Saskatchewan; 6%

Reddish copper of hue, this slightly strong Vienna lager/*märzen* quaffer has a caramel apple-ish aroma with a whiff of nutmeg and a nutty, faintly spicy toasted-malt body. Lovely structure with an appetizingly dry finish.

ROBOHOP IMPERIAL IPA

Great Lakes, Toronto, Ontario; 8.5%

With an aroma of fruit cocktail mixed with pine tar, this is a big and unapologetic ale that still manages to cram in sufficient malt that the bitterness never grows overwhelming. The picture of balance in a double IPA.

ST-AMBROISE OATMEAL STOUT

McAuslan, Montréal, Québec; 5%

One of Canada's longest-surviving craft stouts is all that an oatmeal stout should be – pitch black with a silken mouthfeel and a whisper of mocha sweetness to balance the roasted malt.

STOUT

Postmark, Vancouver, British Columbia; 4.8%

Deep brown and highly quaffable, this excellent, not-too-dry stout has a chocolate-brownie aroma and a nutty, faintly burned and gently bitter body

BREWERIES TO WATCH

BLACK BRIDGE

Swift Current, Saskatchewan

Solid new arrival to the relative beer desert of the Prairies, with the perfumey, herbal–citrus–piney **IPA!** (7%) and spicy caramel **Rye Ale** (5.3%), among several others.

BRASSEURS DU TEMPS (BDT)

Gatineau, Québec

Long-standing brewpub that broke ground on a full production brewery in early 2017, aiming to bring its summery **La Saison Haute** (8.5%) and resinous **Diable au Corps** (10%) double IPA to a wider audience.

DAGERAAD

Burnaby, British Columbia

Belgian-style specialist in the Vancouver suburbs, featuring a **Blonde** (7.5%) cast in the Duvel genre and an appetizingly spicy **Lake City Farmhouse** (5.2%).

BREWERIES TO WATCH

NEW LIMBURG

Simcoe, Ontario

Brewery run by a Belgian family transplanted to southwestern Ontario, producing home-country-inspired ales like the peppery **Belgian Blond** (7.2%) and plummy **Dubbel** (6.5%) with a dry finish.

TOOTH AND NAIL

Ottawa, Ontario

Within its first year, this brewery managed to create contenders for both Canada's top pilsner with the crisp, dry-finishing **Vim and Vigor** (5.2%), and best *saison* in the spicy, four-grain **Valor** (6%).

UNFILTERED

Halifax, Nova Scotia

Irreverent outfit helmed by irascible veteran brewer Greg Nash, specializing in hop-forward beers like the richly fruity but decidedly balanced pale ale **Hoppy Fingers** (4.8%) and flagship double IPA, the grassy-fruity, citrus-and-spice **Twelve Years to Zion** (8%).

accented by traces of star anise and espresso, finally finishing quite dry.

SUMMIT SEEKER

Banded Peak, Calgary, Alberta; 6.5%

Unusual for a Canadian IPA, this moderately bitter ale is defined as much by its malt as it is by its hops, with a deep amber colour and a mix of berry, citrus and toasted caramel in the taste.

LA VACHE FOLLE IMPERIAL MILK STOUT

Charlevoix, Baie-Saint-Paul, Québec; 9%

A bold take on a usually gentle style, sweet with notes of burned brown sugar in the aroma, with a chocolaty body boasting elements of sugary espresso and burned caramel and a warming, slightly bitter finish.

WITCHSHARK

Bellwoods, Toronto, Ontario; 9%

The opening of a second brewery in late 2016 brings hope for more regular production of popular brews like this inspired double IPA with a fruit basket of citrusy aromas and flavours backed by dryly toffee-ish malt.

YAKIMA IPA

Le Castor, Rigaud, Québec; 6.5%

A Québécois favourite, the late and dry-hopping of this beer has it exploding with fruity–floral aromas, while the body begins with fruit-cocktail sweetness before sliding into a more hoppy and bitter, citrus-accented body.

LATIN
AMERICA

MEXICO

Due to the oligopolistic tendencies of Mexico's two largest brewers, it took quite a while for craft beer to establish a firm footing in the country. Eventually, though, Guadalajara and Baja California began to see a rise in breweries, followed in short order by the capital city. Aided by some changes in federal law, Mexican craft beer is now not only thriving but improving at an almost exponential rate.

ASTILLERO

Agua Mala, Ensenada, Baja California; 8.5%

Citrus fruit abounds in this bright copper-coloured IPA, with spicy orange backed by lemon zest in the nose and a crisp, lemony and grapefruity body buttressed by herbal notes that carry through to the finish.

BÁGHA SUPER IPA

Propaganda, Monterrey, Nuevo Leon; 9%

Mexican breweries such as this are still feeling their way where highly hopped beers are concerned, which makes this double IPA with a big peppery, orange-citrus aroma and flavours of tropical fruit, citrus zest and lemon oil all the more impressive.

BOCK

La Blanca, Guadalajara, Jalisco; 7.3%

Mexico's leading and perhaps only wheat beer specialist, this heavily German-influenced operation crafts several fine ales, including this *bock* with a fragrant banana nose and lightly phenolic, sweetish body.

BRUTAL IMPERIAL STOUT

Border Psycho, Tijuana, Baja California; 10.5%

Over-the-top brewery making over-the-top beers such as this dense and rich stout with a tar-ish maltiness, cocoa- and aniseed-accented body and restrained sweetness.

CROSSOVER IPA

Urbana, Mexicali, Baja California; 6.5%

From Cerveza Mexico's large brewery of the year for 2016 comes this well-balanced IPA with broad floral and citrus notes in the aroma and a body that is hop-forward and grapefruity without being overdone.

HÁZMELA RUSA

La Chingonería, Mexico City; 7%

Another in the country's growing range of cocoa-and-spice Mexican Imperial stouts, this is also among the best, with a large nose of molasses, dark chocolate and port wine, and a subtle pepper element within a robust chocolate flavour.

LÁGRIMAS NEGRAS

Rámuri, Tijuana, Baja California; 10%

Billed as an oatmeal stout, the elevated strength and chocolaty intensity of this

CAN'T-MISS BREWERIES

CALAVERA

Tlalnepantla, State of Mexico

Located in the suburbs of the capital, this brewery turned heads early with solid Belgian abbey-style ales, including the milk chocolaty **Dubbel de Abadía** (6.4%) and slightly candied but dry-finishing **Tripel de Abadía** (9%), as well as what might have been the country's first **Mexican Imperial Stout** (9%), with lovely smoked chilli notes accenting flavours of dark chocolate. Not to be overlooked are the brewery's solid quaffing beers, like the tropical-fruit and citrus **American Pale Ale** (5.4%).

MINERVA

Zapopan, Jalisco

Low-key brewery located near Guadalajara and producing solid interpretations of mostly classic and lower-strength styles. Typical of this approach are **Viena** (5%), a lovely quaffer with toasted malt tones throughout, and **Rila** (4.88%), an occasionally brewed burgundy-hued ale with notes of toasted malt, berry and cinnamon. Veering slightly from the brewery's norm are the also fine **I.T.A.** (7%), or Imperial Tequila Ale, with a distinctly peppery body, and a rather restrained, slightly astringent **Imperial Stout** (6%).

CAN'T-MISS BREWERY

● ● ● ● ● ● ● ● ● ● ● ● ● ● ●

PRIMUS

San Juan del Río, Querétaro

Brewers of two lines, the original Tempus range of ales and a pair of lagers under the Jabalí name. Of the former, **Alt Clásica** (5.2%) is well named, being classically enough of its *altbier* style that it could be at home in Düsseldorf; **Doble Malta** (7%) has a similar appeal but with richer yet still balanced hops and malt; and **Dorada** (4.3%) is a golden ale with an appealingly light peachy fruitiness. In the Jabalí family, the **Hellesbock** (8.1%) stands out with its biscuit malt and creeping warmth.

beer make it more akin to an Imperial stout, albeit one with a rich and silken mouthfeel. Cherry and vanilla notes round out its appeal.

LA LUPULOSA

Insurgente, Tijuana, Baja California; 7.3%

Five varieties of hops are used in this highly fruity, berry-ish IPA with a chewy maltiness and a drying, bitter and somewhat grapefruity finish. One of Mexico's best straightforward IPAs.

MAÍZ AZUL

La Brü, Morelia, Michoacán; 4.2%

A special beer developed to highlight the local blue corn, which quite unsurprisingly gives it a distinct yet also distinctive corn flavour, backed up by a light spiciness.

MERCEDES FAUNA

Mexicali, Baja California; 5%

From one of the northwest's most accomplished brewers comes this wonderfully earthy brown ale with a cinnamon-accented aroma and an appealing dryness that lasts from the molasses front to the roasted nutty finish.

MEZCAL IPA

Chaneque, Mexico City; 6.5%

Ageing beer in tequila and mezcal barrels could be a growing trend in Mexico, and if they all turn out like this superbly balanced ale with a smoky, dryly fruity and spicy hop character, so much the better!

BREWERIES TO WATCH

COLIMA

El Trapiche, Colima

Fast-growing brewery south of Guadalajara, known for flagships like the floral, quenching **Colimota Lager** (4.2%) and the perfumey, citrusy **Páramo Pale Ale** (5.2), as well as a number of collaborations.

WENDLANDT

Ensenada, Baja California

Multi-award-winning brewery and pub south of Tijuana, excelling at a variety of styles including **Harry Polanco** (5.5%), a dryly hoppy aperitif red ale, the best bitter-ish **Vaquita Marina Pale Ale** (5.2%) and forcefully aromatic **Perro del Mar India Pale Ale** (7%).

SPORT LOBA

Guadalajara, Jalisco; 5%

A classically fashioned Belgian-style wheat beer with a lightly sweet, aromatic and orangey nose and balanced, faintly acidic and refreshing body. Brewed with the hot Jalisco summers in mind.

BRAZIL

Although recent economic and political woes have certainly not made it easy for Brazil's craft brewers, the number of breweries populating the country continues to grow, and so does the quality of the beers being produced. All of which adds up to a rosy picture for beer drinkers from the Amazonian north – source of many of the interesting fruits and woods making their way into a steadily increasing proportion of Brazilian beers – through to the more German-leaning south.

3 LOBOS BRAVO AMERICAN IMPERIAL PORTER

Backer, Belo Horizonte, Minas Gerais; 9%

Aged in amburana wood, this seductive, pitch-black porter has an aroma of spicy vanilla mixed with sweet espresso and a flavour of spice, cinnamon, chocolate and aniseed with hints of roasted chestnuts.

1516

Verace, Nova Lima, Minas Gerais; 4.8%

Bright, light gold in colour, this German-style pilsner has a floral hop aroma, delicate maltiness, well-balanced and assertive bitterness and a dry, refreshing finish.

AMBURANA LAGER

Way Beer, Pinhais, Paraná; 8.4%

One of the first Brazilian beers to employ the flavours of the Amazon, this full-bodied lager uses ambarana wood in conditioning for a cinnamony, spicy, slightly chocolaty and intensely rich-tasting result.

BLACK METAL IPA

Maniba, Novo Hamburgo, Rio Grande do Sul; 7.2%

A black IPA designed for hop lovers, this assertive brew is strongly citrusy on the nose and intensely bitter in the body with balancing roasted malt and a dry and hoppy aftertaste.

CAFETINA

Landel, Barão Geraldo, São Paulo; 5.2%

This seasonal, coffee-enhanced porter is brewed when only the best beans are available. Fresh floral and fruity notes from the coffee are in full harmony with the caramel and chocolate malt flavours.

FELLAS

Dama, Piracicaba, São Paulo; 9%

A coffee-flavoured double IPA, this combines strongly fruity aromas from both the hops and the coffee beans, balancing them with caramelly maltiness in a velvety body with a warming finish.

FOREST BACURI

Amazon, Belém, Pará; 4.1%

From a brewery specializing in beers flavoured with Amazonian fruit, this pilsner has a sweet and faintly tart aroma and sweetish palate that turns tangier and more gooseberry- and pineapple-accented toward the off-dry finish.

CAN'T-MISS BREWERIES

BAMBERG

Votorantim, São Paulo

One of Brazil's most well-established breweries and one very much influenced by German brewing traditions. The citizens of Bamberg would be proud of the gently smoky **Rauchbier** (5.2%), while Müncheners would approve of the fragrant, honey-ish **Maibaum** (6.5%) seasonal *maibock* and the mellow, lightly roasty *dunkel* **München** (5%). Düsseldorf also gets a shout-out in the form of the slightly sweet but dry-finishing **Altbier** (5%).

BODEBROWN

Curitiba, Paraná

Brewery born out of a brewing school operated by Samuel Cavalcanti and popularized on the back of Brazil's first, and still arguably best, double IPAs **Perigosa** (9.2%), and occasional supercharged offspring **Double Perigosa** (15.1%). The big beers sometimes overshadow other fine creations, such as the strongly Scottish-influenced **Wee Heavy** (8%), with attractive cinnamon and molasses notes, and subtle, quenching **Blanche de Curitiba** (5.5%). Inspired creations like **4 Blés** (11.7%), made from four types of wheat and boasting a highly complex, herbal–dried-fruit character, make sporadic appearances.

GORDELÍCIA

Urbana, São Paulo; 7.5%

An intense and warming Belgian-style strong golden ale, this beer has a strongly spicy and fruity character, notably banana and yellow fruit, which is medium- to full-bodied and pleasantly sweet.

HOLY COW 2

Seasons, Porto Alegre, Rio Grande do Sul; 7.5%

First brewed in collaboration with the US brewery Green Flash (*see* page 226), this IPA is intensely hopped to a tropical-fruit aroma, featuring passion-fruit and pineapple, a striking bitterness and a dry finish.

HORNY PIG SESSION IPA

Blondine, Itupeva, São Paulo; 4.5%

This light amber IPA – with a slightly rude label – features a fresh tropical-fruit aroma and a light, refreshing and moderately bitter body with commendable balance.

MADALENA DOUBLE IPA

Premium Paulista, Santo André, São Paulo; 7.5%

At the low end of strength for the style, this ale manages a nice balance between citrusy and resiny hops and ample malt sweetness in a full, strongly bitter body.

MÄRZEN RAUCHBIER

Bierbaum, Treze Tílias, Santa Catarina; 4.6%

Brewed in the "most Austrian city in Brazil", this Bamberg-style smoked beer has a malty sweetness and biscuit notes that are not overwhelmed by its pleasantly balanced smokiness.

MONJOLO IMPERIAL PORTER

Tupiniquim, Porto Alegre, Rio Grande do Sul; 10.5%

Also available on occasion in a whisky-barrel version, this warming, velvety porter embraces the drinker with aromas and flavours of toffee and chocolate, accented by notes of vanilla and roasted malt.

PETROLEUM

DUM, Curitiba, Paraná; 12%

One of Brazil's most recognized beers, originally brewed as a collaboration with Wäls (*see* opposite), this is as inky and black as its name would suggest,

with a silken mouthfeel and chocolaty character from the oats and cocoa used in its making.

RUSSIAN IMPERIAL STOUT

Bierland, Blumenau, Santa Catarina; 8%

This strong stout brewed in the beer capital of southern Brazil has a cheeky sweetness reminiscent of a chocolate liqueur, but in a roasty and dense body that speaks to its "Imperial" status. A thoroughly enticing ale.

SEXY SESSION IPA

Barco, Porto Alegre, Rio Grande do Sul; 4.3%

Hopped with Citra, Simcoe and Centennial, this features citrusy aromatics, an assertive bitterness and a dry, refreshing finish.

SORACHI BERLINER

Perro Libre, Porto Alegre, Rio Grande do Sul; 3.4%

Conditioned on lemon zest and dry-hopped with Sorachi Ace hops, this well-balanced *Berliner weisse* is highly aromatic with predictable lemon notes, pleasantly tart in character and very thirst quenching.

TRIPPEL

Wäls [AB InBev], Belo Horizonte, Minas Gerais; 9%

As traditional a *tripel* as probably exists in Brazil, this boasts a spicy, dryly lemony aroma and a body that begins orange–herbal, proceeds to tropical fruit and finishes with an earthy, drying hoppiness.

CAN'T-MISS BREWERY

MORADA CIA ETÍLICA

Curitiba, Paraná

Not a nomadic brewery per se, but rather one sharing a facility with other breweries, this home-brewer–turned-professional operation impresses with a wide variety of beers. Their foundational brand is the clever **Double Vienna** (7.6%), a big-bodied take on the Vienna lager style, while newer **Hop Arabica** (5%) impresses with layered coffee and hop flavours. Clean and faintly fruity **Kölsch** (5%) is designed for the Brazilian summer heat, and **Gasoline Soul** (6.7%) is an amber ale drawing inspiration from the Brazil Motorcycle Show.

BREWERIES TO WATCH

DOGMA

São Paulo

Born in 2015, the brewery was earning plaudits early for beers such as the self-explanatory **Mosaic Lover IPA** (8.5%), the double IPA **Rizoma** (8.3%) and **Sourmind** (4.4%), a refreshing *Berliner weisse* with guava and mango juice.

HOCUS POCUS

Rio de Janeiro

A young and innovative brewery that is already considered among Brazil's best whose accomplishments include the spicy, Belgian-esque **Magic Trap** (8.5%), the caffeinated amber ale **Coffee Hush** (5.5%) and newer **Overdrive** (8.2%), a cloudy, fruity double IPA brewed with oats.

VELHAS VIRGENS MR. BROWNIE

Invicta, Ribeirão Preto, São Paulo; 5%

An English-style brown ale brewed with vanilla pods, this mahogany ale boasts caramel, toasted bread and chocolate notes in its aroma and a good balance between toasted malt and sweetness on the palate.

VIENNA LAGER

Da Mata, Embu das Artes, São Paulo; 4.9%

A fine amber-coloured lager that balances a fine spicy–leafy hop aroma with a body that highlights toasted malt without becoming overly sweet, drying with gentle bitterness to its dry finish.

VIXNU

Colorado [AB InBev], Ribeirão Preto, São Paulo; 9.5%

With a nose reminiscent of fruit salad steeped in brandy, this double IPA attracts the drinker into a fruity (apricot especially) and spicy body that turns progressively bitter toward a lingering bitter and warming finish.

VÓ MARIA E SEU LADO ZEN

Avós, São Paulo, São Paulo; 4.9%

Perfectly suited to the strong heat of the Brazilian summer, this golden, well-hopped hoppy lager features balanced bitterness and a pleasant citrusy hop aroma in an impressively refreshing quaffer.

ARGENTINA

Argentina is unusual in that craft brewing first gained its foothold not in any of the country's major cities but rather in the Lake District of northern Patagonia. As breweries have come and gone through the years, however, more and more have made a home in the nation's capital and it is there that we now find the greatest promise for the future.

AMERICAN IPA

Sir Hopper, nomadic; 7.2%

Brewed with imported US hops rather than Argentina-grown versions, this has a pungent, citrusy-fruity aroma and full, citrus and tropical-fruit hoppiness in the body leading to a lingering and dry finish.

BARLEY WINE

Antares, Buenos Aires and other locations; 10%

This brewpub chain, now bottling their beer as well, was a pioneer in Argentina and is still a leader with beers like this boozy, fruity, round and full strong ale with sugary notes and a long finish.

BEAGLE NEGRA CREAM STOUT

Fuegian, Ushuaia, Tierra del Fuego; 6.2%

A full, sweetish, caramel roasted and well-balanced stout, with dabs of chocolate, coffee and bitter hop, made at the tip of the Andes in the world's most southerly brewery.

BLACK MAMBA

Grunge, Buenos Aires province; 6.5%

Perhaps a bit light in strength for its "Foreign Stout" billing, this nonetheless enticing beer combines dark chocolate, dried fruit, coffee and a hint of liquorice on the nose with a complex, full and chewy body and off-dry finish.

BRIGIT

Kraken, Caseros, Buenos Aires province; 5.6%

Billed as an "Irish red", this is appropriately amber in colour with a clean caramel and toffee aroma that extends to the palate as well, although there combined with hints of coffee and a drying yet still caramelly finish.

CHOCOLATE PORTER

Anna-C, Llavallol, Buenos Aires province; 6.5%

Brewed with coffee beans as well as cocoa, this has a forcefully chocolaty nose backed by coffee notes and a mildly bitter, velvety, chocolaty body.

DUBBEL 6

Abdij Deleuze, Avellaneda, Buenos Aires province; 7%

From a brewery crafting exclusively Belgian styles of ale comes this convincing take on an abbey *dubbel*, with a toasty and caramelly aroma backed by hints of prune and a rich, sweet and full palate.

GROSA

Jerome, El Salto, Mendoza; 9%

An unapologetically big beer that spends 18 months inside a wine barrel prior to its release, emerging with a grapey palate, spicy finish and lingering warmth. Ownership of the brand is unclear – it is variously attributed to the company "Cerveza Grosa".

MIVER

Darwin, Buenos Aires; 5.5%

A lovely looking *weissbier* with a good balance between banana and clove notes, accented by light citrus and acidity that enhance the dry finish and overall refreshing character of this beer.

OAK AGED DOPPELBOCK

Juguetes Perdidos, Caseros, Buenos Aires; 10.5%

Aged in barrels previously used for Malbec wine, this offers elements of cherry, vanilla and coconut on the nose, and a full and sweet body accented by hints of orange peel and apricot, leading to a warming finish.

OLD ALE

Berlina, Bariloche, Río Negro; 7.5%

A nice coppery brown ale with complex aromas balanced between fruity and caramel notes. Rich and malty in its viscous mouthfeel with good structure and balance.

RUSSIAN IMPERIAL STOUT

Nihilista, Cipolletti, Río Negro; 9%

Aged at the brewery for six months prior to its release, this gold-medal-winning stout from Nihilista boasts a sherry-ish nose with prune, raisin and mocha tones and an oily, complex and robustly bitter body.

CHILE

Having spent years as the number three craft beer country in South America – after Brazil and Argentina – at last Chile now seems poised to make a bigger name for itself. If a more stable supply of fresh hops can be found, the sky may wind up being the only limit for its increasingly creative brewers.

BLACK IPA

Zigurat, Santiago; 7%

A complex mix of cocoa, chocolate and piney hoppiness characterizes the aroma of this ale, while further intrigue is provided by the blend of coffee, dried fruit, liquorice and spice in the body.

IMPERIAL STOUT

Hernando de Magallanes, Punta Arenas; 7%

The country's southernmost brewery produces this sweet and blackcurrant-y stout that adds port wine and prune notes in front of a creamy, slightly roasty and warming finish.

IPA

Kross, Curacaví, Santiago; 6.5%

An interesting mix of aromas in this beer – passion-fruit, melon, floral, pine and citrus. Together with a quenching bitterness and a good malt backbone, they produce a beer that is creamy, balanced and refreshing.

RAUCHBIER

Grosse Gerste, Pirque, Santiago; 5%

A deep copper lager with balanced smokiness on the aroma, the body strays to the sweet side but does so with a keen understanding of the beer's smoky character, the overall effect being that of a nicely structured smoked malt beer.

CAN'T-MISS BREWERY

● ● ● ● ● ● ● ● ● ● ● ● ● ● ● ● ●

GRANIZO

Olmué, Valparaíso

Located in the Reserve of the Biosphere La Campana-Peñuelas (UNESCO) and using solar energy, Granizo has won awards for beers such as **Tue Tue** (10.5%), a deeply complex and robust black ale fermented in French oak barrels that previously held Pinot Noir; **IRA** (7%), a refreshing India Red Ale flavoured with rosemary; **Foxy Lady** (12.1%), an Imperial stout also fermented ex-Pinot Noir oak but with additions of Puta Madre chilli peppers; and **Quercus** (8.5%), a complex strong ale fermented and matured in French and US oak previously used in Syrah wine production.

BREWERY TO WATCH

HESS

Valparaíso

Dedicated to creating highly hopped ales fashioned in the US style, including the strongly hoppy **Bozko Barakus Brown Ale** (7.5%) and the creamy, balanced stout **Lykantrop** (7%).

SESSION IPA

Jester, Santiago; 4.6%

New for the summer of 2016, this is full of piney, resinous and tropical-fruit aromas with the flavour following suit and adding herbal and citrusy hop notes leading to a dryly bitter finish.

STOUT

Emperador, Santiago; 6%

Impressive and still-improving stout with an almost clotted-cream-like aroma accented by chocolate and soft roasty notes, and a similarly sweet and creamy body with more chocolate and a slight burned woodiness.

STOUT

Szot, Talagante, Santiago; 5.8%

Deep mahogany with a roasty, biscuity aroma holding hints of vanilla and chocolate, this nicely rounded ale has a strong roasted malt character to it, finishing dry, roasty and slightly boozy.

TÜBINATOR

Tübinger, Pirque, Santiago; 8%

The almost port-like sweetness of this intensely ruby-coloured ale is complemented well by the dried fruit and nuttiness of the nose, Christmas cake and sweet plum flavours and warming, toasted brown sugar notes in the finish.

URUGUAY

Only a few years ago, an aficionado of flavourful beer would have had a hard time slaking her thirst in Uruguay, so sparsely populated was the country's craft beer market. But lately, breweries have been opening at a fairly fierce rate, and furthermore, some have been producing ales and lagers of impressive quality.

BELGIAN DARK ALE

Volcanica, Las Toscas, Canelones; 8%

A gorgeous mahogany brew with a fruity, slightly spicy aroma with hints of caramel, toffee and chocolate. Brewed from Belgian malt and fermented with Belgian yeast, it will only get better as it ages.

BELGIAN DUBBEL WITH ARRAYÁN

Oceánica, Playa Hermosa, Maldonado; 6.5%

Brewed with foraged native *arrayán* berries, this blends the spicy, caramel characteristics of a Belgian *dubbel* with the fruity yet slightly minty taste of *arrayán*, producing vivacious flavours that dance in the mouth.

CAN'T-MISS BREWERY

DAVOK

Montevideo

Chief brewer Alejandro Baldenegro is a pioneer in the Uruguayan craft beer scene and generally regarded as a catalyst for the growth in quality of Uruguayan craft beer in general. The brewery's thirst-quenching, superbly balanced **American IPA** (6.2%) is a local icon, while the deep copper **Barley Wine** (12%) is a full-bodied, malty yet not overly sweet beer, brewery-aged for at least six months after bottling. The new flavour bomb, **Choco Canela Stout** (7%), with oatmeal, cacao, US oak chips and cinnamon, is a superlatively chewy beer.

BREWERY TO WATCH

INDICA

Montevideo

A young duo of former home-brewers producing hoppy beers that frequently sell out within a week of arriving at stores. Their citrusy, tropical-fruity **West Coast IPA** (6.8%) and award-winning **Californian Common** (5.2%) are both ground-breaking entries to the local market.

CITRA HIBERNATION

Oso Pardo, Montevideo; 5.3%

Produced by a newcomer to the Uruguayan beer scene who is making very hoppy beers very well, this single hop (Citra, as per the name) US-style pale ale has a strong passion-fruit aroma and a quaffable and highly sessionable character.

DRY STOUT

Montevideo Brew House, Montevideo; 4.7%

Sold exclusively at Uruguay's only brewery–restaurant, this dry stout will transport the drinker instantly to Ireland with its black hue, dense and creamy head and aromas of coffee with dark chocolate undertones.

GUAYABO BLONDE ALE

Ibirá Pitá, San Luis, Canelones; 5%

Produced on a small, family-run farm, this organic pale ale is brewed with an indigenous fruit called *guayabo del país*, resulting in a quince and tropical-fruit aroma and a refreshing flavour of hoppy bitterness mixed with fruity tartness.

REST OF LATIN AMERICA

Outside of the larger countries, craft brewing has come to Latin America in fits and starts, with tourist-oriented breweries here, home-brew clubs there and everywhere a mix of fly-by-night operations, which open only to close almost as quickly, and more stable, long-term-leaning breweries, often helmed or assisted by ex-pats from the USA and elsewhere. Here we present some of the brighter lights.

COLOMBIA

SEPTIMAZO IPA

Bogotá Beer Company [AB InBev], Tocancipá, Bogotá; 6%

An IPA characterized by a thick and enduring collar of foam. Its citrusy, piney aroma presages a citrus–herbal quality in the body and a balanced, clean and dry finish.

COSTA RICA

FUNKY JOSEPH

Calle Cimarrona, San José; 7.2%

A well-integrated mix of aromas with notes of peppercorn, fruit and *Brettanomyces*, supplemented on the palate by spicy, oaky and winey flavours. An interesting and complex beer with a good balance of sweetness and tartness.

MAMACANDELA

Treintaycinco, San José; 7.8%

A deep black stout from Treintaycinco with a creamy and persistent head and attractive aromas of roasted malts, dark fruits, cacao and coffee. The flavour follows suit, with an intense and complex balance of chocolatly malt, fruity esters and floral hops, all finishing with a pleasing warmth.

SEGUA RED ALE

Costa Rica's Craft Beer, Cartago; 5%

From the country's leading small brewery, a coppery-orange ale with an aroma of walnut and ripe apricot and mango, and a nutty, bready, faintly spicy palate that finishes mildly bitter and off-dry.

ECUADOR

HELLER WIEZENBOCK

Pãramo, Quito; 5.8%

Golden with an enduring ivory foam, this not-so-strong *weizenbock* offers rich malt, caramel and bready notes in the nose and a full and malt-forward body with balanced banana and clove flavours.

IRISH RED ALE

Santana, Quito; 5.2%

A complex mix of caramel, biscuit, toffee and toasty maltiness can be found in both the aroma and flavour of this red ale, with hops providing a drying bitterness and dark malts bringing a roasty character to the finish.

WEE HEAVY

Sinners, Quito; 10%

Intense chilli, caramel, toffee and floral aromas introduce this original take on a strong Scottish-style ale, with the heat in the body well integrated with the sweet maltiness and dried fruit character. This is a fine balance of spice and malt.

PANAMA

COCO PORTER

La Rana Dorada, Panama City; 5%

A rich and satisfying variation on the brewery's core line-up porter, this has expressive aromas of chocolate, coconut, vanilla and toasted malts, with a toasty, fruity, coconut-accented body and mild to moderate bitterness.

TULIVIEJA

Casa Bruja, Panama City; 8.4%

An intense double IPA from Casa Bruja with a resinous aroma carrying notes of tropical fruit and citrus, a balanced flavour profile of caramelly malt and moderate, citrusy hoppiness and finally a warming, dry finish.

PARAGUAY

ESPRESSO PALE ALE

Sajonia, Sajonia, Asunción; 5.5%

A special version of the brewery's citrusy Pale Ale, fuelled with coffee from the local Café Consulado for a surprisingly refreshing, coffee-forward and lightly resinous result

PARAGUAYAN ALE

Herken 1885, Cañada de Ybyray, Asunción; 4.7%

Brewed with cassava, kapi'i cedron (a herb similar to lemongrass) and apepú (a sort of sour orange), this is a well-constructed, bright golden, strongly citrusy and highly quaffable ale.

PERU

CH'UNPI SOUR

Valle Sagrado, Pachar, Cusco; 4.6%

An interesting mix of fruity (berries), floral and caramel aromas precedes a complex mélange of maltiness, bitterness and sourness on the palate and a very dry finish.

SHAMAN IPA

Sierra Andina, Huaraz, Ancash; 8%

On the nose this shows a classic citrusy US hop profile, while the flavour adds floral and tropical-fruit notes to the citrus, creating a clean, refreshing and dry-finishing beer.

AUSTRALASIA

AUSTRALIA

Although Australian brewers have gone through a rather halting progression with respect to their craft beer evolution, all indications suggest that they are now firmly set in full-speed-ahead mode. Future developments may well find their raison d'être in the nation's emerging indigenous hop culture, led by the Galaxy hop but with numerous others following.

AMBER ALE

Prancing Pony, Totness, South Australia; 5%

An amber that tips its hat to the USA with multiple hop additions layering textured bitterness over a complex caramel malt.

BALTIC PORTER

Redoak, Sydney, New South Wales; 8.7%

Old rope, rich dark chocolate, figs and demerara sugar all figure in the aroma and flavour of this highly awarded version of a beer style that the brewer discovered in a Polish café early on in his brewing career.

CHEVALIER SAISON

Bridge Road, Beechworth, Victoria; 6%

One of the first locally brewed versions of a *saison* (*see* page 23) and still a reference point for this classic style. Spicy and dry with a grassy hop character and very quenching.

CLOUT STOUT

Nail, Bassendean, Western Australia; 10.5%

First brewed to celebrate the brewery's 10th anniversary and now an annual special release, this chocolate-, aniseed- and tobacco-redolent beast is a yearly highlight from Nail.

CRANKSHAFT

BentSpoke, Braddon, Australian Capital Territory; 5.8%

As with many Australian IPAs, this carries mild bitterness for the style, but still delivers on flavour with a resiny blend of five hops producing notes of tropical fruit salad carried along by caramel malts.

ENGLISH ALE

3 Ravens, Thornbury, Victoria; 4.5%

A classic English-style pale ale, made from Maris Otter malt and Fuggles hops and first brewed for cask-conditioning. Earthy and slightly jammy hops mix with a base of gentle toffee-ish malt edging toward chocolate.

FORMER TENANT

Modus Operandi, Mona Vale, New South Wales; 7.8%

Mosaic and Galaxy hops lend strong tropical aromas to this savoury red IPA, which won the title of Champion Australian Craft Beer in 2014 just three months after the brewery opened.

GOLDEN ALE

Two Birds, Spotswood, Victoria and contract; 4.4%

Highly approachable but still nuanced and rewarding, delicate stone fruits mingle with a honey malt profile in this summery ale from Australia's first female-owned brewery.

GROWLER

2 Brothers, Moorabbin, Victoria; 4 7%

One of the first US-style brown ales commercially brewed in the country and still one of the best, with American-grown Cascade hops adding aromatic light to a crystal-malt shade.

HAZELNUT BROWN

Bad Shepherd, Cheltenham, Victoria; 5.9%

There is no mistaking the nut in question in this rich brown ale, made with hazelnuts, hazelnut extract and even Frangelico with a touch of vanilla. It all works beautifully, right to the smooth, dry finish.

HEF

Burleigh, Burleigh Heads, Queensland; 5%

Classic banana and clove aromas define this award-winning and stylish *hefeweizen*, followed by a light and spritzy mouthfeel and classically refreshing finish.

HIGHTAIL ALE

Mountain Goat [Asahi], Melbourne and Laverton, Victoria; 4.5%

Pioneering beer and brewery, now Japanese-owned but still delivering earthy malt characters and spicy hop bitterness in an ale that should be considered a modern classic.

HOP HEAVEN EASY IPA

Barossa Valley, Tanunda, South Australia; 4.8%

Australia's climate and punitive alcohol taxes see brewers creatively getting more flavour into lower-strength versions of popular styles, including "session IPAs" such as this lemon-tinged zinger from Barossa Valley Brewing.

HOP HOG

Feral, Swan Valley and Bassendean, Western Australia; 5.8%

There are many hoppier pale ales on the market these days, but few better than this perennial critical and consumer favourite. Burnished gold, it assaults the nose with citrus and pine.

HOPSMITH

Akasha, Five Dock, New South Wales; 7.2%

An IPA in the US West Coast style, triple dry-hopping with Amarillo and Simcoe gives a lifted aroma to an already hop-heavy but stylish ale.

IPA

Fixation, Byron Bay, New South Wales; 6.4%

An independent offshoot of Stone & Wood (see page 259) produces this robustly hopped ale delivering a pronounced grapefruit aroma and punchy bitterness over a solid malt base, bold yet emphasizing aroma and flavour over sheer aggression.

ICONIC BREWERY

COOPERS

Adelaide, South Australia

Family owned since its foundation in 1862, and for the second half of the 20th century a bulwark against brewery consolidation despite many fluctuations in fortune, Coopers kept alive Australia's only indigenous beer style, the sparkling ale. Now enjoying a renaissance, that historic **Sparkling Ale** (5.8%) remains the gold standard for the now-resurgent style, joined in the brewery's line-up by its younger, cloudier sibling **Pale Ale** (4.5%), the rich classic **Extra Stout** (6.3%) and an annual highlight **Vintage Ale** (7.5%), which showcases interesting hop character when fresh, but is brewed for ageing.

LITTLE DOVE

Gage Roads, Palmyra, Western Australia, 6.2%

From Australia's only publicly listed craft brewery – with a 25% share recently repatriated from shopping giant Woolworths – comes this fine "New World pale ale" boasting pineapple and orange aromas over a sweet malt body.

LOVEDALE LAGER

Sydney, Lovedale, New South Wales; 4.7%

While Australia loves lagers, its craft brewers have tended to eschew them, a notable exception being Sydney Brewery's luscious Munich-style *helles*, with complexity from three malts and an elegant bitterness.

MOONSHINE

Grand Ridge, Mirboo North, Victoria; 8.5%

With its delicious mélange of burned sugar, dried fruit, chocolate, caramel and just a hint of Vegemite on the nose, this richly malty ale has been delighting Australian beer drinkers for more than 20 years.

NINE TALES

James Squire [Kirin], Camperdown, New South Wales; 5%

The marketing stories may be tortured and contrived, but this English-style brown ale is still highly worthy and rewarding with its rich toffee maltiness and nutty finish.

PALE

Mornington Peninsula, Mornington, Victoria; 4.7%

This rock-solid version of a very common style – pale ale – witnesses passion-fruit and pine aromas atop a refreshing malt base, lightened with wheat malts and a quenching hop bite.

PALE ALE

Little Creatures [Kirin], Fremantle and other locations, Victoria; 5.2%

The brewery's purchase by Kirin in 2012 has seen no loss of quality in this solid and spot-on US-style pale ale from a pioneer of the Australian craft movement.

PENNY PORTER

Green Beacon, Brisbane, Queensland; 6.1%

Subtropical Brisbane's climate makes it an unlikely home to such a delectable porter, with coffee, mocha and liquorice notes mingling on the palate in advance of a drying finish.

PILSNER

Hawkers, Reservoir, Victoria; 5%

With floral and grassy hop characteristics, a bready and honey-ish malt base and a beautifully clean finish, this lager needs little more description than "classic German-style pilsner".

RAMJET

Boatrocker, Braeside, Victoria; 11.4%

Coffee and tobacco are softened with more than a hint of figs and vanilla in this whisky-barrel-aged Imperial stout from one of the country's most extensive barrel-ageing programmes.

ROBERT

Stomping Ground, Collingwood, Victoria; 8.9%

A straight-up-and-down double IPA, with classic pine and grapefruit notes, elevated by the sublime balance for such a big beer.

SEEING DOUBLE

Brew Boys, Croydon Park, South Australia; 8%

A solid whack of peated malts gives this Scotch ale a fair reek of smoky iodine with Vegemite and banana over a syrupy malt base.

STOUT

4 Pines, Brookvale, New South Wales; 5.1%

While it is reputedly being tested to become the first beer to travel into space, for the terrestrial-bound this is a classic dry stout with coffee and chocolate aromas and flavours, and a touch of aniseed at the finish.

TEMPTRESS

Holgate Brewhouse, Woodend, Victoria; 6%

A classically styled porter tricked up with Dutch cocoa and vanilla pods to add caramel smoothness to a sharply espresso-accented body, from a regional brewery that is one of the country's "must-visit" venues.

CAN'T-MISS BREWERIES

● ● ● ● ● ● ● ● ● ● ● ● ●

LA SIRÈNE

Alphington, Victoria

Few Australian breweries attempt Belgian-inspired beers and fewer do it well, which makes La Sirène unique. Launching with a sublime **Saison** (6.5%), and following with several variations, the brewery also excels at other styles, including malt-driven **Farmhouse Red** (6.5%), infused with fresh rose buds, hibiscus and dandelions, and **Praline** (6%), a Belgian-style stout brewed with organic vanilla pods, cacao nibs and hazelnuts.

STONE & WOOD

Byron Bay and Murwillumbah, New South Wales

When others were turning out bitterness-driven pale ales, Stone & Wood launched **Pacific Ale** (4.4%), an aromatic New World take on a British-style summer ale, helping to popularize the indigenous Galaxy hop. **Jasper** (4.7%) is a twist on the German *altbier* and a core brand, while the annual **Stone Beer** (6.4%) is a dark, malty delight and **Cloud Catcher** (5.5%) riffs on the Australian pale ale style while maintaining the brewery's love of colouring outside of the stylistic lines.

THANKS CAPTAIN OBVIOUS

BrewCult, nomadic; 5.8%

Citra, Centennial and Simcoe give a classically citrusy US-style IPA edge to this mainstay of Australia's leading brewery without a home.

TWO TO THE VALLEY INDIA PALE ALE

Newstead, Newstead, Queensland; 5.9%

A tight bundle of Citra, Centennial, Cascade and Simcoe hops serves up an assertive and bold bitterness beneath a grapefruit and melon cloud, while a healthy amount of biscuity malt keeps it all in check.

WEST COAST IPA

Batch, Marrickville, New South Wales; 5.8%

The only permanent offer from this inner-city Sydney operation sees Mosaic, Centennial and Chinook hops pound out a pineapple beat driving malt rhythm in this encore-demanding ale.

WILLIE WARMER

Seven Sheds, Railton, Tasmania; 6.3%

Cassia bark and star anise add greater depth to the already complex and mocha-ish maltiness of this densely rich, rustic and warming dark ale, structured with a nod toward Belgian brewing traditions.

XPA

Wolf of the Willows, Cheltenham, Victoria; 4.7%

The style space between pale ale and IPA has proved a sweet spot for a number of Australian brewers, and this wolf prowls it well. Australian and US hops with Maris Otter and wheat malts provide a cleverly balanced ale.

BREWERIES TO WATCH

BALTER

Currumbin, Queensland

The first release from this brewery – founded by a quartet of champion surfers – a fragrant and balanced pale ale called **XPA** (5%), and the follow-up brown ale **ALT** (4.8%), immediately quashed concerns about image possibly besting quality.

PIRATE LIFE

Adelaide, South Australia

Influenced by Scotland's BrewDog (*see* page 91), where the brewers apprenticed, hoppy ales abound here, with **Throwback IPA** (3.5%), **IPA** (6.8%) and **IIPA** (8.8%) each pushing the lupulin limit while managing a measure of balance.

NEW ZEALAND

If ever there were a craft beer market that has embraced its own uniqueness, it is that of New Zealand. It has defined its style through the use of native hops, welcomed nomadic or contract brewing in order to further the market in a logistically challenging land and, in the early 21st century at least, grabbed the Australasian craft brewing lead from its much larger neighbour. This combination of audacity and creativity is what has made New Zealand a potent force in Southern Hemisphere brewing.

AMBER

North End, Waikanae, Wellington; 4.4%

A New World twist on a quaffable US-style amber ale made by substituting local hops for US ones, creating a beer that is surprisingly full-bodied with dominant notes of caramel, coffee, marmalade and grapefruit.

(NUCLEAR FREE) ANZUS IPA

Croucher, Rotorua, Bay of Plenty; 7%

Named after a defunct defence alliance, this ale employs hops from the three participants – Australia, USA and New Zealand. Hop-forward and resinous, with an early taste of toffee followed by grapefruit, mango, more toffee and pine.

BOOKBINDER

Emerson's [Lion], Dunedin, Otago; 3.7%

The first beer from this veteran and venerated brewery is still a bestseller. Inspired by English best bitter and named after an early customer, Booky (as it known) is soft and balanced, with touches of caramel and stone fruit.

CAPTAIN COOKER

The Mussel Inn, Nomadic; 5%

Easily one of the most distinctive and interesting beers produced in New Zealand, enhanced with tips from the native manuka tree for a unique flavour combination of Turkish delight, honey, rosewater, caramel and ginger.

CITRA

Liberty, Riverhead, Auckland; 9%

Sharing space with Hallertau (*see* page 264) in scenic Riverhead, Liberty's Joseph Wood has developed a brewing style that is unabashedly about big aromas, flavours and bitterness, as demonstrated by this Imperial IPA behemoth exuding grapefruit, orange peel, resin, passion-fruit and pine.

COALFACE STOUT

Eagle, Christchurch, Canterbury; 6.2%

A decadent stout that utilizes nine malts, US and Kiwi hops and the famously pure Canterbury water. Roasted coffee on the nose and in the body, joined by chocolate, burned toast crusts and dark fruit.

DEADCANARY

ParrotDog, Wellington; 5.3%

Despite the outrageous name, DeadCanary is a contemporary Aotearoa pale ale (APA; *see* page 265) combining English malt with Kiwi hops, yielding ample aromas and flavours of tropical fruit, caramel, digestive biscuits and citrus zest.

DEATH FROM ABOVE

Garage Project, Wellington; 7.5%

Super-creative and prolific brewery making this "Indochine Pale Ale", which is brewed with mango, chilli, Vietnamese mint and lime juice. Fascinating flavour combination of orange, lime and herb garden, underwritten by a warming heat.

DUMP THE TRUMP

Behemoth, nomadic; 7.2%

Brewed as a protest against the US President, but this beer is no gimmick. A well-balanced US-style pale ale with a landslide of grapefruit and mango hoppy notes before a strong, clean finish.

THE DUSTY GRINGO

Deep Creek, Silverdale, Auckland; 6.8%

A rare New Zealand example of an India brown ale, with chocolate, toffee and nutty sweetness from the malt upfront, and hoppy citrus, lemongrass and fresh grass as complements.

ENFORCER

Baylands, Petone, Lower Hutt, Wellington; 6%

Balanced black IPA from a brewery that started in a suburban garage. First come notes of chocolate, vanilla and coffee along with a whiff of smoke, before a late charge of citrusy hops completes the equation.

CAN'T-MISS BREWERIES

8 WIRED

Warkworth, Northland

Brewing in a style described as "New World interpretations of Old World styles", this once New Zealand Champion Brewery pushes boundaries with beers like **iStout** (10%), a big Russian Imperial stout, luxurious with notes of chocolate, liquorice, smoke and citrus hops; **The Big Smoke** (6.2%), a porter brewed from Bamberg (Germany) smoked malt that shouts chocolate, molasses and smoke; **Tall Poppy** (7%), a balanced caramel, nutty, food-friendly red ale; and **Super Conductor** (8.88%), a punchy grapefruit and ripe orange double IPA. Look for vintage and barrel-aged releases – a speciality.

EPIC

nomadic

Making "really hoppy beers for the world to enjoy", usually with US hops, and lots of them. **Pale Ale** (5.4%) is a genuine ground-breaker with tangerine and pine, while **Armageddon I.P.A.** (6.66%) ups the ante with a gorgeous combination of grapefruit, orange and ginger over a long, dry finish. Only a 90 IBU **Hop Zombie** (8.5%) double IPA will survive Armageddon, protected as it is by layers of grapefruit, pine and toffee, while a decided change of pace is provided by **Epic Lager** (5.4%), which is balanced with floral, citrus and grain prominent.

TUATARA [DB BREWING]

Paraparaumu, Wellington

Started in a farm shed, it became the first two-time Champion Brewery of New Zealand and was purchased in early 2017. Highlights include **Mot Eureka** (5%), a fruity, grassy pilsner using four hops from the Motueka region; US-style pale ale **Tomahawk** (5.6%), which showcases orange peel and pine needles; dark hoppy ale **Amarillo** (5%), which emphasizes chocolate, peach and coffee instead; and **ITI** (3.3%), from the Maori for "small", a leader in the mid-strength category with a surprisingly flavourful character boasting tropical-fruit and toffee notes.

Blue Flower tea to create a dry and quenching brew, with grapefruit, lemon and, naturally, bitter tea to the fore.

HOPHEAD IPA

Brew Moon, Amberley, Canterbury; 5%

Operating near the small North Canterbury township of Amberley, Brew Moon is known for producing English-inspired beers. Hophead has notes of smooth orange marmalade with balance at a time when many others are going heavy on the hops.

KAURI FALLS

Hot Water, Whenuakite, Waikato; 5.2%

From a brewery located near the popular Hot Water Beach, the first Kiwi operation only to can its beer, this Aotearoa pale ale bursts with grapefruit, pine, orange and caramel flavours while remaining balanced.

FOR GREAT JUSTICE

Kereru, Upper Hutt, Wellington; 4.5%

Chris Mills created this "Wood-Fired Toasted Coconut Porter" as a celebration of beer and pizza. Pizza-oven-roasted coconut results in a mix of flavours of chocolate, burned toast and surprisingly subtle toasted coconut.

GOLD MEDAL FAMOUS

Fork & Brewer, Wellington; 4.9%

Veteran brewer Kelly Ryan is highly regarded, and his Aotearoa golden ale is a showcase for his talents, featuring punchy Kiwi hops that deliver notes of grapefruit, mango skin and pine.

LONGBOARDER

McLeod's, Waipu, Northland; 5.2%

With a name that reflects the area's surf culture, the flagship of this small brewery winning big awards is a crisp and quenching lager with subtle fruitiness, a biscuity malt backbone and lingering bitter finish.

LUXE

Hallertau, Riverhead, Auckland; 4.5%

Sometimes called Number 1 because it was the first beer produced, Luxe is a very rare example of a New Zealand *kölsch*-style beer, straw coloured with grassy notes, biscuity malt and floral hops.

GUNNAMATTA

Yeastie Boys, nomadic; 6.5%

Brewed partly in light-hearted protest against the proliferation of coffee beers, this "Tea Leaf IPA" uses Earl Grey

MILD

mike's, Urenui, Taranaki; 4%

Once lauded by Michael Jackson on a tour of the country, this long-standing dark mild is subtle and silky and certified organic, with flavour tones of coffee, nuts and toffee.

OH LORDY!

Funk Estate, Grey Lynn, Auckland; 5.5%

Funky name and funky branding for a seriously funky brewery. This Aotearoa pale ale is made with local NZ hops for a balanced and quaffable brew complete with prominent notes of passion-fruit, grape skin, grapefruit, pine needles and malt biscuits.

OYSTER STOUT

Three Boys, Christchurch, Canterbury; 6.5%

A beer that the brewer often struggles to convince people contains actual oysters, and the famous Bluff oyster at that. Complex with elements of coffee, liquorice, chocolate, smoke, molasses and leather, but never salty.

STYLE SPOTLIGHT

AOTEAROA PALE ALE

A debate rages over the proper name for pale ales made solely with New Zealand hops, contenders being Kiwi pale ale (KPA), New Zealand pale ale (NZPA) and Aotearoa (the Maori name for New Zealand) pale ale (APA; confusingly also a popular designation for the US style of pale ale).

There is, however, agreement on the critical element – the use of unique New Zealand hops, described as the key to the present and future of New Zealand craft beer. Enjoying the mild climate, rich soil and natural resistance to pests and disease, hops have flourished mainly on the South Island, including new breeds such as Nelson Sauvin, Riwaka, Motueka and Wakatu, all with notable tropical-fruit characteristics. New Zealand hops are globally popular, the amount exported having doubled in recent years.

Tuatara Kapai uses four Kiwi hops to produce notes of orange peel, grapefruit and pine, the name being Maori for "good". One of the first and best Aotearoa pale ales is **8 Wired's Hopwired** with flavours of orange, lime and the country's famous Sauvignon Blanc. **Townshend's Aotearoa Pale Ale** highlights dark stone fruit and grape skin, while **Behemoth CHUR!** bursts with grapefruit, lemon and sherbet, its name being New Zealand slang for "cheers".

PITCH BLACK

Invercargill, Invercargill, Southland;
4.5%

The country's southernmost brewery is renowned for its darker beers, including a *bock* made from malt smoked over native manuka wood. This creamy stout, on the other hand, offers flavours of burned toast crusts, milk chocolate and chewy caramel.

RED IPA

Hop Federation, Riwaka, Tasman; 6.4%

Brewers fled the rat race of Auckland for the idyllic country town of Riwaka to create this wonderfully balanced, rich mahogany brew showcasing caramel, passion-fruit, resin, melon and citrus.

RESURRECTION

Galbraith's, Auckland; 8.7%

New Zealand's first modern brewpub is renowned for traditional cask ales served on handpump. However, Resurrection is a strong, dark, abbey-style ale with a distinctly fruity, spicy Belgian nose and resplendent with burned caramel, raisin, sugar and spice.

SPARKLING ALE

Good George, Hamilton, Waikato;
4.5%

From a brewer also working for the Green Dragon pub in the "Hobbiton" *Lord of the Rings* attraction, this sparkling ale is balanced and sessionable with notes of lime peel, warm malt biscuits and fresh nectarine.

SPRUCE

Wigram, Christchurch, Canterbury; 5%

Using the 1771 recipe of Captain James Cook, explorer and first to brew in New Zealand, this is an unhopped ale flavoured by manuka and spruce. A unique and challenging beer with strong pine, molasses, honey and sherry elements.

BREWERY TO WATCH

ROCKY KNOB

nomadic

Husband and wife Stu and Bron Marshall brewing big-tasting beers like **Snapperhead** (7.4%), a double IPA rich with grapefruit and passion-fruit; **Oceanside Amber** (5.6%), with citrus and straw notes; and IPA **Hop Knob** (6%), with flavours of peach, currant and passion-fruit.

SUTTON HOO

Townshend's, Upper Moutere, Nelson; 4.7%

Previously a one-man operation that famously won the Champion Brewery of New Zealand award, but could not attend because he was working. The brewery is now growing and its amber ale offers a treasure trove of caramel, vanilla, sweet orange and nuts.

ST JOSEPHS

Moa, Blenheim, Marlborough; 9.5%

Located next to the family's Scott vineyard and helmed by Josh Scott, this larger New Zealand craft brewery produces this *tripel* with a classic flavour profile of banana, cloves, spice, caramel, citrus and funky Belgian yeast.

THREE WOLVES

Mac's [Lion], nomadic; 5.1%

Part of the Mac's range of beers, the craft brand of industry giant Lion. Approachable rather than extravagant, this accessible US-style pale ale offers notes of tropical fruit, pine and caramel.

STONECUTTER

Renaissance, Blenheim, Marlborough; 7%

Incredibly complex Scotch ale from a former Champion Brewery of New Zealand, pouring pitch black with intriguing aromas and flavours of coffee, chocolate, whisky, tanned leather, vanilla, oak, cigar ash and plum.

TWISTED ANKLE

The Twisted Hop, Wigram, Christchurch, Canterbury; 5.9%

In 2011 this brewpub had to move after the devastating Canterbury earthquakes, but it is thriving in its new location. Styled as an old ale, this pours an attractive chestnut and exhibits complex notes of roast coffee with hints of toffee and citrus.

SUPERCHARGER APA

Panhead Custom Ales [Lion], Upper Hutt, Wellington; 5.7%

Explosive growth saw the brewery purchased in 2016. Quality remains high with this flagship using US hops to produce a quaffable, bitter but balanced ale with lashings of orange peel, grass and grapefruit.

THE WOBBLY BOOT

Harrington's, Wigram, Christchurch, Canterbury; 5%

Silky-smooth, dark English-style porter from a sizeable brewery that consistently produces the largest range of beers in the country. The Boot (as it is known) exudes chocolate, cocoa and a gentle nuttiness.

ASIA & THE MIDDLE EAST

JAPAN

For most of its almost century and a half of existence, Japanese brewing has been dominated by German methods and styles, all concentrated in the hands of an ever-shrinking coterie of large breweries. That all changed in the mid-1990s, however, when an alteration in the law allowed the establishment of smaller breweries, and since that moment two waves of craft beer expansion and innovation have transformed the land of "dry beer" into Asia's most interesting beer market.

BAY PILSNER

Bay Brewing Yokohama, Yokohama, Kanagawa; 5%

A Bohemian Pilsner with crisp Saaz hops almost balancing the rich, biscuity malt. The most impressive beer so far from a small brewpub that is soon to be a much larger brewery.

BENIAKA

Coedo, Kawagoe, Saitama; 7%

Labelled an "Imperial Sweet Potato Amber" and using locally grown Kintoki sweet potatoes, Coedo's most original year-round ale is sweet and rich, with caramel and sweet potato flavours balanced mostly by the slightly high alcohol content.

BLACK ONYX

Devil Craft, Shinagawa, Tokyo; 4.8%

This oatmeal stout is one of more than 60 beers made in the first year by this trio of US brewers. Full but light, it has smooth chocolate and coffee flavours and a perfect level of roast.

CALIFORNIA COMMON

Brimmer, Kawasaki, Kanagawa; 5%

Released as an autumn seasonal, this offering from Brimmer is a rather hoppy, full-bodied version of the steam beer style, with a malty, bready nose leading to lemony hoppiness and a dry, pleasantly bitter finish.

CHAMOMILE SAISON

Talmary, Yazu, Tottori; 4.8%

Brewpub and bakery opened in 2016 in which all bread and beer is made using wild yeasts. The beers are not sour, but display a barnyard spiciness perfect in Belgian styles, as in this balanced, crisp *saison*.

CHRISTMAS ALE

Minami Shinshu, Komagane, Nagano; 7.5%

This deep amber-coloured English-style strong ale is very malty and rich, with lots of caramel, cherry and dried-fruit flavours, becoming even silkier in its aged versions.

COFFEE AMBER

Marca, Osaka; 4.7%

This brewery started in 2015 and has shown promise with IPAs and saisons, but this deep brown aromatic ale has been the most consistently impressive. Sweet notes of caramel and chocolate are enhanced by cleanly infused coffee.

CORIANDER BLACK

North Island, Ebetsu, Hokkaido; 5%

A rich stout with flavours of chocolate, coffee and tart fruit accentuated by just the right amount of coriander. A roasty and sweet but well-balanced treat from Hokkaido's most innovative brewery.

EISBOCK

Otaru, Otaru, Hokkaido; 13.5%

Oak barrel-aged to a rich, fruity and port-like character with soft carbonation and high quaffability. Brewed only for the New Year.

FRAMBOISE

Atsugi, Atsugi, Kanagawa; 8%

Established as the Japanese leader in abbey-style beers, Atsugi turned to spontaneous fermentation, beginning with this not-quite-authentically lambic-style beer. Raspberries surround a lightly sour, lactic base with a bit of emergent barnyard funk.

FUYU SHIKOMI PORTER

Oh! La! Ho, Toumi, Nagano; 5%

A hotly anticipated winter seasonal that punches far above its weight. Its hoppy, fruity aroma leads to a chocolate malt taste with cherry and grape notes and a slight roastiness.

GOYA DRY

Helios, Gushikami, Okinawa; 5%

From the largest craft brewery in Okinawa, this original lager uses local bitter melon to complement its hops,

resulting in a massive bitterness that is not for everyone, but ideally suits the Okinawan climate.

GRYESETTE

Songbird, Kisarazu, Chiba; 4.5%

Spicy, crisp *saison* with rye and some barnyardy notes, from a tiny two-year-old brewery producing mainly Belgian-inspired beers that extend to the very funky.

HARE NO HI SENNIN

Yo-Ho, Karuizawa, Nagano; ~9%

English-style barley wine from Japan's largest craft brewery, it changes every year but is typically sweet and malty with notes of toffee and treacle and light English hops. Finds its way into various barrels for ageing as well.

HARU URARA

Moku Moku, Iga, Mie; 5%

Made at an agricultural park between Nagoya and Kyoto, this is labelled an "American-style Hefeweizen". It is creamy and fruity, fragrant with citrus hops and has a crisp hoppy finish that keeps everything in order.

HEIHACHIRO

Locobeer, Sakura, Chiba; 7.5%

A rich, full-bodied Baltic porter with lots of chocolate-fudge flavour accented with cherries, soy sauce umami and a touch of smoke, from a brewery experimenting with almost every style imaginable.

BREWERIES TO WATCH

KYOTO

Kyoto

Run by three non-Japanese brewers, this brewery adeptly blends US and Belgian influences, as in **Ichii Senshin** (6.5%), IPA-like but with a Belgian sensibility, and **Ichigo Ichie** (5.9%), a well-hopped *saison*.

Y. MARKET

Nagoya, Aichi

Their abundant use of dry-hopping took Japan by storm in 2014. **Purple Sky Pale Ale** (5.6%) has a big citrus and grassy nose, while **Meiyon Lager** (5.2%) proves they can handle hugely dry-hopped lagers, too.

YOROCCO

Zushi, Kanagawa

Small but expanding brewery focused on hoppy ales like **Skywalker IPA** (5.9%), and Belgian-inspired saisons such as **Cultivator** (6%), also with standout hopping.

IMPERIAL CHOCOLATE STOUT

Sankt Gallen, Atsugi, Kanagawa; 8.5%

Released for Valentine's Day, although with no added chocolate. Six malts and four kinds of hops give a luscious chocolate and coffee taste with an exceptionally strong hop bite.

IMPERIAL STOUT

Swan Lake, Agano, Niigata; 10%

This is an impressive and surprising powerhouse from a brewery that usually does low-alcohol ales to perfection, exhibiting lots of chocolate and berry flavours with rather light roastiness and some gin-like notes.

IMPERIALITY

Anglo Japanese (AJB), Nozawa Onsen, Nagano; 9.5%

English husband and Japanese wife opened the barrel-ageing-orientated AJB in 2015, and this Imperial stout has been the star of a so-far fascinating line-up. Aged in bourbon barrels, with elements of chocolate, vanilla, coffee, pears and soy sauce.

INNKEEPER BITTER LAGER

Outsider, Kofu, Yamanashi; 6%

A brewer well known for barley wines, but this rich, full pilsner, well hopped with Tettanger hops, is the best of their everyday beers, with a herbal, grassy nose and a prickly, bitter finish.

IPA

Oze no Yukidoke, Iatebayashi, Gunma; 5%

Deep golden colour, huge grapefruit hop nose and light, crisp malts made this a winning session IPA before the style was even named. Easier to find in the USA than Japan lately.

KAGAYAKI WHEAT 7

Johana, Nanto, Toyama; 7%

The first super-hoppy beer from a brewery specializing in colourful fruit blends, this convinces with a rich, wheaty backdrop to big grapefruit, orange and tropical-fruit hop aromas and a long, bitter finish.

KARUMINA

Hida Takayama, Takayama, Gifu; 10%

From a little-appreciated brewery in a popular tourist town, this is a black barley wine with Belgian yeast, a spicy and flowery nose and flavour notes of raisins, ginger, orange, chocolate and a touch of liquorice.

BOURBON BARREL AGED RUSSIAN IMPERIAL STOUT

KAZAMATSURI STOUT

Hakone, Odawara, Kanagawa; 7.5%

A potent winter stout from just outside the Hakone National Park near Mount Fuji, with creamy chocolate and coffee tones, faint hints of tart berries and a moderately strong hop bitterness.

KIN'ONI

Oni Densetsu, Noboribestsu, Hokkaido; 5%

Brilliantly hoppy and fruity American Pale Ale, pale of hue with a crisp malt character. New batches are made with different hop combinations and can be fun to compare.

LUSH HOP IPA

Ise Kadoya, Ise, Mie; 6%

From a very experimental brewery, this ale uses US hops for huge fruitiness, spanning citrus to tropical to stone fruits, while a light sweetness and medium bitterness make it very lush and quaffable.

MAROYAKA HYUGANATSU

Hideji, Nobeoka, Miyazaki; 5%

From a brewery that focuses more on yeast and local fruits than hops, and lagers more than ales, this citrus-fruit lager exemplifies their keen ability to harmonize fruity additions with a rich, bready lager base.

CAN'T-MISS BREWERIES

BAIRD

Shuzenji, Shizuoka

Brian Baird has been brewing US ales the Japanese way since 2000. **Suruga Bay Imperial IPA** (8.5%) is a perennial favourite among Japanese hop fanatics, double dry-hopped and fermented to total dryness, while **Natsumikan Summer Ale** (6%) shows Baird's brilliance with fruit, as mandarin orange enhances the ale rather than overwhelming it. **West Coast Wheat Wine** (10%) is sweet, fruity and wine-like, but finishes dry and strong.

FUJIZAKURA HEIGHTS

Kawaguchiko, Yamanashi

From *weizen* to *rauchbier* to pilsner, no one in Japan does German beer styles better than Hiromichi Miyashita at Fujizakura. **Weizen** (5.5%) is creamy and sweet, fruity and spicy, whereas **Roppongi Draft #1** (6.6%), a pale *weizenbock*, is hoppier with notes of orange and peaches, and winter seasonal **Rauch Bock** (7%) is smoky, sweet and meaty. A new taproom in Tokyo's Roppongi district makes the brewery easily accessible to travellers.

MIOBIKI WHEAT IPA

Ushitora, Shimotsuke, Tochiqi; 6.4%

Ushitora made over 150 mostly dry and hoppy beers in its first two years. This wheat IPA, while bursting with tropical-fruit aromas from the hops, is set apart by its juicy sweetness and fuller body.

MUISHIKI NO SHOUNIN

Kazakami, Kawasaki, Kanagawa; 8%

"Unconscious Assent" is a generously spiced Imperial porter from a young brewery specializing in strong and mostly spiced beers. Christmassy with notes of chocolate brownie, clove and orange.

NAGOYA AKAMISO LAGER

Kinshachi, Inuyama, Aichi; 6%

A *dunkel* with local miso paste added, it tastes lightly roasty and meaty with lots of umami and body from the miso.

NINE-TAILED FOX

Nasu Kohgen, Nasu, Tochigi; 11%

This expensive, long-aged barley wine has a sherry-like aroma with caramel and lots of fruity esters. Remarkably smooth with an alcoholic heat that diminishes with ageing.

NIPPONIA

Hitachino Nest, Konosu, Ibaraki; 6.5%

Golden lager made with native Kaneko Golden barley and Sorachi Ace hops, with a lemony, oaky, vanilla character. Perhaps the best of this well-known brewery's originals, and one of the first beers to popularize the hop.

OYSTER STOUT

Iwate Kura, Ichinoseki, Iwate; 7%

First and best of the Japanese oyster stouts, this is a creamy, velvety brew with ample umami from the oyster meat and shells in the boil. Silky and full mouthfeel, with elements of coffee, chocolate and cream.

PHARAOH SMOKED PORTER

Bell, Tokorozawa, Saitama; 5.5%

Whoever thought that malt-produced flavours of bacon, smoked salmon and chocolate could go together so well? A beer with strong smoke, great umami and high drinkability from a brewery opened in 2015.

PILSNER

Inuyama Loreley, Inuyama, Aichi; 5%

A sake maker that started with German-style beers and is now also making US-style ales, but whose best beer is still this standard pilsner, with lemony, grassy noble hops supported by a bready malt backbone.

PILSNER

Nihonkai Club, Noto, Ishikawa; 5%

A very Bohemian-style pilsner made by a Czech brewer at the tip of the Noto Peninsula. Rich biscuity malt character via decoction mash is balanced excellently by the aroma of plentiful Zatec hops.

CAN'T-MISS BREWERIES

MINOH

Minoh, Osaka

Kaori Oshita and her two sisters have been brewing Osaka's best-loved home-town beers for 20 years, including the soft, chocolaty, multi-award-winning **Stout** (5.5%). **W-IPA** (9%), pronounced "Double IPA", was the first high-alcohol hoppy beer in Japan, and its caramel maltiness is still convincing. **Yuzu White** (6%), a *witbier* made with locally grown citrus, is a fruity winter favourite.

SHIGA KOGEN

Yamanouchi, Nagano

Has been making dry, hoppy beers in US and Belgian styles since 2004. **Sono Juu** (7.5%), their 10th Anniversary IPA, uses Miyama-nishiki sake rice (*see* page 276) for a crisp, light palate that lets the hops shine. **Takashi Imperial Stout** (9%) is dark and fruity, with notes of soy sauce and chocolate; versions aged in Ichiro's Malt barrels are especially coveted. **Yamabushi Saison 1** (6.5%), sold in 75cl bottles, has Miyama-nishiki replacing Belgian candi sugar and is also made in occasional, and much-desired, fruit-, brett- and barrel-aged versions.

SHONAN

Chigasaki, Kanagawa

Based at the Kumazawa Sake Brewery, Shonan makes three German-style beers year round, but their vast array of seasonals and one-offs is more in the US mould. **Imperial Stout** (8%) carries a big punch, with roasted, oily, umami-laden malts and a burned, bitter finish; **Belgian Stout** (7%) is a bit milder, focusing more on sweet chocolate and balanced spicing; and **IPA** (6%) appears variously in different guises, with over 35 versions mixing hops, yeasts and even grains and fruits.

STYLE SPOTLIGHT

JAPANESE BEERS WITH A SAKE INFLUENCE

Sake, the original beer of Japan, has been made from rice for over 2,000 years, yet even as drinkers around the world are discovering today's better-than-ever sake, it is losing market share domestically. Hence the reason that many sake breweries are expanding into craft beer, leading to the emergence of a new domestic style of sake-influenced beers.

Various aspects of sake making can be employed in beer production. Possibly the easiest is the use of sake rice as an additive, where it plays a more prominent role than when employed as an adjunct in industrial lagers. **Yago** from Daisen G is made with sake rice and Belgian yeast for a crisp, spicy and fruity take on a *witbier*. Similar is **Konishi Howaka**, a delicate and fruity low-alcohol *wit*. Sake yeast can ferment beer as well, imparting distinct flavours in the process, as in **Umenishiki Sokujo**, which uses ginjo yeast with barley malt and tastes more like a sake than a beer. **Orochi**, a "rice barley wine"

from Shimane Beer Company, uses both sake rice and yeast, the brewery collaborating annually with a different sake maker to produce a startlingly different brew each time. **Hitachino Nest Japanese Classic Ale** is an IPA aged in cedar sake barrels, and in the extreme case, sake and beer can be blended, as in **Kuninocho Kijo Gold**, wherein dry-hopped junmai sake is added to their golden ale.

In the near future, sake-influenced beers may well be seen as the first original Japanese beer style.

PLUM WHEAT

T.Y. Harbor, Shinagawa, Tokyo; 4%

An older brewery that is making waves with fruit beers and kettle-soured ales. Although traditionally fermented, the plums provide a tart juiciness similar to that of a *Berliner weisse* balanced by mild, fruity sweetness.

PORTER

Campion, Asakusa, Tokyo; 4.9%

This small brewpub in touristy Asakusa serves British-style ales straight from bright tanks, low in carbonation and very authentic, like this black, light porter with a bit of tangy fruit and roasty chocolate malt.

PRINZ

Bayern Meister, Fujinomiya, Shizuoka; 5%

Made close to Mount Fuji by a Bavarian brewer who does all things German well, this flagship pilsner is in the southern German style with rich, sweet, bready malt being well balanced by grassy hoppiness.

RASPBERRY

Harvestmoon, Maihama, Chiba; 6%

An original fruit beer, dry but not sour, that uses Champagne yeast in a secondary fermentation. Its rich, jammy raspberry nose becomes unexpectedly dry, clean and minerally with just enough fruit sweetness to keep it fun.

RAUCH

Tazawako, Senboku, Akita; 7.5%

Nearly *bock*-like richness and body make this one of the nicest rauchbiers in Japan, with a smoky caramel and molasses aroma and a lovely smoky, woody flavour. Ageing renders it as smooth as silk.

SAKURA KOBO ALE

Chateau Kamiya, Ushiku, Ibaraki; 7%

Fermented with yeast from cherry blossom, this is fruity and also funky, with cherry notes and a wild, tart, barnyard character. Cherry yeast beers are multiplying in Japan.

SEYA NO KOMUGI

Yokohama, Yokohama, Kanagawa; 5.5%

An ale using local wheat, this is neither exactly German, Belgian nor US in style, with clove notes from the yeast, biscuity wheat malt, and citrus from the hops.

SHIMANOWA

Kure, Kure, Hiroshima; 5%

A lager hopped as an IPA from a brewery adept at lagers of all sorts, the lemon, orange and peach aromas coming from US hops, which are backed up by crisp, crackery pilsner malt.

STEAM LAGER

Aqula, Akita, Akita; 5%

From a brewery adept at both lagers and ales, hybrid fermentation reveals deep orange, grapefruit and peach flavours in a relatively full-bodied beer that showcases spicy, peppery hops.

STOUT

Chatan Harbor, Chatan, Okinawa; 4.5%

From a promising brewery that opened in 2016 at a beach resort near Japan's US military base, this thick oatmeal stout has a full body with rich chocolate and soy sauce notes, making it seem stronger than it really is.

TROPICAL WEIZEN STRONG

Mojiko Retro, Kitakyushu, Fukuoka; 7.5%

A massively fruity blond *weizenbock* from a brewery doing German styles well. Rich tropical-fruit flavours from generous amounts of Nelson Sauvin and Cascade hops are almost shocking in their ability to blend with banana and clove tones.

URSUS

Baeren, Morioka, Iwate; 7%

A velvety smooth blond *weizenbock* with rich notes of cream, melon, banana and clove. This northern Honshu brewer is a local favourite that is an expert with German styles, and experiments with many others as well.

VOLCANO

Kisoji, Kiso, Nagano; 9.7%

Strongest beer made to date from this brewery in a hot springs hotel, toffee-apple red with sweet cherry and citrus tones and a hugely bitter and earthy finish. The one-year-aged version is silkier and less sweet.

WEIZEN

Zakkoku Kobo, Ogawa-Machi, Saitama; 5%

This "Miscellaneous Grains" brewery uses home-grown rye and millet to give a tart, grainy edge to their rich wheat beer's typical banana and clove notes.

WHEAT WINE

Daisen G, Sailiaku, Iottori; 9%

A winter special from Daisen G in western Honshu, this golden brew is wine-like and powerful, with spicy aromas of wheat, pears, bananas and cloves, and a strongly hoppy finish to balance its sweetness.

WORLD DOWNFALL STOUT

Thrash Zone, Yokohama, Kanagawa; 7.6%

As yet the only dark beer from a thrash metal bar and brewery specializing in IPAs. A roasty, chocolaty foreign-export-sized stout with sweetness upfront and a roasted, bitter finish.

YUKYU NO TOKI

Akashi, Akashi, Hyōgo; 5%

A creamy, dry *schwarzbier* from a brewery right on the Seto Inland Sea specializing in German-style beers. With lots of chocolate and coffee flavour, this finishes dry and softly bitter.

CHINA

The world's largest producer of beer by a great margin, brewing as much as the next three largest brewing nations combined, China is also potentially the great disruptor, since the country's per capita consumption is still low compared with the developed beer lands. If the initial stirrings of craft beer interest blossom into more widespread appeal, the strain it could put on hop and malt supplies might be considerable.

CAPTAIN IPA

Urbräu, Handan, Hebei; 6.8%

An IPA built in the classic US style, this has a complex, hop-fuelled aroma featuring floral and citrus–spicy notes before a body that boasts a soft maltiness, layered over the top with crisp hop bitterness.

DUGITE VANILLA STOUT

The Brew, Shanghai; 5%

Black in colour, this creamy stout mixes a rich maltiness with flavours from real vanilla pods to produce a smooth, full-bodied, creamy vanilla character with hints of dark chocolate to round it all out nicely.

CAN'T-MISS BREWERIES

• • • • • • • • • • • • •

BOXING CAT [AB INBEV]

Shanghai

China's first and still most influential craft brewery, and also the country's first international medal winner, with the toffee-ish **Ringside Red** (5%) amber lager winning a silver medal at the World Beer Cup 2016. Other year-round beers include **Contender Extra Pale Ale** (4.9%), golden and lightly hopped with a fruity character; the light and thirst-quenching **Right Hook Helles** (4.5%), with a pleasingly soft bitterness; and **TKO IPA** (6.3%), aromatic and, for Chinese beer, both strong and well hopped.

SLOW BOAT

Beijing

One of the Chinese capital's first breweries – the main brewery is on the city's outskirts, the newer brewpub and taproom both more central – and one of its most reliable. Regular brands include the sweet, floral and dry-finishing **The Helmsman's Honey Ale** (6%), flagship **Captain's Pale Ale** (5.5%), with preserved-lemon notes and a very dry finish, and **Monkey's Fist IPA** (5.75%), with mango and other tropical-fruit tones. Watch for seasonal specialities like densely cocoa-ish **Sea Level Chocolate Sea Salt Stout** (7.1%).

KOJI RED ALE

Jing-A, Beijing; 5.5%

Innovative approach by a pair of expat brewers, one American and the other Canadian, using koji rice, wasabi and ginger to create a unique, lightly sweet, earthy, spicy-peppery ale.

KUDING PALE ALE

Panda Brew, Beijing; 6.5%

Made with the Traditional Chinese Medicine herb that gives the beer its name, this has a strongly herbal aroma and a fascinating bitterness, different than one would get from the use of hops alone.

KUNGFU PEPPER

Zinnbath, Jinan, Shandong; 5.2%

An unusual lager brewed with Chinese Sichuan peppers to produce a unique peppery aroma and a clean and

BREWERY TO WATCH

SHANGRI-LA HIGHLAND

Shangri-la, Yunnan

Producing six different beers at over 3,300 metres (10,800 feet) above sea level, including **Yalaso** (3.1%) and **Son Gha** (5.2%), both lagers brewed from heirloom Qingke barley.

surprisingly unpeppery, malty palate accompanied by medium bitterness.

LITTLE GENERAL IPA

Great Leap; Beijing; 6.5%

Made with whole cone hops from China, of a variety known as Qingdao Flower, which give it a vaguely citrus-peel but mostly floral hoppiness that blends well with the fruity malt.

TENGYUN WHEAT ALE

Fengshou, Chengdu, Sichuan; 5%

A gentle fragrance of banana and coriander announces this summery thirst-quencher, with yeasty notes of bitter orange and other strongly aromatic fruits occupying the body.

TIAO DONG HU

No 18, Wuhan, Hubei; 5.5%

Award-winning US-style IPA featuring tropical-fruit hop aromas and fruity malt supporting a gradually growing hop bitterness that culminates in a flavoursome bitter and lingering finish.

SOUTH KOREA

Hampered for years by laws that limited their number rather severely, South Korean craft breweries have flourished since the repeal of those laws and are now beginning to catch up in terms of quality, consistency and creativity as well. A bet against the country's beer scene yet developing into one of Asia's most interesting would be ill-advised indeed.

KUKMIN IPA

The Booth, Seongnam-si, Gyeonggi-do; 7%

Born as a small alleyway pub with a single contract-brewed beer, this growing operation now boasts an expanding portfolio of own beers and collaborations, including this IPA with a crisp malt palate that lets its well-structured hoppiness shine.

MOONRISE PALE ALE

Galmegi, Suyeong-gu, Busan; 5%

This brewery with four taprooms in Busan is known for its uncompromisingly hoppy beers, but credit is also deserved for their well-balanced pale ale with a peppery citrus nose and zesty, quenching palate.

SLOW IPA

The Hand and Malt, Hwado-eup, Gyeonggi-do; 4.5%

At the high end of strength for its declared "session IPA" style, this is nonetheless a fragrant, appealingly floral and eminently quaffable ale from an already sound and still fast-improving brewery.

STOUT

Gorilla, Gwanganhaebyeon-ro, Busan; 6.3%

In any young craft beer culture there is a need for breweries that present straightforward beers like this somewhat light-bodied, well-structured ebony ale with mocha notes layered over a simple base of roasted maltiness.

THE LAST TRAIN

Magpie, Jeju-si, Jeju-do; 8%

Born a nomadic brewer, Magpie found a permanent home for their fine ales in a disused fruit packaging plant on Jeju Island in 2016, including this silky, rounded, sweetly chocolaty and stronger take on their core Porter.

BREWERY TO WATCH

GOODMAN

Guri-si, Gyeonggi-do

A young brewery outside of Seoul making creative beers from the get-go, such as a Pinot Noir–barrel-aged **Garden Saison** (5.5%), a chocolate–caramel, London-style **Seoul Porter** (5.1%) and an aromatic **Table Beer Pale** (3.1%) made with a rotating schedule of hops.

TAIWAN

Of all Asia's still-underdeveloped beer lands, Taiwan and perhaps South Korea hold the greatest promise for the future, with active and collaborative home-brewing cultures giving rise to ambitious commercial-brewing concerns. That said, Taiwan is also, like most of Asia outside of Japan, significant more for its potential than for its creative and impressive present.

#1 PALE ALE

23, New Tapei City; 5.5%

From an expat US brewer, this offers tea-like hop aromas with earthy qualities and a citrusy, floral complexity with a firm, lingering bitterness – although deliberately made slightly less bitter to suit the Taiwanese palate.

AMBER ALE BREWED WITH DRIED LONGAN

55th Street, Taoyuan City; 5.5%

One of Taiwan's smallest breweries produces this amber ale with prominent smoky fruit flavours from the use of smoked and dried longan fruit. Smooth and nutty in its maltiness, with a pleasant minerality in the finish.

THE CACAO FOUNTAIN CACAO PORTER

Indie Brew, Taoyuan City; 6.9%

A well-crafted porter from Indie Brew providing layers of roasted malt and complex chocolate notes, a rounded mouthfeel and a sweetness that avoids becoming cloying.

GOKUAKU WHEAT BEER

Shodoiji, Taoyuan City; 5%

This slightly hazy wheat beer pours with a generous foam and bready aromatics. Despite a slightly grainy profile, it is well balanced with medium acidity and a somewhat creamy texture.

HONEY LAGER

Dingmalt, New Taipei City; 7%

Companion to the brewery's German-style *kellerbier* specialities, this lager is deep gold with alluring honey aromas, piney, fruity complexity and a warming finish.

LONGAN HONEY LAGER

Radiant, New Taipei City; 6%

Made in small quantities due to the limited availability of the speciality honey used in its recipe, this has a fragrant and floral nose, firm yet smooth bitterness and a drying, thirst-quenching finish with long, honeyed malt flavours.

MANEKI NEKO PUMPKIN ALE

Sunmai, New Taipei City; 5–5.5%

From Sunmai, one of the leading brewers in Taiwan, this beer has a spicy complexity, yet remains refreshingly light for the style – a summery interpretation of an autumnal beer.

PANGU ALE

Prost 12, Zhubei City; 6.7%

Slightly hazy with fresh citrusy hop aromas, this offers firm bitterness in balance with gentle malty flavours and fruitiness, drying on the finish with grapefruity notes. Crisp, delicate and highly quaffable.

PASSION MOSAIC

A Brewers Team, nomadic; 5.6%

Created under contract by a talented home-brewer, this summer thirst-quencher has attractive citrusy and passion-fruit aromas, gentle herbal tones and a light, refreshing body with firm fruitiness in the finish.

330ml
ALE 5.5%

REALITY AMERICAN PALE ALE

WAXY RICE ALE

Taiwan Ale, New Taipei City; 4.5%

From a brewery with a focus on creating original recipes using local ingredients, including various kinds of rice, comes this ale with a smooth and creamy texture, fruity and bready body and lingering, off-dry finish.

WOO BEER – SANDALWOOD FLAVOUR BEER

North Taiwan, Taoyuan City; 6%

Initially brewed for the Woobar cocktail lounge bar and made available commercially, this speciality amber ale has smoky, woody, spicy complexity, and is remarkably refreshing.

REALITY AMERICAN PALE ALE

Beer Farm, Taoyuan City; 5.5%

Based on a home-brewing competition winner, this is a refreshingly light pale ale with citrusy and piney hop flavours, moderate bitterness balanced by biscuit malt and a drying, lingering finish.

SOUTH GATE SCHWARZBIER

3000 Brewseum, Hengchun, Pingtung; 4.9%

Produced at a brewpub below a beer museum, hence the brewery name, this is refined, balanced, long and complex, close to a world classic in quality and one of Brewseum's best.

TAIWAN RAUCHBIER

Taiwan Head Brewers, nomadic; 5.5%

With refined smoky flavours well balanced by sweet and nutty maltiness, this beer finishes dry without any undue harshness from the smoke and a lingering minerality.

VIETNAM

Alongside traditions of brewing "yellow" and "black" beers, effectively interpretations of *světlý ležák* and *tmavý ležák* imported from the Czech Republic, and the country's own light, fresh *bia hoi* beers, Vietnam is now beginning to witness impressive growth in craft brewing. While it is still early days, we will watch anxiously to see what distinctly Vietnamese beers may yet emerge.

BIA HOI

HABECO, Hanoi; 3.5%

The name for both Vietnam's famous light beer, brewed from malt, rice, sugar and hops, and the street-side establishments that serve it. One of the best of the many brands available in Vietnam.

BLACK BEER

Goldmalt, Hanoi and other locations; ~5%

For over 10 years, this company has been opening small brewpubs around the country, now 20 in number, all of them brewing this Czech-inspired lager with notes of coffee and chocolate and a dry, nutty finish.

CAN'T-MISS BREWERY
● ● ● ● ● ● ● ● ● ● ● ● ● ● ●

FURBREW

Hanoi

Opened in 2016 and with plans for up to 40 different beers in 2017. Danish brewer Thomas Bilgram produces experimental beers like the seasonal **Yuletide 2016** (8.3%), complex with sweet maltiness and a spicy nose, and **Boston Rose** IPA (7.3%), flavoured with rose pellets for Valentine's Day, as well as more conventional ales, such as **Hoa IPA** (7.3%) with lightly malty and citrus notes, and nine other regular offerings.

BLONDE LAGER

Hoa Vien, Hanoi and other locations; ~5%

From a brewery producing Czech-style lager in multiple locations; amber and floral with hints of grapefruit.

FAR EAST IPA

East West, Ho Chi Minh City; 6.7%

A full-bodied IPA with aroma and flavour notes of citrus, tropical fruit and pine, courtesy of the Nelson Sauvin and Centennial hops used.

FARMER'S WEIZEN

Barett, Hanoi; 5.5%

From Siebel-Institute-educated brewer Quang Van comes this fruity and effervescent *hefeweizen* with a light body, fruity character and lemongrass and apricot finish.

BREWERY TO WATCH

EAST WEST

Ho Chi Minh City

Head brewer Sean Thommen's US roots are evident in beers like **Coffee Vanilla Porter** (7%), with toffee-ish coffee and vanilla flavours, the darkly fruity **Independence Stout** (12%) and raspberry and citrus **Saigon Rosé** (3%).

JASMINE IPA

Pasteur Street, Ho Chi Minh City; 6.5%

As true to type an IPA as Vietnam has to offer; malty with notes of citrus and a bitterness that you expect from a US-style IPA.

LOST-AT-SEA DOUBLE IPA

Lac, Ho Chi Minh City; 8.5%

A rare Vietnamese double IPA, this juicy ale is suffused with hops for an aroma and flavour thick with lemony, grapefruity and orangey tones.

LÙN MÀ LÁO BLONDE ALE

BiaCraft, Ho Chi Minh City; 5.2%

The name translates to "Short but Arrogant", which sums up the gentle yet firm approach of this golden ale with a lightly malty body and floral hop notes.

PALE ALE

Platinum, Ho Chi Minh City; 4.6%

One of Vietnam's first widely available craft beers, initially marketed in trendy clubs, this is an approachable ale with a light body and modest hoppiness.

PATIENT WILDERNESS WHEAT ALE

Heart of Darkness, Ho Chi Minh City; 4.5%

A recent arrival to the local beer scene, one of this young brewery's first efforts was this banana-y *hefeweizen* with a gentle bitterness and fruit-forward flavour.

ISRAEL

For obvious reasons, there is not a lot of brewing underway in the Middle East. Of what relatively little there is, however, Israel is the undisputed leader, its way paved over the past decade or so by US-influenced breweries like Dancing Camel.

ADMONIT

Malka, Yehiam, Upper Galilee; 5.5%

One of Israel's most popular and widely available craft beers, this quaffable, medium-bodied pale ale has considerable caramel malt sweetness, mellow bitterness, lively carbonation and a touch of coriander.

BAZELET PILSNER

Golan, Katzrin, Golan Heights; 4.9%

This German-style pilsner from Golan Brewery is crisp and refreshing, with a floral aroma, clean malt flavours, sharp but tamed bitterness and a light body. Not completely filtered and highly thirst quenching.

BLACK

Alexander, Emek Hefer, Central Israel; 7%

This acclaimed robust and chocolaty porter is a winter seasonal that carries a full body, creamy texture and a couple of international gold medals. Rich malt character and earthy hops help define this hearty beer.

DARK LAGER

Jem's, Petach Tikva, Central Israel; 5%

This amber-hued Munich-style *dunkel* is light-bodied and balanced, with pleasant toasty and biscuity malt flavours and a gentle noble hop aroma. Clean, mellow and quaffable.

DARK MATTER

HaShakhen, nomadic; 5.5%

Even with occasional hop substitutions based upon availability, this black IPA features a bold but well calculated hoppy character, balanced with highly roasted malt flavours and an agreeable approachability.

EMBARGO

Herzl, Jerusalem; 6%

A unique porter based on an award-winning home-brew recipe, brewed with Cuban tobacco leaves. Loaded with cocoa and vanilla aromas, powered by fresh herbal flavours and with a moderately full body.

JACK'S WINTER ALE

Shapiro, Beit Shemesh, Jerusalem; 8.2–8.5%

Probably the country's most anticipated winter seasonal is a strong Belgian-inspired ale conditioned on Jack Daniels-soaked oak chips. Lots of woody and bourbon-ish flavours add complexity to the rich maltiness and fruity banana esters.

PATRIOT

Dancing Camel, Tel Aviv; 5.2%

A citrusy US-influenced pale ale brewed since the very early days of this first-ever Israeli craft brewery. Rich with American hop aromas and flavours, backed by a clean biscuity body.

PUMPKIN ALE

Galil, Moran, Lower Galilee; 5.1%

This sought-after autumn seasonal from Galil Brewery is Israel's only pumpkin beer, released once a year on Hallowe'en. Brewed with baked pumpkin chunks, pumpkin-pie spices and floral hops, it is sweet without being cloying and highly enjoyable.

RONEN THE UGLY BEER

Srigim, Li On, Jerusalem; 6.5%

A heavily hopped IPA that combines the attractive fruity and piney aromas of US hops with high bitterness and enough caramel malt to support it all. Intentionally somewhat out of balance, but quite irresistible.

REST OF ASIA & THE MIDDLE EAST

Most Asian nations aside from those already featured are notable more for their potential than their current craft beer reality. They range from countries with nascent though laudably ambitious brewing markets, such as India, to those with established, superior mass-produced brands that may in time beget the growth of even more interesting beers from a new generation of craft breweries, for example Cambodia. Until such potential is realized, we highlight a few of the important existing labels.

CAMBODIA

ABC EXTRA STOUT

Cambodia [Heineken], Phnom Penh; 8%

Brewed under licence to varying strengths in at least five Asian countries, this thick, sweet, somewhat burned-tasting and aniseed-accented stout paved the way for similarly styled beers from several as yet not as accomplished breweries.

SRI LANKA

STOUT

Lion (Ceylon), Biyagama, Western Province; 8.8%

Widely exported, this inky black stout is characterized by notes of tar in the aroma and a sweet, faintly lactic body offering flavours of chocolate, aniseed and burned herbs. Also known Sinha Stout.

THAILAND

DUNKEL

Tawandang, Bangkok; 4.5%

The best of the trio of beers produced at this showstopper brewery and beer hall with three locations of varying enormity. Chocolaty and off-dry, it has a broadly toasty character with a nuttiness that emerges as the beer warms.

LEBANON

LEBANESE PALE ALE

961 Beer/Gravity, Mazraat Yachoua, Mount Lebanon; 6.3%

Brewed with Lebanese flavours such as sumac, sage and mint, the dry, almost woody entry of this unique pale ale leads to a balanced body with a bracing, herbal dryness and a nutty maltiness.

AFRICA

SOUTH AFRICA

Far and away the African continent's leader in brewing, South Africa is not only the birthplace of part of what is now the world's largest brewing company – the former SABMiller part of AB InBev – but also the sole African nation that can boast rapidly developing craft beer culture. Hopes are that its influence will continue to spread north.

1912 APA

Clarens Brewery, Clarens, Free State; 4.5%

Of the extensive range of beers served in this small-town brewpub, this US-style pale ale, with peach, passion-fruit and toffee flavours vying for top spot, is the most memorable.

COCONUT IPA

Afro Caribbean, Cape Town, Western Cape; 6%

While experimental, one-off beers are the speciality here, and their flagship ale, with plenty of body, a subtle hit of toasted coconut and a long bitter finish, is the go-to pint.

BONE CRUSHER

Darling Brewery, Darling, Western Cape; 5.2%

Of the vast range produced at this not-to-be-missed brewery, the well-spiced *witbier* stands out for its heady perfumed aroma.

EXTRA PALE UIL

Aegir Project, Noordhoek, Western Cape; 3.8%

The lightest and perhaps cleverest of a strong range from a small husband-and-wife team with real talent. A hoppy, surprisingly full, fruity summer ale.

GUARDIAN PALE ALE

Citizen, nomadic; 5%

The star in the line-up of this Cape Town contract brewery is a well-balanced quaffer, light in body with notes of biscuit, toffee, grapefruit and gooseberries.

THE GUZZLER

Mad Giant, Johannesburg, Gauteng; 4.8%

Johannesburg's must-visit city-centre brewery boasts a solid core range, but this citrusy, dry-hopped pilsner steals the show.

LOXTON LAGER

Humanbrew, Johannesburg, Gauteng; 5.3%

With great whiffs of blackcurrant and mint and flavours to match, this is a singularly South African brew spiced with a secret blend of endemic herbs.

ICONIC BREWERY

DEVIL'S PEAK

Cape Town, Western Cape

Leading the way in the South African craft beer scene, Devil's Peak has legendary status among local beer aficionados. The exceptional **The King's Blockhouse IPA** (6%) is packed with grapefruit and lychee aromas, while the **Pale Ale** (4%) offers an approachable taste of hops. The superlative **Black IPA** (6%), with its pungent pine aroma, is usually only available at the Devil's Peak taproom, where you can also sample barrel-aged experimental brews, including the outstanding **Vannie Hout** (7.5%), a complex *Brettanomyces*-influenced *saison* with characteristic barnyard character.

MJÖLNIR IPA

Anvil Ale, Dullstroom, Mpumalanga; 6%

One of the country's most highly regarded IPAs, this packs a tropical-fruit punch, with the passion-fruit and peach backed up by a subtle but noticeable touch of toffee.

MR BROWNSTONE

Woodstock, Cape Town, Western Cape; 5.2%

The showstopper in this inner-city Cape Town brewery's much-lauded seasonal range is an almost chewy autumnal ale offering equal doses of chocolate, hazelnut and long-lasting hop bitterness.

PALE ALE

Striped Horse, nomadic; 5.2%

Contract brewed in the Winelands region and served at a seaside pub in Cape Town, toffee, breadiness and tangerine notes are served up in equal amounts in this refreshing amber brew.

SOWETO GOLD SUPERIOR LAGER

UBuntu Kraal, Soweto, Gauteng; 5.2%

Produced in one of the most culturally and historically important cities in South Africa, this amber-coloured lager is darker and sweeter than many of its peers, but still delivers a crisp, refreshing finish.

CAN'T-MISS BREWERIES

CAPE

Paarl, Western Cape

Best known for its German-style brews, this award-winning brewery also produces highly hopped ales plus seasonal and speciality beers. The go-to is the **Pilsner** (5.2%), beautifully balanced with biscuity aromas and a bitter, spicy finish, while of the various weissbiers, **Krystal Weiss** (5%) stands out for its banana-bread character and clean, crisp finish. In season, try the caramel-laden **Oktoberfest** (6.1%), or year round seek a coveted bottle of **Cape of Good Hops** (7.5%), a double IPA with heavy hits of gooseberry and passion-fruit.

JACK BLACK'S

Cape Town, Western Cape

After nine years of contract brewing, one of South Africa's largest and best-established brands has opened its own brewery. The flagship **Brewers Lager** (5%) is a quaffable and accessible all-malt brew, while the new **Keller Pils** (5%) offers complexity and superb balance. At the boozier end of the scale, **Skeleton Coast** (6.6%) is a more malt-forward IPA than most.

VALVE RIOT

Cape Town, Western Cape; 5.0%

Lashings of grapefruit, a mild hint of caramel and a long bitter finish are the hallmarks of this medium-bodied, golden-hued IPA showcasing South Africa's Southern Passion hop.

WEIZEN

Brauhaus am Damm, Rustenburg, North West; 4.5%

Orange-gold and topped with a crown of fluffy white foam, this is one of the country's top weissbiers, with a prominent banana aroma and background notes of spice and freshly baked bread.

BREWERIES TO WATCH

DRIFTER

Cape Town, Western Cape

Passionate owner Nick Bush brings a level of inspiring innovation to a core range that includes the excellent **Scallywag IPA** (6%) and the subtle, biscuity **Stranded Coconut** (4.5%), plus a series of experimental brews.

FRASER'S FOLLY

Bredasdorp, Western Cape

Owned by a boutique winery but brewer-led, making a light but big-tasting Anglo-pointing **Pale Ale** (3.7%) and **Stout** (5.4%), with new efforts in the pipeline, heralded by **Dark Continent Moer Koffie Condensed Milk Stout** (5%).

MOUNTAIN

Worcester, Western Cape

Brewery destination in an idyllic rural setting, already turning heads with off-style winners like Belgian *alt* **Cape Kraken** (4.8%), *tripel-hefeweizen* **Madala's Gold** (6.8%) and wheaty porter **Black or White** (5.2%), with more to come.

REST OF AFRICA

While the first rumblings of craft beer development have been felt in various parts of Africa, we have found little thus far that excites beyond the simple pleasure of discovering a moderately characterful summer ale or wheat beer among a sea of remarkably pedestrian light lagers. It is our hope and cautious belief that the beers below are merely the harbinger of much better and more exciting things to come.

ETHIOPIA

GARDEN BRÄU BLONDY

Beer Garden Inn, Addis Ababa; 4.5%

The country's older better-end brewery produces a reliable and fulsome, *Reinheitsgebot*-compliant, Hallertau-hopped, hazy light draught *helles* from handsome German coppers.

MOZAMBIQUE

LAURENTINA PRETA

Cervejas De Moçambique [AB InBev], Maputo; 5%

In a sea of pale lagers, this deep brown *dunkel*, with a dose of caramel, a note of chocolate and a palate-cleansing bitterness, stands out as Mozambique's most flavourful beer.

NAMIBIA

URBOCK

Namibian Breweries, Windhoek; 7%

Brewed just once a year, this rich wintry brew is brimming with treacle toffee, toasted bread, a touch of liquorice and just a hint of alcoholic warmth.

INDEX

CONTRIBUTOR BIOGRAPHIES

Christian Andersen is a journalist, communications consultant and beer blogger at durst.nu/. He also writes and reviews for various print media, serves as a member of the board for the Danish Beer Enthusiasts consumer group and is an instigator of the New Nordic Beer movement.

Max Bahnson was born in Argentina and moved to the Czech Republic in 2002. He blogs under the pen name of Pivní Filosof, "Beer Philosopher", and is the author of *Prague: A Pisshead's Pub Guide* and co-author with Alan McLeod of *The Unbearable Nonsense of Craft Beer*.

Jay R Brooks has been writing about beer for over 25 years and currently writes a syndicated newspaper column, "Brooks on Beer". His most recent book is *California Breweries North* . He is also president of the North American Guild of Beer Writers.

Phil Carmody and **Anna Shefl** sample, review, judge and enjoy beers, while also striving to advance the Baltic beer landscape through their consulting with breweries, restaurants and other businesses. They aim to encourage awareness of the developing landscape and appreciation of tradition.

Lucy Corne has written two books on South African beer and pens a popular blog documenting all things beer in southern Africa at brewmistress.co.za/. Lucy lives with her husband and son in Cape Town where she also helps to run the local home-brewing club.

John Duffy lives in Dublin and has been blogging as The Beer Nut since 2005. When not engaged in the Sisyphean task of keeping track of the modern Irish beer scene, he travels and writes about what he finds to drink there.

Per Forsgren is a Swedish beer enthusiast and ratebeer. com administrator who has been documenting beer on the web and in magazines since the early 1990s, both in his home country and during his worldwide travels now spanning more than 100 countries.

Jonathan Gharbi is the author of *Beer Guide to Vietnam* and has also written articles about beer for various magazines. He opened the first craft brewery in Burkina Faso (Brasserie Artisanale de Ouagadougou), but is now brewing in Morocco.

João Gonçalves is the owner of Portugal's leading craft beer site, Cerveja Artesanal Portuguesa (cervejaartesanalportuguesa.pt), and a contributor to Cerveja Depressão (cervejadepressao.wordpress.com), a humorous beer review blog. In his free time, he works as a Project Manager for a Portuguese Internet company.

Shachar Hertz is a UC Davis brewing graduate and owner of Beer & Beyond, a beer promotion company based in Israel. He is the author of two editions of *The Beer Brands in Israel* and a beer tour operator and guide.

Stan Hieronymus is a lifelong journalist who has been writing about beer since 1992. As his most recent book *Brewing Local: American-Grown Beer* suggests, he is

an advocate of terroir, and comments about it at www.appellationbeer.com/.

Matt Kirkegaard is one of Australia's most experienced beer writers and commentators. He is founder of leading online beer news and discussion site Australian Brews News, and in 2014 won the inaugural Beer Media trophy at the Australian International Beer Awards.

Rafał Kowalczyk and **Jan Lichota** are Polish beer judges. Rafał is a journalist and educator on beer who owns the Warsaw beer pub Jabeerwocky, while Jan is a beer lawyer, reporter and researcher who works in the tourism sector.

Maurizio Maestrelli is a professional journalist who has focused on beer, wine and spirits since 1997, and is author of *Birra and Thomas Hardy's Ale: the Story, the Legend*, as well as contributor to *1001 Beers You Must Try Before You Die* and *Baladin. La Birra Artigianale è Tutta Colpa di Teo*.

Mark Meli is senior writer for the *Japan Beer Times* and has written two books about Japanese craft beer. He lives in Kyoto, and is professor of ecocritical cultural studies at Kansai University in Osaka.

Neil Miller was the Brewers Guild of New Zealand Beer Writer of the Year 2014–15. His work has appeared in *Beer & Brewer*, *The Shout*, *Cuisine*, *New Zealand Liquor News*, *Sunday Star Times* and *Dominion Post*. He is also a regular on Radio New Zealand's The Panel.

Des de Moor is the author of The *CAMRA Guide to London's Best Beer, Pubs & Bars*, a contributor to *Beer Magazine*, *Beer Advocate* and *Time Out* among others, a respected international beer judge and a regular host of tutored tastings and brewery walks and tours.

Lisa Morrison began writing about beer professionally in 1997 and has authored or contributed to more than six books on beer. After two decades writing, speaking and teaching about beer, she is now co-owner of Belmont Station Bottle Shop & Taproom in Portland, Oregon.

Laurent Mousson is a Swiss beer activist and the former vice-chair of the European Beer Consumers Union (2008–11). He is also an international beer judge and active in beer education.

Alexander Petrochenkov has written seven books and many articles about beer, in so doing becoming Russia's most prolific beer writer. His latest book is *Крафтовое пиво*, translating to "Craft Beer".

Élisabeth Pierre is a French beer writer and the author of five books, including *Choisir et Acheter sa Bière en 7 Secondes*. She is also an international judge and founder of the Paris-based *L'Académie Bierissima*, offering beer training for brewing and hospitality professionals.

Daniel Rocamora and **Karen A Higgs** are Uruguayan beer and travel authorities. Daniel is probably the country's foremost beer expert and a frequent beer judge, while Karen is the author of *The Guru'Guay Guide to Montevideo* and creator of the English language Uruguay website guruguay.com/.

Conrad Seidl, known as the Bierpapst, or "Beer Pope", is a beer writer based in Vienna, Austria. He has published several books on beer in German, including the annual *Conrad Seidls Bier Guide to Austria*, and has a website at www.bierpapst.eu/.

Tim Skelton is the author of two beer books – *Beer in the Netherlands* and *Around Amsterdam in 80 Beers* and – and three editions of the *Bradt Travel Guide Luxembourg*. He is a regular judge at beer competitions.

Espen Smith is a well-known Norwegian beer critic who regularly appears on television and talk radio, and writes for newspapers and magazines.

He also teaches classes on beer and brewing, guides frequent beer tours, has authored several books and consults on brewery development.

Ricardo Solis is the Academic Director of the Instituto Cervezas de América in Santiago, Chile, and a professor on the Diplomado en Microcervecería course at the Universidad Católica de Valparaíso. He has more than 15 years of experience in the brewing industry.

Péter Takács is a craft beer specialist in Hungary who, in various guises, supplies hops and exclusive grains mostly to craft brewers from Bratislava to Bucharest. He is a beer judge, a nomadic brewer, an advisor to aspiring brewers and an occasional beer writer.

Joan Villar-i-Martí (aka "Birraire") is a Catalan writer, consultant and beer enthusiast. He writes mainly in specialized media and at his blog birraire.com, is co-author of *Guia de Cerveses de Catalunya* and part of the organization team of the Barcelona Beer Festival.

Michelle Wang was editor-in-chief of China's first beer magazine before she founded The Beer Link, a magazine, media and technical services company. She is also organizer of the annual China Craft Beer Conference and travels widely as China's unofficial craft beer ambassador to the world.

Paul Peng Wang（王鵬）is a Taiwanese specialist in beer, wine and spirits. He is the author of two beer books written in Mandarin and a beer judge and educator who also consults for producers and importers.

Kathia Zanatta is food engineer, beer sommelier and brewmaster. During 12 years in the brewing segment she has worked for big and small breweries and now runs the Instituto da Cerveja Brasil, the largest school focused on beer education in Latin America.

Thanks also to **Alejandra Abrodos, Francisca Gabarro, Daniel Goh, Erik Lu, Bill Miller, German Orrantia, José Ruiz, Adrian Tierney-Jones** and all the friends, industry folk and fellow writers who helped us along the way with information, advice and more than the occasional shared beer.

PICTURE CREDITS

Mitchell Beazley would like to thank all the breweries and their agents who have kindly provided images for publication in this book.

Additional credits
6 Shutterstock Ramon L Farinos/Shutterstock; **10** pattang/Shutterstock; **13** Erdosain/Dreamstime.com; **15** Image Source/Alamy Stock Photo; **16–17** courtesy Nynäshamns, Shiga Kogen, G Schneider & Sohn; **18–19** courtesy Geco, Grist House, Coopers; **20** courtesy Brekeriet, photo Ulf Mellander; **21** courtesy Three Dogs; **22–23** courtesy Srigim, Brasserie DuPont, Kneitinger; **24–25** courtesy Riegele, Allagash; **25b** courtesy Microbrasserie Les Trois Mousquetaires, Quebec; **26** Brent Hofacker; **28–29** courtesy Ballast Point, The Alchemist, Stowe; **31** Jim Holden/Alamy Stock Photo; **32** Alexander Zemlianichenko Jr/Bloomberg via Getty Images; **35** courtesy Almond '22; **37** Mira/Alamy Stock Photo; **48** Arterra Picture Library/Alamy Stock Photo; **63** Knut Niehus/Zoonar/Alamy Stock Photo; **136** Lphoto/Alamy Stock Photo; **165** Michael Juno/Alamy Stock Photo; **198** Ian Dagnall/Alamy Stock Photo; **235** Lucas Vallecillos/Alamy Stock Photo; **254** Dinozzaver/ Dreamstime.com; **268** Prasit Rodphan/Dreamstime.com; **293** René Mattes/hemis.fr/Alamy Stock Photo.